The Short Oxford History of Europe

# Europe 1900–1945

# The Short Oxford History of Europe

General Editor: T. C. W. Blanning

NOW AVAILABLE

**Classical Greece**
*edited by Robin Osborne*

**The Early Middle Ages**
*edited by Rosamond McKitterick*

**The Seventeenth Century**
*edited by Joseph Bergin*

**The Eighteenth Century**
*edited by T. C. W. Blanning*

**The Nineteenth Century**
*edited by T. C. W. Blanning*

**Europe since 1945**
*edited by Mary Fulbrook*

IN PREPARATION, VOLUMES COVERING

The Romans
The High Middle Ages
The Late Middle Ages
The Sixteenth Century

The Short Oxford History of Europe

General Editor: T. C. W. Blanning

# Europe
## 1900–1945

Edited by Julian Jackson

OXFORD
UNIVERSITY PRESS

# OXFORD
## UNIVERSITY PRESS

Great Clarendon Street, Oxford OX2 6DP

Oxford University Press is a department of the University of Oxford.
It furthers the University's objective of excellence in research, scholarship,
and education by publishing worldwide in

Oxford  New York

Auckland  Bangkok  Buenos Aires  Cape Town  Chennai
Dar es Salaam  Delhi  Hong Kong  Istanbul  Karachi  Kolkata
Kuala Lumpur  Madrid  Melbourne  Mexico City  Mumbai  Nairobi
São Paulo  Shanghai  Singapore  Taipei  Tokyo  Toronto

with an associated company in Berlin

Oxford is a registered trade mark of Oxford University Press
in the UK and in certain other countries

Published in the United States
by Oxford University Press Inc., New York

British Library Cataloguing in Publication Data

Data available

Library of Congress Cataloging in Publication Data

Data available

ISBN 0–19–820757–3 (hbk)
ISBN 0–19–924428–6 (pbk)

10  9  8  7  6  5  4  3  2  1

Typeset in Minion
by RefineCatch Limited, Bungay, Suffolk
Printed in Great Britain by
T.J. International Ltd, Padstow, Cornwall

# General Editor's Preface

The problems of writing a satisfactory general history of Europe are many, but the most intractable is clearly the reconciliation of depth with breadth. The historian who can write with equal authority about every part of the continent in all its various aspects has not yet been born. Two main solutions have been tried in the past: either a single scholar has attempted to go it alone, presenting an unashamedly personal view of a period, or teams of specialists have been enlisted to write what are in effect anthologies. The first offers a coherent perspective but unequal coverage, the second sacrifices unity for the sake of expertise. This new series is underpinned by the belief that it is this second way that has the fewest disadvantages and that even those can be diminished if not neutralized by close cooperation between the individual contributors under the directing supervision of the volume editor. All the contributors to every volume in this series have read each other's chapters, have met to discuss problems of overlap and omission, and have then redrafted as part of a truly collective exercise. To strengthen coherence further, the editor has written an introduction and conclusion, weaving the separate strands together to form a single cord. In this exercise, the brevity promised by the adjective 'short' in the series' title has been an asset. The need to be concise has concentrated everyone's minds on what really mattered in the period. No attempt has been made to cover every angle of every topic in every country. What this volume does provide is a short but sharp and deep entry into the history of Europe in the period in all its most important aspects.

T. C. W. Blanning

*Sidney Sussex College*
*Cambridge*

# Contents

# List of contributors

RICHARD BESSEL is Professor of Twentieth Century History at the University of York. His publications include *Germany after the First World War* (Oxford, 1993), (ed.) *Fascist Italy and Nazi Germany: Comparisons and Contrasts* (Cambridge, 1996), (ed., with Ralph Jessen) *Die Grenzen der Diktatur* (Göttingen, 1996), and (ed.) *Life in the Third Reich* (revised edition, Oxford, 2001). He also is co-editor of the journal German History.

RAJNARAYAN CHANDAVARKAR is Reader in the History and Politics of South Asia, and Director of the Centre of South Asian Studies, University of Cambridge, and Fellow of Trinity College, Cambridge. He is the author of *The Origins of Industrial Capitalism in India: Business Strategies and the Working Classes in Bombay, 1900–1940* (Cambridge, 1994) and *Imperial Power and Popular Politics: Class, Resistance and the State in India, 1850–1950* (Cambridge, 1998).

MODRIS EKSTEINS is Professor of History at the University of Toronto at Scarborough. His books include *The Limits of Reason: The German Democratic Press and the Collapse of Weimar Democracy* (London: 1975), *Rites of Spring: The Great War and the Birth of the Modern Age* (London, 1989), and *Walking Since Daybreak: A Story of Eastern Europe, World War II, and the Heart of the 20th Century* (London, 2000).

JULIAN JACKSON is Professor of French History at the University of Wales, Swansea. His publications include *The Politics of Depression in France 1932–1936* (Cambridge, 1986), *The Popular Front in France 1936–1938: Defending Democracy* (Cambridge, 1988), *De Gaulle* (London, 1990), and *France: the Dark Years 1940–1944* (Oxford, 2001).

HAROLD JAMES is Professor of History at Princeton University and the author of *International Monetary Cooperation Since Bretton Woods* (Oxford, 1996), *The End of Globalization: Lessons from the Great Depression* (Harvard, Mass., 2001), and *The Deutsche Bank and the Nazi Economic War Against the Jews* (Cambridge, 2001).

KEVIN PASSMORE is Lecturer in History at Cardiff University. His publications include *From Liberalism to Fascism: the Right in a French Province 1928–1939* (Cambridge, 1997) and *Fascism: A Very Short Introduction* (Oxford, 2002). He has edited *Women, Gender and the Extreme Right in Europe, 1919–1945* (Manchester, 2003).

DAVID STEVENSON is Professor of International History at the London School of Economics and Political Science. He is the author of *French War Aims against Germany, 1914–1919* (Oxford, 1982), *The First World War and International Politics* (Oxford, 1988), *Armaments and the Coming of War: Europe, 1904–1914* (Oxford, 1996), and *The Outbreak of the First World War: 1914 in Perspective* (Basingstoke and New York, 1997).

# Introduction

## Julian Jackson

## Writing twentieth-century history

Writing the history of the first half of the twentieth century poses its own particular problems. This period is now undeniably the 'past', but it is close enough for our perspective on it to be constantly shifting. As we move away from the events, different parts of the landscape come into sharper relief; as we try to answer questions, the very questions themselves seem to change. This is true of all history writing, but especially of a period which still inhabits a twilight zone between history and memory. How can we possibly achieve the necessary critical distance from a period whose contested meanings are still part of contemporary political and social debates in a way that is not true of, say, the Albigensian crusade, the Thirty Years War or even the French Revolution?

Nothing demonstrates these problems better than the changing ways in which we have viewed what has come to be called the 'Holocaust'. When in the autumn of 1947 the Italian chemist Primo Levi published *If this is a Man*, an account of his experiences at Auschwitz, the book aroused little interest and was a commercial flop. Two thousand five hundred copies of the book were printed, and the unsold ones rotted in a storage warehouse until they were destroyed by a flood of the Arno River in 1966. An English translation in 1959 met with similar indifference. Dispirited by his failure, Levi stopped writing for thirteen years. It was only during the 1960s that his reputation began to grow. Now his writings on Auschwitz are viewed as classics, and Levi himself is considered one of the significant literary voices of the century. Levi's journey from obscurity to celebrity was part—both cause and symptom—of a general shift in perception in which

the Holocaust has become central to our understanding of the twentieth century. Now we *see* the Holocaust; for about twenty-five years
we did not. It now seems remarkable to us that when the French
filmmaker Alain Resnais made the first documentary film about the
concentration camps, *Night and Fog*, in 1956, he almost entirely
ignored the fate and presence of the Jews in the camps; it took
another French filmmaker, Claude Lanzmann, twenty-nine years
later, to make another documentary, *Shoah*, entirely devoted to the
extermination of the Jews. In Alan Bullock's biography of Hitler,
which appeared in 1952, the Holocaust only merits three pages; in Ian
Kershaw's biography forty-eight years later it is a central theme.

The Holocaust is now generally deemed to have been unique in its
horror. Recently, however, some historians have questioned whether
our contemporary obsession with the Holocaust has not caused new
kinds of distortion just as misleading as our previous neglect of it. It
has been pointed out that every historical event or series of events is
in its own way unique, and there is no reason why one particular set
of unique circumstances should necessarily be elevated above any
other. If the uniqueness of the Holocaust was that it represented a
deliberate policy aimed at the extermination of every member of a
single ethnic group, does that mean that gypsies and homosexuals,
who were also killed by the Nazis, cannot be included among its
victims? If they can be included, how would the definition be revised
to accommodate them? Other historians wonder if the 'sacralization'
of the Holocaust causes us to underplay other horrors, such as the
camps of the Soviet Union? Others wonder if it would be possible,
without in any way denying the horror of the Holocaust, to write
an account of the Nazi regime which did not ascribe centrality to the
Holocaust. For example, might it be possible, from a different perspective, to see the regime's social policies as part of a longer term
development of the welfare state which extends from Bismarck,
through Weimar, and into the post-1945 period? Or would such an
attempt to 'historicize' Nazism in this way be to miss what was essential about it in favour of what was peripheral? How are such kinds of
judgement to be made?

There are indeed some for whom the events of the twentieth
century call into question the whole enterprise of historical writing.
If, as Modris Eksteins writes in the present volume, the nineteenth
century was the great age of history writing—with history becoming

'the principal intellectual tool for interpreting existence'—the twentieth century shattered the confidence, the sense of certainty, which made historical narrative possible. What words can explain the seemingly senseless horrors which the first half of the century witnessed? Eksteins reminds us of the famous remark of Theodor Adorno about the impossibility of writing poetry after Auschwitz. Yet already in 1916 the Armenian poet Avetik Ishakian had written in a similar vein of the sufferings of his people in the Armenian genocide which took place in the Ottoman Empire from 1915: 'So great is the anguish . . . of the Armenians, so hideous and unprecedented, that the infinity and fathomlessness of the universe must be considerate in gauging it; there are no words in the dictionary to qualify the hideousness of the terrors. Not a single poet can find words.'

The twentieth century has certainly made us more sceptical of narratives of progress; it has made us aware, as Richard Bessel puts it in his essay in this volume, of the 'Janus face of modernity'. This is very evident, for example, in the varied fortunes of the so-called science of eugenics—improving the racial stock. In the early years of the century, eugenics had a considerable following in progressive and left-wing circles among such figures as the Webbs, Keynes, Shaw, and H. G. Wells; the first Chair of Eugenics was established at University College London in 1909; and an Institute of Racial Biology was founded at Uppsala in Sweden in 1922. Sterilization of mentally handicapped people was introduced in sixteen American states starting with Indiana in 1899; by 1941 it had affected 36,000 people. These 'progressive' intellectual origins of eugenics are something that we would rather forget in the light of the horror to which the idea of racial improvement was to lead under Hitler who moved from sterilization in 1933 through euthanasia in 1939 to genocide in 1941. But it should not be forgotten either that the Nazis were pioneers in organizing health prevention campaigns, particularly against cancer. They launched intensive anti-smoking campaigns—propaganda pointed out that Roosevelt, Churchill, and Stalin smoked while Franco, Mussolini, and Hitler did not—limited the use of asbestos and encouraged the production of whole-grain bread. The Nazis were so 'modern' that they even produced election literature written in Braille. This is not to say that in some respects the Nazis were 'progressive' and in others 'barbarous', but that what was most 'progressive' about them was intertwined with what was most 'barbarous'. Doctors and medical experts were as central to Nazism as torturers and secret policemen.

One certainly does not have to be an extreme post-modernist to be dissatisfied with some of the polarities which once presented themselves as a way of organizing a narrative of twentieth-century history. One such polarity might, for example, be the conflict between liberal democracy, on the one hand, and varieties of fascism, on the other, culminating in the triumph of the humane values of the liberal democratic model in most of Western Europe after 1945. But, as Kevin Passmore's chapter argues, liberal democracy was not always pluralist or tolerant, especially of ethnic and religious difference. Ironically, anti-feminist conservative movements often offered more significant opportunities for female activism than did their liberal opponents (providing the women abandoned solidarity with women of other races); and fascism could open up opportunities to social groups who had been excluded from traditional liberal politics. The frontiers between democracy and fascism could be blurred. Much of the political conflict of the century was not between democrats and anti-democrats but about what democracy should mean in the first place. Although it might have been axiomatic among 'progressive' opinion at the beginning of the century that the future lay with liberal democracy, this was not the assumption in the inter-war years of many artists and intellectuals in the vanguard of modernism. It would not have been the view of figures as diverse as T. S. Eliot, D. H. Lawrence, Le Corbusier, Maurice Blanchot, Guiseppe Marinetti, Salvador Dali, and W. B. Yeats, to name but a few. Democracy looked fragile and exhausted in Europe in 1939; it did not look 'new' or 'progressive'.

It is interesting to see how some recent historians have attempted to make sense of the twentieth century. For Eric Hobsbawn (1994) it was an 'age of extremes', with the period up to 1945 being an 'age of catastrophe'. His central narrative is the conflict between fascism and democracy, with Communism paradoxically coming to the rescue of democracy. For Mark Mazower (1998) whose title 'dark continent' is an argument in itself, the lines are fuzzier: he sees the triumph of democracy in 1945 as contingent, and devotes much space to uncovering the darker side of liberal democracy. For Clive Ponting (1998) the century 'demonstrated that progress and barbarism could exist alongside each other'. Most recently, Richard Vinen (2000) eschews an overall interpretation and offers a 'history in fragments' while warning against viewing the history of the century only in terms of catastrophe.

It is interesting also to see where these historians choose to start their twentieth century: Hobsbawn in 1914, Mazower in 1918, Ponting and Vinen in 1900. Other dates could be proposed. Virginia Woolf once famously remarked that 'On or about December 1909 human character changed' (she was thinking about the post-Impressionist exhibition of that year). The Futurist Manifesto of 1909 declared that 'Time and space died yesterday'. More prosaically one could suggest 1917 as a major turning point. This was the year in which the chance of a negotiated peace was definitely scotched, America entered the war, and the Bolsheviks took power in Russia.

## The shadow of war

Whatever year we choose to start the 'short' twentieth century, it is generally accepted that the Great War represents some kind of watershed, the end of a world: 'Never such innocence again' as Philip Larkin put it in his poem 'MCMXIV'. As the liberal British historian G. M. Trevelyan wrote after the war: 'we are at present no better than a company of ante-deluvians who have survived the fire deluge, sitting dazed among the ruins of the world we knew. The certainty of permanence has gone'. The French poet Paul Valèry wrote in 1919 that the war had demonstrated the 'mortality' of civilizations.

But if there is agreement that the war represents some kind of rupture, it is not so clear what kind of rupture. In the arts, for example, the break with the nineteenth century—indeed with a tradition of western art going back to the Renaissance—occurred before 1914, in those extraordinary seven years between 1905 and 1912 which saw the arrival of Fauvism, cubism, futurism, abstraction, Vorticism, and atonality. In this perspective, the period after the war to some extent represented a return to tradition by some artists: Picasso and Stravinsky sought inspiration from classicism in the 1920s. One effect of the war was to cast a hazy glow of nostalgia over pre-1914 Europe. But it would be a mistake to underestimate the class tensions, structural instabilities, and political violence of Europe's *belle époque*. Passmore's chapter dissects the barely contained tensions between left liberals, nationalists, feminists, socialists, and liberals in European politics before 1914. As for the tranquility of pre-1914 Europe, what about the massacre of 500 miners in the Lena Goldfield in Russia in 1912; or the simmering violence between peasants and landowners in Andalucia in Spain or in Latvia on the Baltic; or the uprising of Romanian peasants in December 1907 suppressed at the cost of over 11,000 lives; or the massacres of Armenians in the Ottoman Empire in 1905 and 1908 in each of which about 20,000 perished; or the Balkan Wars of 1912–13 which set a new standard for horror; or the anti-Jewish pogroms in Russia; or the horrors inflicted on native populations by the Germans in their conquest of South-West Africa in 1904, not to speak of the Belgian atrocities in the Congo? As Raj Chanda-varkar observes in his chapter, 'historians have insufficiently explored the violence which sustained Europe's civilizing missions'. For all the *douceur de vie* of the period before 1914 Europe was also a continent from which many people wanted to escape. Some 3.5 million Poles left for the United States in the two decades before 1914; 1.9 million Italians between 1900 and 1909. The number of British casualties in the Great War was smaller than the number of British citizens who emigrated to America in the previous three decades.

Many of the developments which would transform daily life in the twentieth century—the motor car, the moving picture, the telephone, the aeroplane, the mass circulation newspaper—made their first appearance well before 1914. The late nineteenth century also saw the rise of organized labour, the emergence of the white collar tertiary sector, the development of a new style of right wing populist anti-semitic nationalism, and an intellectual revolt against positivism and rationalism. Nietzsche died in 1900, but the twentieth century was in some sense to be his. The French writer Charles Péguy wrote in 1900: 'the world has changed more in the last thirty years than in the last two millennia'. One historian famously dated the 'strange death' of liberalism in Britain to the period before 1914; but this would also be true of the rest of Europe. Hitler, it should be remembered, was already 25 in 1914, Mussolini was 31 ; Lenin was 34. Their view of the world had to a large extent already been formed at the outbreak of war.

Wherever one chooses to start the twentieth century, there can be no doubt that one of the central facts of European history in its first fifty years has been the experience of war—after a century which saw no major international European conflict. One of the central threads of this period must be a narrative of catastrophe and destruction. Apart from the two world wars which engulfed almost the whole of the European continent (only Spain, Sweden, Holland, Norway, Denmark, Portugal, and Switzerland stayed out of the First War; only Spain, Portugal, Sweden, Switzerland, and Turkey out of the Second), there was also the Russian Civil War (1918–21), which owing to the halfhearted intervention of the British and French, was not only a civil war; the semi-forgotten Russo-Polish War of 1919–21, which was a vast war of movement involving about one million combatants; and the Greco-Turkish War (1921–3).

War, then, gives a grim unity to this period. De Gaulle talked of a 'Thirty Years War' starting in 1914 and ending in 1945. He meant by this the conflict between Germany and France, but the term could be more accurately applied to the conflict between Germany and Russia, where by far the largest number of casualties occurred. Others have talked of a 'European Civil War', and this designation is useful in pointing up the ideological dimension to international conflict, already present in the First World War ('civilisation' against 'Kultur', an 'existential conflict' in the words of the Kaiser) and even more in the Second (fascism against Bolshevism, race war, Weltanschauungs-krieg). The international 'European Civil War' also unleashed a series of internecine conflicts—ethnic, ideological, and religious. It was superimposed upon a series of civil wars, or turned pre-existing ethnic, social, and political tensions into civil wars. In Armenia the Turks massacred Armenians in 1915–16; in Yugoslavia the Croatian Ustaše massacred hundreds of thousands of Serbs, Jews, and gypsies in 1941; in Bukovina and Bessarabia the Romanians massacred some 200,000 Jews in 1941 on a scale and with a savagery which shocked and impressed the Nazis: Romania's leader Antonescu talked in October 1941 of 'cleansing' his country of Jews. This inter-relationship between international conflict and internal conflict was exemplified in Spain where an internal Spanish conflict was internationalized in the Civil War (1936–9) during which Germans and Italians and Russians fought each other by proxy, rehearsing for the international war to come. The 'Spanish' domestic conflict itself was a bundle of other conflicts between landless peasants and landlords in Andalucia, between miners and bosses in the Asturias, between monarchists and Republicans, between anarchists and Communists, between Catholics and anti-clericals, between autonomists and Castilian centralists. Other Europeans could certainly recognize themselves in these conflicts. As Auden put it: 'In Spain, soldered so cruelly to inventive Europe/Our fever's menacing shapes are precise and alive.' Europeans in this period found limitless reasons to hate each other.

The human toll of these conflicts was immense: 9 million deaths in the Great War, about 1 million (on the Bolshevik side alone) in the Russian Civil War, 1 million in the Spanish Civil War, 55 million in the Second World War. There was also a massive human cost in uprootedness: this was the century of the refugee. There were estimated to be approximately 9.5 million refugees in Europe in 1926. This did not include the massive exchange of population, affecting approximately 1.5 million people, between Greece and Turkey under the terms of the Lausanne Convention of 1923 which put an end to the Greco-Turkish War. Of the 2 million Greeks living in Turkey in 1914, 1 million perished, and the rest were forcibly uprooted in 1923. There were possibly 30 million displaced persons in Europe in 1945; what was to become West Germany absorbed some 10 million refugees of whom 3.5 million had been expelled from Czechoslovakia.

Of the two world wars, the second was bloodier than the first and witnessed greater physical destruction, and yet the first haunts our imaginations in a way that the second—apart from the Holocaust—does not. Almost from the start of the conflict there was the sense that something irremediable was about to occur. When German bombardments destroyed the famous library at Louvain, Henry James commented that this was 'the most heinous crime ever perpetrated against the mind of man'. The immediate legacy of the Great War was one of upheaval, fragmentation, and insecurity. The key modernist text of the post-war years, T. S. Eliot's *The Wasteland*, reads like a collection of fragments, the shards of a lost world. The first half of the 1920s were overshadowed by inflation and the fear of revolution, both of them born out of the war. But even when some kind of economic stabilization and prosperity had been achieved in the second half of the decade, war continued to cast its shadow: each society invented rituals of memory and mourning; war veterans claimed a moral authority which they aspired to turn into political influence. It proved in the end harder to demobilize minds than to mobilize them; the culture of war could not suddenly be unthought. War had brought about a brutalization of politics; Europeans had

been up to a point desensitised to horror and violence. The industrialized killing of the First World War prefigured—perhaps made
imaginable—the 'militarized genocide' (Omar Bartov) of the Holocaust. Indeed there was already much anti-Jewish violence in the First
World War since much of the fighting in eastern Europe occurred in
the Pale of Settlement where large numbers of Jews had been concentrated for over a century. Now Jews, suspected of being spies, were
expelled from their homes or massacred. Anti-semitism was not born
in the First World War but it was certainly aggravated by it. The two
new ideologies of the first half of the century—fascism and
Communism—were born out of war. Fascism represented in some
sense a transposition into peacetime politics of the cultural values of
war. In Italy, fascism represented the attempt to achieve in peacetime
the kind of kind of mobilization of minds that had been tried, but
never fully achieved, in war. Fascism is suffused with the imagery and
aesthetic of war: its rhetoric of struggle and battle and combat ('Mein
Kampf', 'the battle for births'), its slogans ('believe, obey, fight'), its
violence, its hierarchical forms of organization.

Similarly, the experience of the First World War and the Civil War
militarized the political culture of Bolshevism: army boots and tunic
became almost a uniform of the Party in the early 1930s. One third of
the members of the 1927 Bolshevik party had joined in 1917–21. Many
Bolsheviks got their first experience of administration during the
Civil War; they forged bonds as comrades in arms. Early Bolshevik
economic planning was inspired to a considerable extent by the war
economy of Germany where the government had expanded control
over industry to an unprecedented degree: this was at the time the
only 'socialist' economic model available.

Outside the Soviet Union the mood after 1919 was in favour of
deregulation and dismantling wartime controls, but everywhere the
war had awakened governments to the need to draw on greater
technical expertise and demonstrate greater efficiency. Wichard von
Moellendorff, one of the officials in charge of the German war economy, had been influenced by the American scientific management
techniques of Taylorism. In the 1920s there was a general fascination,
and in some cases fascinated horror, with the possibilities of mechanization and technology. Technocratic models of social management
seemed especially attractive at a time when representative institutions
seemed to be working badly. The engineer and the supposedly

non-political 'expert' were the new heroes of the age. The modern
production methods of what came to be called 'Fordism'—assembly
lines, standardization—were viewed by many as a way of absorbing
class conflict through prosperity, and dissolving class hatred in the
Werksgemeinschaft. Mussolini appealed for an alliance of 'producers'
and 'veterans'. War offered lessons for peace. André Citroën had
started his career in 1915 applying modern methods to the production
of shells; after the war he turned the same methods to the production
of cars.

# The advance of the state

Citroën, the epitome of the brash new world which technology and
modernity seemed to portend—in 1929 he famously installed neon
advertisements on the Eiffel tower—was also one of the most spectacular examples of the collapse of that brief flurry of optimism when
he went bankrupt in 1935 as a result of the economic crisis which hit
Europe after 1929. The Great Depression of the early 1930s was, along
with war, the other great calamity of the first half of the twentieth
century. The economic and social aspects of this catastrophe are
described in this volume by Harold James and Richard Bessel. In
cultural and political terms, the Depression seemed to represent the
final bankruptcy of laissez-faire liberalism. Governments responded
to the Depression in ad hoc, improvisatory, and contradictory ways—
imposing tariffs and quotas to hold up prices, distributing social
benefits to save the unemployed from starvation, and providing state
investment for bankrupt industries. The most sophisticated analysis
of what governments might do to alleviate the Depression occurred
in Britain under the influence of Keynes. At this stage his ideas had no
bearing on policy in Britain although what later came to be known as
'Keynesian' measures were applied by the social democratic government in Sweden. Mostly, however, Socialists rejected Keynesian style
solutions either because they did not believe it to be their role to
make capitalism work or because they believed, as good Marxists,
that it was impossible to do so.

The economic recovery which started after 1933 probably owed
little to any of the policies which had been applied. But assumptions

about the relationship between state and society had been altered once and for all. In Italy, for example, fascism, which was always reinventing itself, became economically interventionist in a way that it had not been in the 1920s. Thus fascism, born out of the first catastrophe of the century, was shaped by the second, only to collapse in the third. Out of the extraordinary mobilization of resources which took place during the Second World War developed the idea that the state would have a significant role to play in economic management and welfare. 'War and welfare went hand in hand' to quote the historian Michael Howard. Economic planning reached its apotheosis in Britain during the Second World War when Churchill's coalition government became the example of the most successfully planned modern economy in history. After that war, those like the liberal economist Hayek who tried to stand against this new tide, warning of a *Road to Serfdom*, were isolated voices. 'We are all planners now' declared the British economist Evan Durbin in 1949.

The increasing role of the state in this period offers us another possible narrative of the twentieth century—not catastrophe but the progressive extension of economic interventionism and state sponsored social welfare—pensions, health insurance, affordable housing, and organized leisure. This would apply to social democratic Sweden, conservative Britain, Nazi Germany, Fascist Italy, Soviet Russia. The development of the welfare state had many roots and many ramifications. It was inspired by conservative fears about the challenge of labour, by technocratic desire to increase workplace efficiency and by nationalist ambitions to promote healthy and expanding populations. In Italy the regime developed the Dopolavoro ('after work') organization which provided leisure activities and holidays; the German version was called Kraft durch Freude (Strength through Joy). In France the democratic Popular Front government provided free paid holidays to the working class. Along with welfarism came the policing of morality and sexuality. Abortion and homosexuality were repressed throughout the continent in both liberal and dictatorial regimes—though more harshly in the latter.

In its wake, then, welfare brought regulation. Thus any discussion of the increasing power of the state in the twentieth century also needs to consider briefly the word 'totalitarian' which was another of the inventions of the first half of the century. For many people, the emblematic twentieth-century figure might be Franz Kafka's Joseph K, an innocent citizen caught up in the nightmare of a pitiless and meaningless bureaucracy. The term totalitarian was used by Mussolini in 1925, and has been endlessly repeated ever since, even if it has gone in and out of favour with historians. One problem is that, although the term emerged in Italy, the totalitarian model does not really apply to Italy—if only because of the enormous social and cultural power of the Catholic Church. Another problem with the term is that it was appropriated by Cold War polemicists, defined in a very unhistorical way, and used as a weapon against the Soviet Union. Another problem is that it seems to render the notion of fascism redundant. If the more significant comparison is between Nazism and Stalinism, as totalitarian regimes, than between Italy and Germany as fascist ones, where does that leave 'fascism' as a generic concept? Another problem is that the term totalitarian is insufficiently sensitive to the dynamic relationship between state and society. It assumes that certain societies are infinitely malleable and posits a one way relationship between state and society. This ignores the extent to which so-called totalitarian regimes genuinely mobilized popular support: even terror rested upon large scale support and complicity either because people shared its goals or because they stood to gain from it. A recent study of the Gestapo has shown that it relied to an enormous extent on tip-offs from the population.

Despite all these caveats, the term totalitarian is useful if employed more loosely as an expression of the limitless utopian *ambitions* of the fascist and Soviet states, their aspiration to take responsibility for all areas of existence, to embody a new civic religion, to create a 'new Man', and to break down the boundaries between private and public. The most radical attempt to remodel a society was undoubtedly the Soviet Union. But did it succeed? There can be no doubting the extent of the Stalinist state's repressive power, climaxing in the terror of 1936–7 (even if it is still unclear how much of this was actually willed from the centre); no doubting its massive destructive power as witnessed in the terrible famine of 1929–30; no doubting its massive creative power as witnessed by the creation within ten years of an industrial economy. Certainly many Soviet citizens did learn to 'speak Bolshevik', in the words of Stephen Kotkin, but did they also think it? Soviet scholars are still in dispute as to the extent to which its citizens internalized the values of the regime. Some see the citizens of Stalinist society only as victims; others argue that the regime redefined individuals' social identities for them and consequently defined the way they thought about themselves. Stalinism was a culture which tried to destroy the conceptual vocabulary for thinking 'outside' the system. Diary evidence suggests that in some cases this succeeded: we have the diary of a son of a Kulak who recasts his identity for himself as a 'true citizen'. One of the great visionary novels of the twentieth century, Arthur Koestler's *Darkness at Noon*, derives its horror not so much from the persecution of the hero Rubashov, who is a Communist on trial for crimes he did not commit, but his incapacity to think that the Party can be wrong. He has internalized his own persecution.

In Nazi Germany also, where the regime, in the words of the labour minister Robert Ley, had decreed 'only sleep will be private', there is some evidence that the regime's values were up to a point internalized. Recent studies of the letters of German Wehrmacht soldiers on the Eastern Front have found that their vision of the world was framed around such concepts as Fuhrer, race, and *Volk*, quite different from the Christian, monarchical, and nationalist world of the First World War soldier. The Jewish academic Victor Klemperer, who survived the Nazi regime, wrote a study of the way in which Nazism corrupted the daily language. In his diary for February 1935 he records a conversation with his last two students whom he described as 'completely anti-Nazi'. They were discussing a recent trial which resulted in the execution of two women in Berlin. Despite the fact the trial had been entirely secret and the defendants had been denied any legal rights, the students saw nothing wrong and believed the verdict to have been 'totally appropriate'. In many respects, then, people may have become more 'Nazi' than they realized.

## The limits of the state

But these arguments about the power of the state should not be pushed too far. As far as the Soviet Union is concerned, when it came to recreating mankind, the Stalinist experiment demonstrated not the power of the state but the limits of its power, or at least the capacity of society to refract and distort the intentions of those who intended to mould it. The notion of totalitarianism seems inadequate to encompass the varieties of daily life under Stalinism. Stalinism was a social revolution possibly unparalleled in history for its rapidity, but the 'new quicksand society', to quote Moshe Lewin, which Stalinism created reacted back against those who tried to transform it: the Russian peasant could be driven into the city but his values could not be transformed overnight. The result was, to quote Lewin again, the 'ruralization of the cities' as much as the urbanization of the peasants, a society of Oblomovs as much as Stakhanovs, of peasants in cities oblivious to official propaganda, recreating a culture of religion, drunkenness, and folklore, subverting official channels through networks of client–patron relationships. As for Nazi Germany, the regime was always more pragmatic than the rhetoric allowed, and individuals who did not fall into one of the categories persecuted by it could carry on their lives largely undisturbed. Even the Nazi campaigns against smoking had no effect: tobacco consumption increased during the first seven years of Nazi rule; only the war reversed the trend.

Over the long term, it is striking how resistant social trends have been to state policy in the century of 'totalitarianism'. Despite their best efforts to encourage women to breed, the Nazis, like the Italian fascists, failed to reverse the long-term secular trend towards decreasing family size. As Richard Bessel observes, whether in Italy or Germany or Britain or France, we see in this period broadly similar patterns in female employment, demography, and family structure. One might therefore suggest a third possible narrative for the first half of the century: the emergence in western Europe of a mass culture of leisure which cuts through our two other narratives of catastrophe and of increasing state power, and prefigures the consumerism of the 1950s and 1960s. Europe after 1918 was already the Europe of the automobile, the radio, the cinema, the illustrated magazine, and mass advertising. It witnessed the beginning of Americanization—and its antithesis anti-Americanism. The most universally known figure in the world between the wars was Charlie Chaplin. The American chewing gum manufacturer Wrigley opened its first plant in Germany in 1925, and Coca-Cola its first German plant in 1929. The Nazis did not like American films but were too sensible to try and ban them all, and instead tried to create their own Hollywood style. The same was true of jazz. The radio, which was of course a potent weapon of State control, was also a weapon against it. Goebbels failed to stop the Germans tuning in to the popular Radio Luxemburg; Vichy France failed to prevent its citizens listening to the BBC.

Conceiving this period in terms of a nascent mass consumer culture clearly does not apply to most of eastern and central Europe or to the Iberian peninsula, but curiously it does up to a point apply to the Soviet Union where after 1935 there was a retreat from the austere cultural values of the first five year plan. Consumerist values were praised by the regime. Macy's department store in New York was held up for praise and there was a campaign to promote and enhance department stores: they were encouraged to decorate with plants, put up white curtains, and have piped music. In 1936 the Soviet Union boasted that it outstripped France in production of perfume; an Institute of Cosmetics and Hygiene opened in Moscow in 1936. Lenin had once said that Socialism equaled 'Soviets plus electrification'; now it seemed to be Soviets plus chintz.

In the end, then, the first half of the twentieth century certainly demonstrated to a frightening degree the destructive power of the modern state as well as its potential capacity to improve people's lives, but also, more unexpectedly, and more reassuringly, it demonstrated the subversive potential of modernity, and, even in the most extreme circumstances, the extraordinary capacity of people for evading, resisting, and circumventing the best and worst intentions of those who strive to tell them how to live. If, then, one had to choose an emblematic twentieth-century figure perhaps it should not be Joseph K, but rather the 'good soldier Švejk', the creation of another Czech writer, Jaroslav Hašek. Švejk is a cunning simpleton who is drafted into the Austro-Hungarian army in 1914. It is never entirely clear if he is more simple than he is cunning, or more cunning than he is simple, but there is no doubting that all the best efforts of bureaucrats, judges, army officers, policemen, priests, and army chaplains are powerless to discipline and socialize him.

# 2

# International relations

## David Stevenson

International relations in the first half of the twentieth century were dominated by the two world wars. No other series of political events touched the lives of Europeans more deeply. Rather than recounting the detailed history of these conflicts, this chapter will focus on a series of crucial questions. Why did war break out in 1914? Why did it intensify and escalate, and end in victory for the Allies? Why did the post-1918 settlement disintegrate and a second war begin in 1939? And why did that war also escalate and end with a defeated Germany and a divided Europe? The period falls naturally into four sections: the years before 1914, the First World War and the 1919–20 peace settlement, the inter-war years, and the Second World War.

## The road to World War I, 1900–1914

The decisions of the Great Powers for war in 1914 reverberated for the rest of the century. They were taken by two opposing alignments: the Triple Alliance of Austria-Hungary, Germany, and Italy, dating from 1882, and the Triple Entente of Russia, France, and Britain, formed between 1891 and 1907. In the July 1914 crisis the Central Powers (Austria-Hungary and Germany) took the initiative, but both sides were willing to fight rather than give way.

The July crisis began as a confrontation between Austria-Hungary and Serbia, triggered by the assassination in Sarajevo on 28 June of

Franz Ferdinand, the heir to the Dual Monarchy's throne. The assassins came from Bosnia, which Austria-Hungary had administered since 1878. They wanted union with Serbia in a South Slav federation. Serbian military intelligence had supplied the conspirators with weapons and training in Belgrade and arranged for them to cross the border. Suspecting Serbian involvement, and exasperated by the support for Bosnian separatism from Serbian sympathizers, the Austrian leaders delivered an ultimatum on 23 July that was designed to be unacceptable. It demanded sweeping powers over Serbia's education, media, and courts. As Serbia's reply fell short of full compliance, on 28 July Vienna declared war.

The Austrian leaders believed that peaceful solutions to their Serbian problem were exhausted. After a hostile dynasty seized power in Belgrade in 1903 they had imposed an economic boycott, but Serbia had found alternative export markets. In 1908 they annexed Bosnia, but pan-Serb agitation there merely intensified. In the Balkan Wars of 1912–13 Serbia and its allies defeated and virtually expelled the Ottoman Turkish Empire from Europe before overwhelming Bulgaria, their former partner against Turkey. Serbia doubled in size, and by 1914 Austria-Hungary seemed about to lose Romania, its last Balkan ally. The Dual Monarchy's two dominant nationalities (the Austrian Germans and the Magyars) formed between them less than half its total population, and the authorities feared a Bosnian secession would break it up. But what really frightened them was less internal unrest than Serbian or Romanian aggression with Great-Power backing. Italy was nominally an Austrian ally, but 800,000 Italians lived under Austrian rule and the Vienna leaders regarded Rome as untrustworthy. Russia, the traditional patron of the South Slavs, had been defeated by Japan in 1904–5 and was therefore unable to retaliate against the 1908 Bosnian annexation. But since then its economy and military spending had recovered, and it was outmanoeuvring Austria-Hungary in the rivalry for Balkan influence. Confronting this gloomy outlook, the Austrian leaders concluded in 1913 that war with Serbia was inevitable. Even so, they would not have forced the issue without the 'blank cheque' delivered by the Germans to an Austrian envoy on 5–6 July 1914. The German Emperor, Wilhelm II, and his Chancellor, Theobald von Bethmann-Hollweg, urged Austria-Hungary to use force against Serbia, and promised full support if Russia intervened. This pledge was the precondition for European war.

Only very indirectly is it true that the German leaders risked war to stabilize their regime at home. However, it had been partly to consolidate domestic support that in 1897–8 Wilhelm had inaugurated his so-called *Weltpolitik* or 'world policy', which meant asserting Germany's interests against Britain, France, and Russia outside Europe as well as building up a North Sea battlefleet. The disastrous repercussions of this policy are essential to understanding events in 1914.

First, *Weltpolitik* had helped cause Germany's 'encirclement' by contributing to the formation of the Triple Entente. Russia and France had been allies since 1891–4 but both had extra-European quarrels with Britain. The 1904 agreement known as the 'entente cordiale', however, settled most of the issues between London and Paris, and in the Anglo-Russian entente of 1907 London and St Petersburg agreed on spheres of influence in Central Asia. Britain cooperated with its new partners in the 1908 Bosnian crisis. It did so again in the two Moroccan crises of 1905–6 and 1911 caused by unsuccessful German challenges to France's efforts to gain control over Morocco. When Bethmann-Hollweg tried to undermine the ententes by wooing the British into pledging to stay neutral in a European war in return for slower German naval building, he met with a refusal. Given Italy's unreliability the Germans were left with Austria-Hungary as their one substantial ally. In 1914 they feared that if they failed to back the Dual Monarchy it might either disintegrate or defect to the opposite camp.

Secondly, *Weltpolitik* had made Germany militarily more vulnerable. The German leaders had starved their army of resources and concentrated on the naval race against Britain. Once a land arms race developed between the Austro-German and Franco-Russian blocs, domestic resistance to yet higher taxes hamstrung them. In 1913 they passed the largest ever army bill in German history, but they knew they could not repeat the effort, and the Berlin General Staff believed that by 1917 France and Russia would possess an unchallengeable advantage. Hence, although at no point before July 1914 did the German leaders decide to launch a European war, they increasingly contemplated one as an option. When Austria-Hungary approached them after Sarajevo they urged their ally to attack Serbia, in the hope of propping up the Dual Monarchy and, if Britain and France restrained Russia, of splitting the Triple Entente. The Germans' only war plan (usually if misleadingly known as the Schlieffen Plan after the military planner chiefly responsible for it) envisaged crashing through Belgium to outflank France's border defences and defeat the French within weeks, before turning eastward to deal with the more slowly mobilizing Russians. Wilhelm and Bethmann-Hollweg knew this, which is why if Russia started military preparations, they were prepared to start a European war at once before they lost all chance of winning it.

Whether the Austro-Serb war started a general European conflict therefore depended largely on Tsarist Russia, which responded to Vienna's ultimatum to Serbia by ordering military precautions against Austria-Hungary and Germany on 26 July and mobilizing against both on the 31st. The Germans warned Russia to stop mobilizing and France to pledge neutrality in a Russo-German conflict, and when neither complied they declared war and activated the Schlieffen Plan. Tsar Nicholas II had been advised that war might unleash revolution in Russia, but his Foreign Minister, Sergei Sazonov, insisted that he would face a nationalist backlash if he abandoned Serbia. Sazonov realized that Germany supported Austria, and argued that if Berlin were determined on a showdown Russian weakness would only postpone it. Russia's rearmament remained incomplete but the French were optimistic about the military prospects and their ambassador affirmed that they would stand by the alliance. Nicholas II knew general mobilization was tantamount to war, but by the time he ordered it he believed that war was coming anyway and the imperative was to be ready.

Once the French received Germany's ultimatum, there was no doubt they would fight rather than repudiate a Russian alliance which they deemed essential to their independence. For the sake of national unity, however, they preferred to seem the victim of aggression and to wait until Germany declared war. Britain had more freedom of action. The German leaders did not want war with Britain but they were willing to accept it rather than back down after Russia mobilized, and the Schlieffen Plan provided the trigger. Britain and Germany were signatories to the 1839 Treaty of London guaranteeing Belgium against attack, and it was ostensibly because Germany invaded Belgium that Britain entered the war. In reality, although safeguarding the Channel coast was a traditional British preoccupation and the defence of treaties and small nations an opportune cause for rallying public opinion, the Cabinet did not believe that Britain was legally obligated. For the key figures in the government the issue was less Belgian neutrality than German aggression, after a decade of Anglo-German antagonism had convinced them that Britain had a vital interest in preventing French defeat.

This account of 1914 has focused on the ruling élites. Cheering crowds appeared in Europe's capital cities only after the decisions had been taken. However, it did matter, albeit negatively, that the socialists of the Second International generally rallied behind their governments. Most accepted that self-defence was legitimate, and self-defence was what the war appeared to be. Equally ineffectual was the Concert of Europe, the approximate pre-1914 precursor of the League of Nations and the UN. Its essence was a willingness by the Powers to meet in conferences at times of crisis, but when Britain proposed a conference Germany and Austria-Hungary blocked it. The Concert was dependent on a Great-Power consensus that had evaporated. All the same, the division of Europe into opposing blocs did not in itself cause war. Rather, the development of the land arms race since Russia's recovery from its defeat by Japan upset the balance between the blocs, the Triple Entente growing stronger while the Triple Alliance grew weaker. By 1914 the Russians and French felt less need to be conciliatory, while the German military advised that victory was still possible but not for much longer. Bismarck's wars had demonstrated that gambling with the use of force could solve political problems. Now Germany gambled again.

# World war and peace settlement, 1914–1920

Recent research has undermined the traditional view that the German military foresaw a speedy victory. None the less, most political leaders and ordinary citizens expected a short war. The ensuing conflict's impact was so devastating because these expectations proved unfounded. Governments failed to halt it even after it evolved into a slaughter without precedent, and of a character radically different from anticipated. We need to analyse the political and military stalemate that dominated the first three years of hostilities, before considering how after 1917 that stalemate was broken and the bloodshed came to an end.

The first reason for the stalemate was that the opening offensives failed. The French army was mobilized as quickly as Germany's and was almost as big, and in General Joseph Joffre it possessed a resilient commander. Even if the Germans had reached Paris the French would have had no reason to yield. Neither were the hastily executed French and Russian offensives of August 1914 likely to achieve a breakthrough. The reasons why the war in Western Europe became bogged down after 1914 were partly technological and logistic. Entrenched defenders with magazine rifles, machine guns, and quick-firing field guns could overwhelm attacking infantry. Armies that were much larger than in 1870 and supplied by a dense rail network could establish a continuous front, and despite the enormous casualties both sides could plug the gaps by sending in young men as they came of age and by rehabilitating the wounded. By late 1915 both could manufacture immense quantities of military equipment. By expanding the note issue and by borrowing at home and abroad both could finance the war. Germany's purchases from neutrals undermined the Allies' blockade, while American protests restrained U-boat attacks on Allied shipping. Although other fronts, in Poland and the Balkans, were more mobile than the Western one, until Russia collapsed in 1917 neither side knocked out an opposing Great Power.

A further precondition for stalemate was cohesion on the home front. The political truces formed in most belligerent countries when war broke out survived until 1917–18. Governments on both sides pleaded that the war was necessary and defensive, and must continue until aggression had been punished. They prolonged it by successive incremental decisions to fight on for the next few months, and public opinion shared their hope that victory would come quickly. The initial 'short-war illusion' did not die in 1914.

Furthermore, incompatibility between the two sides' political objectives, or 'war aims', thwarted negotiation. The German leaders wanted to set up buffer states under their military and economic domination in Belgium, Poland, and along the Baltic coast; to annex France's Briey-Longwy iron ore basin, Luxemburg, and a 'frontier strip' on their eastern border; and to establish a Central European customs union, an African colonial empire, and a worldwide chain of naval bases. As Chancellor, Bethmann-Hollweg was willing to compromise in the interests of a separate peace with one or other enemy, but after Paul von Hindenburg and Erich Ludendorff took over the

High Command in 1916 they opposed such concessions and in 1917 they ousted him. Conversely, by the Pact of London signed in September 1914 the Triple Entente became an alliance, its members committed to reject any separate peace and quickly formulating war aims of their own. Britain wanted to take Germany's colonies, destroy its navy, and liberate Belgium; France to regain the provinces of Alsace-Lorraine (lost to Germany in 1871) and set up Rhineland buffer States; Russia to bring all Polish-inhabited territory into a satellite kingdom under its control. After the Ottoman Turkish Empire entered on Germany's side in November 1914 the Allies agreed to partition between them its Near Eastern possessions (now Syria, the Lebanon, Israel, Jordan, and Iraq). In return for Italy joining the Allies in May 1915, they promised it gains from Austria-Hungary in the Alps and Dalmatia. The Germans tried to divide their enemies in 1915 by driving Russia out of Poland and in 1916 by 'bleeding white' the French army (in the words of their commander) at the battle of Verdun. In 1917 they launched a campaign of 'unrestricted' submarine warfare (i.e. sinking merchant shipping without warning) that they hoped would starve out Britain. Not only did it fail to do so, but it prompted intervention by the American President, Woodrow Wilson, who had decided that victory over Germany would provide him with the influence that he needed to impose on both sides his projects for a new international order based on the principles of collective security and self-determination.

In contrast to the pattern in 1914–17 of escalating violence, in 1917–18 the war was terminated, first in the east and then the west. Following the March 1917 uprising that ousted Tsar Nicholas II, the refusal of the short-lived Russian Provisional Government to make a separate peace did much to seal its destruction. After the Bolsheviks overthrew it in November their first acts included signing an armistice, before they submitted to dictated German and Austrian peace terms in the March 1918 Treaty of Brest-Litovsk. They ceded Poland, the Baltic coast, and the Ukraine. The collapse of discipline in the Russian army had made resistance impossible, and Lenin's priority was to save his regime. Yet within weeks of signing the treaty (and in part because of doing so) he faced civil war against his 'White' (i.e. anti-Bolshevik) opponents as well as Allied landings at Archangel and Vladivostok aimed at reconstituting an anti-German front.

In contrast, although in 1917 the French army mutinied and Italian soldiers surrendered en masse at the battle of Caporetto, the Western Allies escaped a Russian-style collapse. The British and French leaders reckoned on winning with American aid, and rejected enemy peace feelers. Despite growing internal unrest, the Central Powers also persevered, Hindenburg and Ludendorff seeing Russia's defeat as enabling an all-out assault in France. Whereas the Russian revolution ended the war in the east, in the west the decisive factor was Germany's military defeat. Its five great Western Front offensives from March to July 1918 cost one million casualties, and failed to achieve their objectives. By the autumn massive American troop shipments had restored the Allies' numerical superiority, and their armies were moving cautiously but relentlessly forward. Germany's war economy was seizing up and its cities near to starving. Its partners were exhausted, Austria-Hungary breaking up at the end of October into new states based on its component nationalities. In these circumstances Ludendorff decided to request a peace based on the relatively lenient American principles set out in Woodrow Wilson's Fourteen Points address of January 1918. To an extent this final attempt by Germany to split its enemies succeeded. Wilson pressed his partners into accepting an armistice agreement based on his programme, which included the creation of a League of Nations as well as restrictions on Allied territorial expansion. But the ceasefire's military clauses allowed Britain to control Germany's colonies and navy and France to occupy the Rhineland, while the November 1918 revolution that replaced Wilhelm II by a republic reduced Germany to helplessness. Both America and its allies made significant interim gains, and they postponed the reckoning between them to the peace conference.

The peace conference met in Paris in 1919–20 and set much of the agenda for inter-war European diplomacy. The lesser treaties can be dealt with quickly. The Treaty of Sèvres imposed by the Allies on Turkey proved impossible to implement and was superseded by the Treaty of Lausanne, negotiated with the triumphant new regime of Kemal Ataturk in 1923. The treaties with Austria, Hungary, and Bulgaria were important mainly for delineating the new South-Eastern European frontiers: the Allies could not have reinstated the Dual Monarchy even had they wanted to. A post-war alliance system known as the Little Entente, concluded in 1920–1, linked the new states of Czechoslovakia and Yugoslavia with a much-expanded Romania, and successfully kept Hungarian revisionism at bay. The settlement in the Balkans, surprisingly, proved longer lasting than in the West.

Yet initially the Allies seemed firm enough. Hoping to be treated as equal partners, the new democratic leaders in Germany placed their trust in America, rejecting co-operation with Moscow. But the Allies found agreement amongst themselves so difficult that they dared not risk negotiations round a table with their enemies and the June 1919 Versailles Treaty was essentially a *Diktat* or dictated peace. The only major concession to German representations was a plebiscite that partitioned the disputed province of Upper Silesia rather than assigning it to Poland. Russia was likewise sidelined, the Bolsheviks being excluded from the Paris conference. After half-hearted attempts to negotiate a ceasefire the Allies extended partial recognition and military assistance to the Whites, only to disengage when the Russian Civil War turned in Lenin's favour. Finland, Poland, and the Baltic States consolidated their independence, leaving the newly emergent Soviet Union with much reason for territorial dissatisfaction, quite apart from its ideological hostility to capitalism.

Amongst the victor states, Japan took Germany's Chinese and North Pacific territories but had negligible influence in Europe. Italy gained a frontier on the Brenner Pass and annexed the Adriatic port of Fiume, though in the latter case only after a long and bitter struggle against American-backed resistance from Yugoslavia. Even so, Italy gained much less from the Yugoslavs than it had been promised against Austria-Hungary and the resulting disappointment with the so-called 'mutilated victory' contributed to the rise of Fascism. But Rome had little influence on the German settlement.

America, Britain, and France, represented respectively by President Wilson and Premiers David Lloyd George and Georges Clemenceau, were the key players. Wilson's programme had supposedly been accepted at the armistice and his partners were financially dependent on him. But he was a poor negotiator with vague ideas: even the League of Nations project owed much of its detail to Britain. In economic matters America exerted an important negative influence by insisting on dismantling the wartime controls over commerce and refusing to cancel Allied war debts. This encouraged the Allies to press for reparations from Germany, although they would have done so anyway. The Americans, who had suffered little damage, wanted quick agreement on a modest reparation lump sum that would pave the way for a European reconstruction financed by private American loans. But in fact the Versailles Treaty made Germany liable not only for damage to property but also for war pensions. An inter-Allied Reparation Commission was given until 1921 to fix Germany's reparation debt, which would be discharged by annual payments that could go on for decades. Moreover, the notorious Article 231, or 'war-guilt clause', asserted the Central Powers' liability in principle for the entire loss and damage inflicted by their aggression, an indictment that proved fiercely controversial for years ahead.

Over reparations Britain and France co-operated against America. Over territory and security, France took the lead, Lloyd George and Wilson only rarely combining against Clemenceau. All three agreed that France should regain Alsace-Lorraine, but Wilson resisted Clemenceau's claim to annex the Saar coalfield, which was placed under French administration (and League of Nations supervision) pending a plebiscite after fifteen years. The Germans of the new state of Austria, however, whose parliament had voted to unite with Germany, were forbidden to do so, and the Germans of the Sudetenland were incorporated into Czechoslovakia. As neither of these groups had belonged to Germany before 1914 their fate caused less resentment there than did the territorial 'corridor' created as a Polish outlet to the Baltic, which separated East Prussia from the rest of Germany. In fact much of the corridor was ethnically Polish, and on Lloyd George's initiative it was narrowed by plebiscites, while the port of Danzig at its mouth was not assigned to Poland but made a free city under the League. Moreover, the Fourteen Points had pledged an independent Poland with secure sea access. In general, as regarded the territorial settlement, Germany had few justified grounds for grievance.

The conference underlined the contrast between Clemenceau's premise that Germany could not change and must be weakened: and Lloyd George and Wilson's greater leniency. Yet Lloyd George was not prepared to sacrifice Britain's colonial and naval claims, and in Wilson's thinking Germany should undergo several years of punishment before it could be rehabilitated. In consequence, the Allies invited the charge of following their principles except when doing so would favour Berlin. Versailles was indeed a discriminatory treaty, but to an extent it had to be, given that a fully sovereign Germany would inevitably be stronger than its neighbours. The Allies and Americans were agreed on limiting Germany's army to 100,000 men, confiscating most of its navy, denying it an air force, and creating a disarmament monitoring agency, the Inter-Allied Military Control Commission (IMCC). Clemenceau also wanted a permanent occupation of the Rhineland and French-dominated buffer states there. In return for an Anglo-American offer to guarantee France against aggression, he settled for demilitarization of the Rhineland and an occupation of at least fifteen years' duration. There was still enough here to ensure that Germany could not start another war. On the other hand, the occupation could end earlier and reparations be reconsidered if a democratic Germany convinced its neighbours of its good faith. The Versailles treaty was more flexible than is often acknowledged, and could be used both to keep Germany harmless and as a framework for reconciliation. Much would depend on how it was implemented.

## From war to war, 1920–1939

International politics in the 1920s was overshadowed by the legacies of World War I. In the early post-war years successor conflicts proliferated, the Soviet-Polish war of 1919–21 and the Greco-Turkish war of 1919–22 being prominent among them. The same years saw a Franco-German cold war, whose central issue was the enforcement of the peace settlement. Reparations were the crucial flashpoint. In 1921 the Allies approved the London Schedule of Payments, setting the defeated countries' total liability at 132,000 million gold (i.e. pre-1914) marks, and timetabling cash annuities. The latter would comprise interest and amortization on 50,000 million gold marks of bonds—it being left to the Allies to decide when the remaining 82,000 million would be issued, if at all. The London Schedule annuities would amount to some 7% of Germany's annual national income. Although a large figure, this was not absolutely impossible to pay. But the Germans had no intention of doing so. Their Foreign Ministry orchestrated a propaganda campaign to undermine Article 231 by denying their sole responsibility for the war, and they claimed the Schedule was impossible to implement. By withholding reparations they placed the Allies in a quandary, for no aspect of Versailles divided the victors more.

In attempting to implement the Schedule, France found itself isolated. In 1919–20 Wilson had failed to win ratification of the Versailles Treaty by the American Senate, which objected to the open-ended commitments in the League Covenant. The USA stayed out of the League and the Reparation Commission, and the Anglo-American offer to guarantee France against German aggression fell through. Yet the Republican administration that took over in 1921 was more committed than Wilson to Allied repayment of war debts. The British refused to write off their own war loans to France unless America did likewise, and once the British economy crashed into slump in 1921 Lloyd George's priority was to revive exports to Germany rather than to exact reparations. Benito Mussolini, who headed the Italian Government from 1922 and assumed dictatorial powers in 1925, did not hide his dissatisfaction with the peace treaties and his antagonism towards France. As for the Soviets, they sought to keep the capitalist world divided by co-operating with Germany. German troops practised illegal military manoeuvres on Soviet territory, and under the Rapallo Treaty of 1922 Moscow and Berlin waived financial claims upon each other. Subversion by the Communist International, or Comintern, and the western Communist parties further inhibited good relations with London and Paris. Although France signed security pacts with Belgium in 1920, with Poland in 1921, and with the three Little Entente countries of Czechoslovakia, Romania, and Yugoslavia in 1924–7, these partnerships were a poor substitute for a Great-Power alliance and might become liabilities if Germany revived. The French feared letting Germany recover until their security was safeguarded, and they were in desperate financial straits.

The Germans made only one payment under the London Schedule before appealing for a moratorium. In January 1923 the Reparation Commission ruled that they were in default and a French government under Raymond Poincaré sent in troops to occupy the Ruhr coalfield. Belgium assisted them but Britain remained on the sidelines. In protest, the Ruhr workers went on strike for eight months, supported by the German Government. The cost of subsidizing this policy of 'passive resistance', coming as the last straw after near continuous monetary instability since 1918, drove Germany into hyper-inflation. In September 1923 a new German ministry headed by

Gustav Stresemann called the resistance off. But from this point on France lost the initiative. The Germans introduced a new and stable currency while the French backed abortive separatist uprisings in the Rhineland. Rejecting a German offer of bilateral negotiations, Poincaré agreed to an American proposal for an inquiry by a committee of financial experts, chaired by the Chicago banker Charles Dawes. By the time the committee reported, there had been a run on the franc and Poincaré had been replaced by the inexperienced Edouard Herriot, with the result that when the Dawes Plan was adopted in 1924 the French were outmanoeuvred.

Under the Dawes Plan an international loan to Germany (mostly coming from American private investors) enabled it to resume paying reparations, though at a much lower rate. The French evacuated the Ruhr and lost the power to declare Germany in default again. Their powers to enforce Versailles unilaterally were further weakened by the Locarno treaties of 1925, under which France, Germany, and Belgium agreed to respect their common frontiers and Britain and Italy placed the frontiers under guarantee. Germany's eastern borders were not similarly protected, and as Britain was simultaneously guaranteeing France against Germany and Germany against France, Locarno was far from the Great-Power alliance that Paris craved. None the less, the Dawes Plan and the Locarno treaties temporarily eased France's financial and security dilemmas, and the late 1920s were years of economic recovery, diminishing political extremism, and subsiding international tension. Germany entered the League of Nations in 1926, and the former wartime Allies negotiated with Berlin as an equal partner. Movements in support of collective security and of European union gained strength, and governments gestured towards them. By the terms of the Kellogg–Briand Pact of 1928, most states pledged to renounce aggressive war. The Briand Plan of 1930 was a proposal by the French Foreign Minister for a European confederation and common market, although it foundered on German and British objections.

This optimism had fragile foundations. The German army was already planning for war, and Stresemann, who served as Foreign Minister until 1929, pursued detente with the West essentially as a stratagem. More dismantling of Versailles followed Locarno. In 1926 the IMCC was withdrawn, and in 1930, in exchange for a new and supposedly definitive reparations schedule, the Young Plan, the last

Allied forces left the Rhineland five years earlier than scheduled. The revival after 1924 of Anglo-American diplomatic involvement in Europe was no substitute for Versailles as a basis for French security. The British guarantee given at Locarno was followed neither by British rearmament nor by military contingency planning. America remained politically uncommitted, and although in 1924–8 American investors placed twice as much in Germany as Germany was paying out in reparations, after the Wall Street crash in 1929 American loans were recalled, intensifying Germany's descent into economic depression and helping plunge the banks of Central Europe into insolvency. After Locarno the victor Powers staked European stability on the survival of the German moderates, but well before Adolf Hitler came to power in 1933 their survival seemed improbable. As soon as French troops left the Rhineland, German diplomacy became more assertive. The year 1931 witnessed higher German military spending, an initiative from Berlin for a customs union with Austria (which French financial pressure on Vienna killed off), and a new German request for a reparation moratorium. A one-year standstill on reparation and war debt payments initiated by the American President, Herbert Hoover, was followed in 1932 by the Lausanne conference, at which reparations were effectively abandoned. Yet the very substantial concessions that the Allies made to the Weimar Republic between 1919 and 1933 failed to save it, and it is doubtful whether more such concessions would have kept German democracy alive. In the process the Allies had dismantled most of the machinery created in 1919 to prevent Germany from reopening hostilities, and the consequences of their actions soon became grave.

After 1933 three circumstances led Europe to renewed disaster: Nazi Germany's drive towards war; the 'appeasement' by the other Powers that enabled it to grow strong enough to launch one; and the eventual retreat from appeasement that led to Britain and France guaranteeing Poland in 1939 and declaring war when Hitler invaded it.

Hitler wanted war. He regarded it as inevitable and desirable, the engine of racial regeneration. This does not mean, however, that he planned or desired the war with the West that began in 1939. Since the early 1920s he had looked rather to an assault on the Soviet Union that would eradicate Bolshevism and endow the German people with economic self-sufficiency and territory for settlement. As a man whose profoundest life experience was his 1914–18 military service,

Hitler was driven into politics by Germany's defeat. The foreign policy programme outlined in his *Mein Kampf*, written in 1924–5, was to rebuild Germany's international position by force, while avoiding the mistakes of the last war. By winning over Britain and Italy against France he hoped to break out of the Versailles constraints, prior to conquering eastern 'living space'. As Chancellor after 1933 he declared his aims were peaceful and limited, but privately he reiterated the goal of eastward expansion, and within months of gaining office he embarked on secret and massive rearmament. All the same, in his early years he was less fully in control of policy and less overbearingly confident in his judgement than he became later. He was aware of Germany's vulnerability and feared a Franco-Polish preventive attack. In 1934, when Mussolini moved up troops to the Brenner Pass following an attempted Nazi coup in Austria, Hitler backed off. At least until he remilitarized the Rhineland in 1936 he was capable of being deterred from acts of aggression. The 1918 victors briefly enjoyed a third option between appeasement and fighting another major war. But if pre-emptive action would have been a difficult choice, after 1936 only worse ones remained. There are times, as Machiavelli warned his Prince, when inaction is the riskiest course of all.

The years from 1933 to 1938 witnessed a series of German unilateral actions that met with passivity from the former Allies, not to say encouragement. In 1933 Germany walked out of the League of Nations and the Geneva disarmament conference; in 1935, after regaining the Saar in the promised plebiscite, Hitler announced he was re-introducing conscription and had established an air force; in 1936 he reoccupied the Rhineland and sent combat forces to aid Francisco Franco and the Nationalists in the Spanish Civil War; and in 1938 he annexed Austria in March, and annexed the Sudetenland from Czechoslovakia after obtaining British, French, and Italian acquiescence at the Munich conference in September. Not only did he rearm Germany and win more defensible borders, but also he enticed Japan, Italy, and eventually Soviet Russia into a revisionist front against the post-1918 status quo. The anti-German coalition of World War I appeared smashed beyond remedy, and the new pattern of alignments was far less favourable to the West. To understand the sources of appeasement within Europe, however, it is necessary first to look outside.

The 1929–33 depression weakened the pro-Western forces in Tokyo and strengthened those who desired a Japanese-dominated bloc in East Asia. During the Manchurian crisis of 1931–3 the Japanese established a puppet state in Manchuria and left the League of Nations after it censured them, while the Western Powers confined themselves to diplomatic protest. It is doubtful whether the Manchurian example directly inspired later aggression in Europe, although Japan's withdrawal from the League may have encouraged Hitler's seven months later. But both in the Rhineland crisis of 1936 and the Sudetenland crisis of 1938 the British Chiefs of Staff warned their government that war with Germany would probably mean war with Italy and Japan, and in such a war Britain would lose. Even before the Japanese concluded the Anti-Comintern Pact with Hitler in 1936 they had undermined the prospect of resistance to him.

So had the USA, by passing three Neutrality Acts in 1935–7. The third, and most wide-ranging, provided that in the event of a war or civil war affecting American security the President must ban loans and arms sales to belligerents and travel by Americans on belligerent ships. He could subject trade in other goods to a 'cash and carry' requirement: i.e. they must be paid for on receipt and transported in the belligerents' own ships. Although this latter provision would benefit Britain over Germany, the legislation was intended to prevent America from being drawn into a Second World War as it had been into the First. It reflected a militantly pacifist and isolationist mood in Congress, which President Franklin Roosevelt, who needed approval for his New Deal programme and was sympathetic to the Neutrality Acts in so far as they left him with a free hand, did not resist. Hitler saw America as a long-term enemy but believed it had been enfeebled by the Depression and took little account of it. But the British were in a dilemma, as unaided they could neither win a short war against Germany nor pay for a long one, and the possibility of another long war supported by America seemed now ruled out. This reinforced the arguments against risking war at all.

Within Europe, the decision whether or not to act against Hitler rested in the first instance with the French, but their post-1918 alliance system was in advanced decay. Hitler dealt a heavy blow to it in 1934 when he signed a non-aggression pact with Poland, thus neutralizing the danger of Franco-Polish preventive action against him. The depression lessened France's ability to help its partners economically, and the remilitarization of the Rhineland made it almost impossible to do so militarily. In 1936–7, moreover, partly because of internal pressure from its Flemish population for a more neutral and less Francophile alignment, Belgium withdraw from its 1920 military convention, leaving France exposed to another German invasion from the north. Yet new possibilities of co-operation with Soviet Russia and Fascist Italy potentially offset these developments. Temporarily both seemed willing to join with France and Britain in containing German aggression, but by 1939 both had entered the revisionist camp.

This outcome was probably avoidable. After Hitler came to office the Soviet Union experimented with the policy of 'collective security' advocated by Stalin's Commissar for Foreign Affairs, Maxim Litvinov. It joined the League in 1934 and signed security pacts with France and Czechoslovakia, with the declared objective of deterring aggression. The Comintern endorsed the 'Popular Front' policy of co-operation between communist and non-communist parties against fascism. It is true that the precondition for this change of tack was Hitler's breach with the Soviet–German friendship that had been inaugurated at Rapallo. Stalin continued extending feelers to Berlin, and he may have tolerated Litvinov's initiatives only because Germany's attitude left him with little alternative. But Britain and France's acquiescence in Italian and German expansion, and their failure to join with Stalin in aiding the Republicans in the Spanish Civil War, cast doubt on the value of their partnership even before they settled the Sudetenland crisis in a four-way conference with Hitler and Mussolini to which Stalin, despite his pacts with Paris and Prague, was not even invited.

As for Mussolini, he like Hitler had a foreign policy vision extending back to the early 1920s, centred on Italian domination of the Mediterranean. He still wanted to contain Germany, as was shown by his resistance to Nazi control of Austria and his joining Britain and France in April 1935 in the so-called 'Stresa Front' to condemn German rearmament. But hints that London and Paris were willing to award him portions of Abyssinia may have encouraged him to invade that country in September 1935 on the assumption that he could both absorb it and maintain the Stresa Front. Unfortunately for this calculation the vigour of British public reaction against aggression drove Britain and France into a two-faced policy of secretly offering to partition Abyssinia while publicly promoting economic sanctions by the League of Nations against Italy. Mussolini conquered Abyssinia regardless, and the crisis both stripped the League of its remaining credibility and drove Rome into Berlin's arms. Early in 1936 Mussolini told Hitler that he would no longer honour his Locarno obligation to keep the Rhineland demilitarized and that he was willing to scale down his support for Austria. Even so he might still have rebuilt his bridges with London had it not been for the outbreak of the Spanish Civil War in July 1936 and nearly three years of Italian and German assistance to the Nationalist rebels, in opposition to Anglo-French efforts to maintain a facade of non-intervention. After aligning his foreign policy with Germany's in the Rome–Berlin Axis of November 1936, Mussolini did nothing to save Austria in 1938 and he signed an alliance, the Pact of Steel, with Germany in May 1939. While privately still wary of Hitler, the Italian leader had decided to protect his interests through expansion in parallel with Germany rather than through containment in association with an ineffectual West.

France's response to Hitler's takeover was therefore to seek deterrent alliances rather than intervene pre-emptively. The Rhineland crisis of 1936 spotlighted the reasons for this passivity. After sterling and the dollar were devalued in 1931–3 the franc was left exposed and military action would have caused an even bigger run on the currency than in 1924. The French economy recovered more slowly from the depression than did Germany's, and French public finances were in persistent deficit. At the time of Hitler's Rhineland reoccupation in March 1936 the French Government could pay its bills only with the aid of a recent British Treasury loan. The defence budget had been capped—and such funds as were available went on the frontier fortifications of the Maginot Line rather than on aircraft and tanks—while Germany forged ahead regardless. The economic crisis had intensified domestic conflict, benefiting both the communists and the paramilitary Right, and when Hitler struck France had a caretaker government, weeks away from crucial elections. The French army leaders could recommend only full mobilization, as they had no contingency plans for a standing-start attack, and they overestimated—perhaps wilfully—German strength. They advised that Hitler was already capable of stalling a French attack. War against him would be a long and costly undertaking, in which France must have Britain on its side. As London would risk no effective retaliation against the Rhineland reoccupation, nor would Paris. Since the 1923 Ruhr crisis,

French leaders had learned well the perils of unilateral action. The Locarno agreements were vague enough to allow Britain to evade any commitment to military retaliation, but France had little stomach for it anyway. And after March 1936, now that Hitler could fortify his western border, in future crises France would be even less capable of independent action. Both in abandoning the Spanish Republic in 1936 and the Czechs in 1938, Paris felt obliged to follow London's lead.

In London the arguments for appeasement were no less powerful, and British appeasement meant not simply acquiescence in Hitler's faits accomplis but an active search for agreement, often at third parties' expense. In June 1935 Britain broke with the Stresa Front by concluding a naval agreement with Hitler. Instead of resisting the Rhineland reoccupation in 1936 it engaged in fruitless negotiations for an air pact. After Neville Chamberlain became Prime Minister in 1937 he held out commercial and colonial concessions as well as territorial gains on Germany's eastern borders. This persistent quest for settlement was not simply due to British public opinion, although in the early 1930s the latter took a sharply isolationist turn. By the time of Munich in 1938, in contrast, opinion polls disclosed much scepticism about Chamberlain's policy. Ministers shared the public's abhorrence of war and its Francophobia, but they went much further than public opinion forced them to, using their influence over the press and the BBC to deny anti-appeasement voices a hearing. Nor do economic and strategic considerations suffice to explain appeasement, compelling though they were. Britain's 1920s defence cuts and its worldwide commitments had left it overextended against the 'Triple Threat' of Germany, Japan, and Italy. In the Treasury view, Britain dared not risk exhausting its foreign exchange reserves by premature rearmament. But even if it did rearm, it had no answer to the German bombers that were expected to pound London if war came. Chamberlain therefore had excellent reasons to avoid an unnecessary conflict: but he was also a man with a mission, who cannot be exonerated from the charges of naivety and excessive trust in the Führer. At Munich he railroaded the French and Czechs into a surrender that weakened the West strategically, failed to satisfy Hitler, and alienated Stalin.

If the case for appeasement was so overwhelming, why did Britain and France eventually abandon it in favour of a strategy of containing and deterring Germany, yet without the one factor—a Soviet alliance—that might have made such a strategy effective? On 15 March 1939 Hitler tore up the Munich agreement by occupying Prague and the rest of Czechoslovakia, and two weeks later Britain and France guaranteed Poland's independence. Encouraged by a non-aggression pact signed with Stalin on 23 August, Hitler none the less attacked Poland on 1 September, and two days later Britain and France declared war. We need to consider the German, Western, and Soviet sides in turn.

Hitler did not know when to stop. That he failed to settle for his winnings after Munich was less because of the needs of the German economy (which had suffered greater pressure from rearmament in 1935–6 than it did in 1938–9) than because of the compulsions of his own personality. A restless hypochondriac, who sensed time was against him, he felt that Munich had cheated him out of a war. At the 'Hossbach' conference (named after the officer who took the minutes) in November 1937 he had told his military chiefs that he aimed to 'clear the flank' by overthrowing Austria and Czechoslovakia before dealing with Britain and France, prior to a war for living space in the mid-1940s. After Munich he began negotiating with Poland, not just over Danzig and the corridor but also with a view to aligning Berlin's and Warsaw's foreign policies. When the Poles rejected his terms he decided to use force before the autumn rains. If Austria-Hungary's attack on Serbia triggered the First World War, Germany's on Poland triggered the Second.

Unlike in 1914, however, Britain and France's guarantee of Poland made—or should have made—it unequivocally clear that this war could not be localized. The two Western governments had begun reacting against appeasement almost as soon as Munich was signed, encouraged by a hardening of their public opinion and by a rumour in the winter that the Low Countries might be Germany's next target. The key development, however, was Hitler's occupation of Prague, which had no justification on grounds of self-determination or legitimate treaty revision, and implied that his ambitions had no limit. By now British and French rearmament was coming on stream and radar and monoplane fighters were beginning to offer a credible defence of London, but Hitler's own actions were the main reason why Western policy shifted. As the fall of Prague was followed within days by reports that Germany was threatening Poland and might take over Romania's oil, Britain and France felt that they must act at once and they issued guarantees against aggression to both Warsaw and Bucharest. They aimed, should war break out, to keep an eastern front in being and maintain Germany's vulnerability to blockade, but their preference was to deter Germany from further expansion until circumstances again favoured negotiation. Hitler, however, had little respect for British and French willpower, and the only development that might have made him hesitate was an Anglo-Franco-Soviet alliance. The Nazi–Soviet Pact ruled this possibility out.

By 1939 cumulative disappointments administered by the West had undermined Litvinov, whom Stalin replaced by Vyacheslav Molotov in May, and Munich strengthened Moscow's suspicions that Britain and France intended, as Stalin put it, that the Soviet Union should pull their chestnuts out of the fire for them. But the key difference now was that Hitler wanted a deal. A pact with Stalin would allow him to attack Poland in the hope he could deter Western intervention, and in the knowledge that if deterrence failed he could circumvent a Western blockade. He was willing to promise all the territory Stalin wanted, a secret protocol to the Pact providing that in the event of a 'territorial and political rearrangement' eastern Poland, Finland, the Baltic States, and Bessarabia (in Romania) would fall within the Soviet sphere of influence. Britain and France, conversely, who were negotiating with Moscow simultaneously, hesitated to endorse Soviet intervention in the Baltic States or agree to Soviet forces traversing Romanian and Polish territory. They had no plans for joint military action: and, given the purges of the Red Army since 1937, they doubted Stalin's value as an ally. Hence the Pact was signed, Stalin probably expecting Germany and the West to grind each other down as in 1914–18 while he rearmed in safety.

As in 1914 a local war escalated because the British and French governments believed that further German expansion would destroy the balance of power, and that if they stood by their turn would come next. The Germans again believed they had a temporary advantage in the arms race, while Britain and France were better prepared than previously and could not afford to retain high readiness for long. Hitler probably intended to attack westwards in any case, perhaps as early as 1940, and his forces were prepared for short, sharp localized conflicts while he kept his enemies divided. Conversely, the democracies hoped blockade and bombing would bring them a relatively painless victory. Once they had convinced themselves they must accept the risk of war, they became more confident that they could win it.

# The Second World War and after, 1939–1945

To begin with, the Second World War in Europe appeared a continuation of the First. Whereas in 1914–18 Germany was victorious in the east and narrowly defeated in the west, however, in 1939–45 it was first victorious in the west and then defeated largely by the Soviet Union in the east, although Anglo-American strategic bombing and the campaign in North-West Europe in 1944–5 ensured that this time Germany was comprehensively overwhelmed.

The first spectacular difference in the unfolding of the two conflicts came with France's collapse. The French expected a German onslaught, and their first priority was to halt it. Unlike in 1914 they planned not to engage in futile offensives, and they intended to shield French territory with the Maginot Line. When Germany attacked through the Low Countries in May 1940 the French and British were not much inferior in divisions and the French had more tanks than the Germans, of at least comparable quality, although the Allies were much weaker in the air. After sending many of their best units northwards the French were surprised when the Germans pierced their defences at Sedan. Faced with a much faster pace of warfare than they had expected, they failed to plug the gap until the British and many of their own forces had been cut off or evacuated. If technical, military reasons can account for the French defeat, however, the decision to seek an armistice and to vote full powers to Marshal Philippe Pétain rather than to continue the struggle from abroad resulted from deeper-rooted political and psychological factors. They included the terrible cost of victory in 1914–18, the lack of allies on the Continent, distrust of the British, and fear of revolution at home. Much of the country greeted the armistice with relief. In London, in contrast, the incoming Churchill Government resolved (to Hitler's exasperation) to reject Germany's overtures and carry on, at least to explore whether it could improve its bargaining position. The combination of French defeat with

British resistance set in motion processes that in 1940–1 globalized the war.

In this phase of globalization, three developments stood out. The first was Italy's war entry in June 1940. Mussolini felt unprepared for hostilities in September 1939, and chary of an enterprise over which he had been perfunctorily consulted. In 1940 he declared war only after the French were clearly beaten, and did not attack until they had sued for a ceasefire. He acted neither out of ideological solidarity nor personal regard for Hitler, but as part of his programme of keeping pace with Germany by parallel expansion. As in 1915, in fact, Italy supposed the end of the conflict to be much closer than it really was, and this time it did not even join the winning side. Italian offensives against Greece and Egypt in the autumn failed dismally, and Mussolini could keep fighting only by accepting precisely the dependence on Germany that he had hoped to avoid. None the less, his intervention drew first Britain and then America into a Mediterranean campaign that dominated their strategy until 1944.

Secondly, the fall of France was the precondition for Hitler's invasion of the USSR in June 1941. Operation 'Barbarossa' marked the culmination of ambitions he had nurtured for two decades. Yet *Mein Kampf* had warned of the folly of war on two fronts and Hitler first broached the invasion of Russia with his generals in summer 1940 as a means of forcing Britain to sue for peace. It is doubtful whether he took this argument seriously, or whether his heart really lay in the war in the west: thus he neglected less roundabout means of pressure on Britain, such as stepping up U-boat production or sending more forces against Egypt. More relevant to Hitler's decision was that after the fall of France (which probably gravely upset Stalin's calculations) the Soviet Union accelerated rearmament, and rivalry between Berlin and Moscow spread across Europe. The Soviets had taken eastern Poland, the Baltic States, Bessarabia, and territory from Finland in 1939–40; but they also took the Bukovina (not promised to them by the Nazi–Soviet Pact), which brought them dangerously close to the Ploesti oil fields in Romania. Both these and the Petsamo nickel mines of Finland were vital for Germany's war effort. In the course of 1940 German troops moved into Romania and Finland, and Bulgaria became a German ally. In December, after an unsuccessful effort to renegotiate the two sides' spheres of influence when Molotov visited Berlin, Hitler ordered a 1941 invasion. Yet diplomatic friction with Moscow was probably less crucial in this decision than were Hitler's ideological hostility to the Soviets, his and his generals' overconfidence, and their perception that the fall of France provided an opportunity that might not last. They would be assaulting an adversary that substantially outnumbered them in tanks and aircraft as well as men. They anticipated victory in a battle of envelopment on the frontier although Russia had far more space for manoeuvre than did France. They expected to advance so quickly that they would capture intact the wheat and oil with which Stalin had been so generously supplying them; and they made no provision for a winter campaign.

The third consequence of the Fall of France was an Atlantic alliance between America and Britain. America's 1937 Neutrality Act took effect when war broke out, and (apart from relaxing it to allow arms sales and loans) Washington at first did little to help the Allies. But the Act had been passed in the expectation that Britain and France could prevent Germany from menacing the Western Hemisphere, and France's collapse caused a radical reappraisal. Roosevelt moved to strengthen the Western Hemisphere defences and to keep Britain fighting as in effect an American proxy. In September 1940 he sold London fifty over-age destroyers in return for rights to construct bases on British territory in Canada and the Caribbean; in March 1941 the Lend-Lease Act authorized him to supply up to $7,000 million of goods to a Britain that was nearing bankruptcy; and soon American warships were authorized to escort British convoys and American merchantmen to travel direct to British ports. The Neutrality Act lay in tatters, and at the Atlantic conference in August 1941 Roosevelt and Churchill issued a joint declaration of principles on the post-war settlement. From a low-profile, unprovocative stance the United States had shifted to a position of prominence.

None of this meant that Roosevelt had already decided or wanted to intervene. On the contrary, Lend-Lease for Britain (and for Russia too, after August 1941) was an alternative to an American declaration of war that neither Congress nor the public would yet support. Given that Hitler, with uncharacteristic restraint, hesitated to respond, American intervention was eventually precipitated only by a further consequence of the fall of France: a power vacuum in South-East Asia. With France and the Netherlands prostrate and Britain with its back to the wall, a swathe of resource-rich European colonies lay vulnerable, and the Tokyo leaders decided on a 'southward advance' into the region. The Italo-German-Japanese Tripartite Pact of September 1940, although intended to cover this expansion by deterring the Americans, in fact confirmed suspicions in Washington that the West faced co-ordinated Axis aggression. Both to safeguard British access to the raw materials of Malaya and to relieve the Soviet Union from pressure on two fronts, Roosevelt tightened the screws on Tokyo. The process culminated in a July 1941 trade embargo that threatened Japan with exhaustion of its oil stocks and led to its onslaught in December against Malaya and the oil-bearing Dutch East Indies as well as the American fleet at Pearl Harbor. Hitler, who now believed that war with America was coming anyway, and wanted Japanese goodwill, overruled his advisers and declared war on Washington.

With American entry the globalization of the conflict was completed, and the anti-German coalition of 1917–18 reborn. Instead of re-enacting the deadlock of the previous struggle, however, the Second World War resembled more a flow and ebb: an Axis outsurge followed by a long retreat. In many ways this conflict was more total than its predecessor. Whereas trench warfare, for all its horrors, had concentrated the fighting in a narrow killing zone, in 1939–45 much wider swathes of Europe were occupied and devastated. Civilians were far more likely to suffer bombing from the air, and to take part in Resistance movements and partisan warfare. Characteristic of the conflict in much of the Continent were punishment expeditions into hapless villages. This was also an ideological war, in which the Western, fascist, and communist regimes were far more profoundly at odds than had been the liberal and autocratic states in 1914–18. These circumstances left little scope for diplomacy. The main peace feelers took place in 1939–40, the neutrals attempting to mediate and Hitler sounding out both Western Allies before France fell and the British afterwards. Thereafter the radical incompatibility between the two sides' war aims left little scope for compromise. The Anglo-American 'Unconditional Surrender' doctrine, announced at the Casablanca conference in January 1943, ruled out peace with the existing Axis regimes. Although the Western leaders conceded a ceasefire to a government headed by the Italian king and military after they ousted Mussolini in July 1943, there was no possibility of their negotiating with Germany until they had destroyed Nazi rule. In contrast, it now seems that Stalin, faced with the formidable task of reconquering much of his country at immense cost, did extend feelers to the Germans via Sweden in the winter of 1942–3, but the latter failed to respond.

Not only were the opposing governments in the Second World War more polarized than in the First. The home fronts were more solid. In Germany, the Soviet Union, and Japan this was partly because of repression, but on both sides it also reflected the higher costs of defeat, as well as better management of public opinion and the economy than in 1914–18. Even higher percentages of Gross National Product were devoted to war production, but the British, American, and German economies were more successful in fighting inflation and protecting living standards (albeit in Germany's case with the aid of plunder from the occupied territories and wholesale use of slave labour). In the USSR, on the other hand, living standards fell further from what was already a pitifully low level, but the barbarity of the Nazi onslaught and the desperation of the country's predicament sustained the will to win. Conversely, fear of Russian retribution bolstered German resistance during the long retreat of 1943–5 from Stalingrad to Berlin.

The globalization of the war did not make the Allied triumph inevitable. Such was the loss of territory and industrial capacity inflicted on the Soviet Union, and so unprepared was the United States, that as of 1942 the Axis armies were not much smaller than those of the Allies and were much more effective. Until late in that year the Allied record was of scarcely relieved defeat, and in the battles that turned the tide of conflict they had no overwhelming advantage. For all the Axis leaders' mistakes the Allies had to fight for victory: it was not handed to them (Overy, 1995). None the less, at Stalingrad between November 1942 and February 1943 the Russians stopped and reversed the German drive to the Caucasus, and at Kursk in August 1943 they definitively halted blitzkrieg warfare in its tracks. The Western Allies defeated the U-boats in the Atlantic in May 1943, won air superiority over Western Europe in spring 1944, and cleared the enemy out of North Africa and southern Italy before breaching the Atlantic Wall and destroying the German forces in France in the Battle of Normandy. These Allied triumphs were in part ones of production, for although German military output trebled in 1942–4 it was outpaced by Soviet weapons manufacture and the astonishingly successful military conversion in the United States. In addition, several crucial technological developments greatly assisted the Allies—the decrypting of German 'Enigma' wireless traffic, Russian T-34 tanks, American Liberator bombers over the Atlantic and Mustang fighters over Germany, and the cluster of innovations in amphibious warfare that made possible the Normandy landings. In contrast, German work in jet propulsion, rocketry, and nuclear fission diverted resources unproductively from more crucial sectors of the war effort. None of these factors would have sufficed without the superior statesmanship of the Allied leaders and the courage and endurance of their civilians and combatants, above all in the Soviet Union whose 27 million dead were 100 times more numerous than those of Britain, France, or the US. It is true that Allied strategic bombing drew off German airpower, and that production for the air war absorbed much of Germany's industrial effort, while American Lend-Lease deliveries provided the Red Army with invaluable logistical support. None the less, as late as June 1944 250 German divisions were fighting on the eastern front against only 90 in the west. The Soviet forces, in Churchill's phrase, 'tore the guts out of the German army', and they paid a fearful price.

In the Second World War, unlike the First, it was apparent long before the end that Allied victory was highly likely. Planning for the future of Europe seemed more than just a hypothetical exercise, provided the winners could agree among themselves. But the Allied Governments were divided by ideological and cultural differences dating back at least to 1917, as well as by the rancour left by Munich and the Nazi–Soviet Pact. Only German aggression had brought them together, and they campaigned with one eye on the future. In 1944–5 Stalin pursued a political strategy designed to secure control of the Balkans and Poland. Conversely, Roosevelt promised Stalin a cross-Channel attack as early as 1942, but it was not delivered for two more years. The reasons for this delay were in part technical: until 1944 the Allies lacked troops and landing craft and air superiority. But in addition, although the postponement was not a deliberate attempt to maximize Soviet casualties, it was certainly intended to minimize Western ones, and to conserve British morale and resources. In contrast to Churchill, however, who wanted a Balkan invasion to forestall Soviet domination of south-eastern Europe, the American army leaders believed a landing in the west offered the advantages of following the most direct and easiest supplied line of attack against the enemy's decisive position. Moreover, Operation 'Overlord' might consolidate good relations with Stalin if co-operation with him were feasible, and if it were not at least the Channel ports, the Low Countries, and the Ruhr would fall under Western control. With such ideas in mind the Americans overrode Churchill and agreed with Stalin at Teheran in November 1943 that Overlord would proceed.

If in 1942–3 strategy was the main source of inter-Allied discord, in 1944–5 disagreements over the future of Europe replaced it. These disagreements suggest that the subsequent East–West confrontation was likely, though more because of conflicting conceptions of national security requirements than because either side wished to impose its political and social system on the other. Soviet aims were not simply to export the Stalinist model to every territory available, and might better be envisaged as a series of concentric circles, becoming more negotiable with distance from the motherland. Stalin soon made clear to his new partners that he wanted the Soviet frontier of June 1941, i.e. to push forward his inter-war frontier by annexing the territories he had absorbed in 1939–40. At the end of the war this line, with the addition of the easternmost tips of Germany and Czechoslovakia, was indeed what he gained. Beyond this, his second aim was 'friendly governments' on his western borders, which meant military base rights and control over his neighbours' foreign policies. Subject to these requirements, he was willing to tolerate some political liberties and a mixed economy in, for example, Finland and Czechoslovakia, and even in Poland he urged on the local communists an inclusive, 'broad front' approach rather than a single-party dictatorship. The third circle was Germany itself. In the wartime conferences at Teheran and Yalta Stalin wanted Germany to be partitioned (its eastern quarter going to Poland), its war industries to be dismantled and reparations paid. Yet the exiled German communists in Moscow wanted a united Germany under their control and Stalin himself doubted whether Germany could be kept divided in defiance of nationalist sentiment. After Germany surrendered he proclaimed that he wished to see it reunited. Fourthly, beyond Germany there were signs of opportunist Soviet expansion as victory approached (for example Soviet claims to Spitzbergen and for bases at the Turkish Straits), but Stalin appears to have accepted that his allies would dominate Mediterranean and Western Europe. Whatever his doubts about the sustainability of co-operation with the West, he prioritized it over revolutionary expansion. During the war he signed twenty-year alliances with Britain and France, and became a founder member of the United Nations Organization, the International Monetary Fund, and the World Bank. In the 'Percentages Agreement' that the Soviet leader reached with Churchill in October 1944, the latter accepted Soviet predominance in Romania, Bulgaria, and Hungary, but Stalin assigned Greece to the Western sphere of influence and agreed not to 'stir up' the Italian communists.

The Percentages Agreement testified to Western preparedness to tolerate Soviet predominance in Eastern Europe. Although the Americans were not party to the understanding, Roosevelt and the State Department were privately willing to accept an 'open' Soviet sphere of influence: i.e. that Moscow could protect its legitimate security interests if it did not interfere too blatantly in the region's internal affairs. Much American planning was directed not to Europe specifically but to creating new global institutions such as the IMF and the UN, and Roosevelt believed that the essential task was to hold the wartime victors together. America, Britain, the Soviet Union, and China, he proposed, should be the 'Four Policemen' of the post-war order. Europe would be primarily an Anglo-Soviet responsibility, Roosevelt telling Stalin at Yalta that American troops would be out within two years. He discouraged plans for a European federation, which had won strong support among the Resistance movements, because they were anathema to Stalin and might jeopardize Soviet friendship. It is true he told the Soviets nothing about the atomic bomb project, and that he stalled on their application for a reconstruction loan. Had he not died in April 1945 a Soviet–American rift would probably still have developed, though more slowly. But while he lived, an accommodation with Stalin remained his priority.

It was clear well before VE Day that Roosevelt's project was in trouble. The President failed to win Soviet trust, as Molotov's fury in February 1945 when the Americans discussed a separate armistice with the German forces in Italy demonstrated. And in Poland, which was excluded from the Percentages Agreement, no 'open' sphere arrangement was attainable. The country was vital to Stalin as a German 'invasion corridor': he intended to shift it bodily westwards, so that it would take territory from Germany and cede its eastern provinces to the Soviet Union. Such a rearrangement was broadly acceptable to Roosevelt and Churchill, but not to the Polish government-in-exile. When Stalin created a rival communist government on the ground, and his troops failed to intervene to save an uprising in August 1944 by non-communist Poles in Warsaw, Western confidence was badly shaken. Britain had ostensibly gone to war to protect Poland, and in the USA the issue was sensitive for the six million Polish-Americans as well as for the Catholic Church and the Republican opposition. Stalin's failure to honour the agreements reached at Yalta on an all-party Polish Government caused his first clash with Roosevelt's successor, Harry S. Truman. Even so, neither Britain nor America was willing to fight over Poland, and eventually they recognized a communist-dominated government there. Over Germany, too, all three Powers seemed agreed at the Potsdam conference of July–August 1945 that it should be divided only temporarily into occupation zones pending reunification and a peace treaty with a democratic all-German government. Both America and Britain still hoped for continued co-operation—though not on any terms, and both foresaw the possibility of conflict. Stalin also seems to have wanted friendship at least in the short term, and his determination to dominate Eastern Europe can be interpreted as primarily anti-German rather than anti-Western. This was the state of relations when the Second World War in Europe ended.

The year 1945 might seem an obvious concluding point for this account, but it took over a decade to construct a political settlement in Europe after the Second World War as it had done after the First. Whereas the settlement of the 1920s collapsed almost as soon as it had been created, however, that of the 1950s survived for over a generation, and major elements of it have continued into the new millennium. In retrospect the first half of the twentieth century seems characterized above all by its instability and destructiveness, sandwiched between two long periods of peace. Absence of war between the Great Powers before 1914 and after 1945 did not mean an absence of tension, or of armaments competition and confrontations between opposing blocs. Nor did it mean an absence of internal repression, which to some extent was the precondition for international peace. All the same, the characterization of 1914–45 as an era of exceptional violence still holds good.

Much of this violence can be traced back to the decisions of 1914. Quite apart from the ten million men it killed, the First World War overturned the humanitarian law of armed conflict, destabilized the European economy, and weakened the moderate political centre to the benefit of extremism. Without it, neither Hitler, nor Mussolini, nor Stalin could have held power. The First World War did not make the Second inevitable, but it was the essential precondition for it, and it made a durable peace extraordinarily difficult to regain. It opened a phase of terrible brutality within European societies as well as between them. Of course the decisions of 1914 themselves resulted from a growing sense of insecurity among the Great Powers that dated from a decade or so earlier—from German *Weltpolitik*, the Belgrade coup of 1903, and the Russo-Japanese War. The Balkan Wars of 1912–13 and the European land arms race raised the confrontation to a critical threshold. To some extent violence begat violence, which in turn begat ever more, but peaceful solutions had not been exhausted in Europe in 1914, and an exceptional burden of responsibility falls on the statesmen who rejected them.

If the First World War let the genie of mass violence out of the bottle, could it be put back in again? Conflict did not end in Europe after 1945: the next five years saw civil war in Greece, political strife in France and Italy, and mass deportations and political purges east of the Elbe. International crises erupted over Berlin in 1948–9 and 1958–61. None the less, by the mid-1960s Europe, unlike many other parts of the globe, had attained a strange but enduring international stability for the first time since the turn of the century. At the root of this transformation were two developments that were strongly in evidence before 1914, and in the 1920s and 1930s in comparative eclipse: globalization and integration. Already before the First World War the United States dwarfed the European Powers industrially and Tsarist Russia was growing faster than was Germany, while economic interdependence in Western Europe reached levels not matched until the 1950s. But between the wars trade and investment between the European states declined, while the retreat of the USA into isolationism meant that in the 1930s diplomacy between the European states occupied (for the last time) centre stage in world politics. In contrast, after 1945 the two superpowers, both of them victorious states with little stake in more upheaval, extended their presence to the heart of Europe, while the Western and Central European countries were unprecedentedly weak. This latter applied even to Britain, whose economic difficulties obliged the USA to take on much larger and more permanent overseas responsibilities than Roosevelt and Truman had envisaged. The turning point was less 1945 than 1947, and above all the launching of the Marshall Plan, after which the Soviet Union repressed all political activity within its sphere and most of a greatly weakened Germany was contained by its own consent within the West. American willingness to provide economic aid and security commitments to Western Europe made possible Franco-German rapprochement and launched a drive for economic and political integration, designed to contain both German and Soviet power. The fear of another war with even more powerful weapons underpinned the peace, but that peace rested on a complex series of political accommodations and never on the nuclear missiles alone. Though there have been tragic exceptions (most notably in former Yugoslavia) and there is no cause for complacency, so far events since the fall of the Berlin Wall have underlined the durability of the reconstruction after 1945 even in the absence of the bipolar Great-Power system that gave rise to it. In most of the Continent Europe's inner demons remain the stuff of nightmares rather than of real life.

# 3

# Economy

## Harold James

The beginning of the new century was an age of global inter-connection (today we would say 'globality'), in which integration and progress went hand in hand. At the beginning of his great novel of the last turn of the century, *Der Stechlin*, the German novelist Theodor Fontane describes the remote Lake Stechlin: 'Everything is still here. And yet, from time to time things happen here. When somewhere out there, in the wide world, whether in Iceland or in Java, it begins to rumble, or when an ash cloud from an Hawaiian volcano drifts far out into the Pacific ocean, then this place too comes alive. A water fountain rises and sinks again in the deep of the lake.' Fontane regarded the changes of his age with an elegiac, sometimes nostalgic pathos. He was a very old man. Most of his contemporaries were much more optimistic, and looked 'ever onward and upward'. But this dynamic and self-confident world was soon to break apart. The break-up destroyed the optimistic belief in cooperation across national boundaries, and indeed in human progress.

## The basis of integration

The world was integrated through the mobility of capital, goods, and people. Capital moved freely between states and continents. Trade was largely unhindered, even in apparently protectionist states such as the German Empire. Above all, people moved. They did not need passports, and in Europe there were hardly any debates about citizen-ship. In a search for freedom, security, and prosperity—three values closely related to each other—the peoples of Europe and Asia left their homes and undertook often uncomfortable journeys on foot, by rail, and across the oceans in search of a new life and new fortunes. Between 1871 and 1915, 36 million people left Europe. In the countries of immigration, the inflows brought substantial economic growth. At the same time, in the countries the migrants left behind them, their departure resulted in large productivity gains as surplus (low productivity) populations were eliminated. Such flows eased the desperate poverty of, for instance, Ireland or Norway. The great streams of capital, trade, and migration were linked to each other. Without the capital flows, it would have been impossible to construct the infrastructure—the railways, the cities—for the new migrants. The new developments created large markets for European engineering products as well as for consumer goods, textiles, clothing, and musical instruments.

These inter-related flows helped to ensure a measure of global economic stability. Some forty years ago, the economist Brinley Thomas brilliantly demonstrated an inverse correlation between cycles in Britain and the United States: slacker demand in Britain helped to make the Atlantic passage more attractive. The new immigrants stimulated the American economy, and hence also British exports, and the British economy could revive.

This integrated world bears a close resemblance to our world in which 'globalization' is so hotly debated. Economists who have tried to find a statistical basis for a comparison of this first era of globalization with our own era are usually struck by the degree of similarity. How can we measure international integration? One way is to look at the size of net capital movements. Measured in relation to GNP, both the imports and the exports of capital were much greater than today: between 1870 and 1890 Argentina imported capital equivalent to 18.7% of National Income, and Australia 8.2%. Compare these figures with the 1990s, where the respective figures of these large capital importers are a meagre 2.2% and 4%. The figures for capital exports are even more dramatic. On the eve of the Great War, Great Britain was exporting 7% of its National Income. There is no country in the post-1945 world which has even got near to such a level, not even Japan or the pre-1989 Federal Republic of Germany.

The trade comparison is only slightly less dramatic. For most countries, despite all the intervening improvements in the means of transportation, levels of trade of the pre-war world were not reached

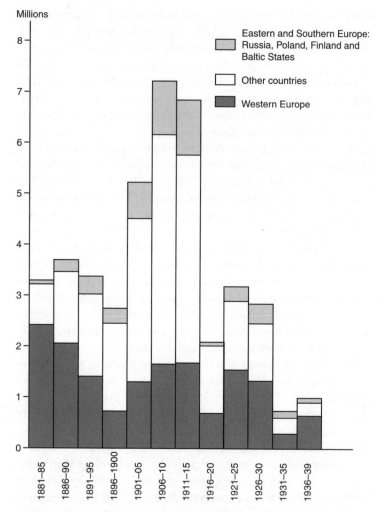

**Figure 3.1** European gross emigration overseas, 1881 to 1939.

Source: Ingvar Svennilson *Growth and Stagnation in the European Economy* (Geneva, 1954).

again until the 1980s. For Britain in 1913, the share of exports in GNP was around 30%. The rather lower German figure in 1913 of 20% was only reached in the 1970s.

But we do not need only to look at figures as an indicator of integration. We may also think of the standardization of the world, where railways in civilized countries ran on a track with a gauge of 4 feet 8.5 inches (the Russian Empire's choice of a wider gauge was an early indication that it did not wish to follow a Western course). But there was also a standardization of products that anticipated the rise of the McDonalds hamburger as the icon of globalism. A whole world clothed itself in the cheap (and hygienic) cotton textiles of the type developed originally in Manchester. Women sewed at home with machines made by the Singer Company.

Another approach to the world's first wave of globalization relies on an examination of attitudes to internationalism. The optimism of the age can be used as a testimony to its internationalism or cosmopolitanism. Some analysts believed that the dynamic of integration was so great that it could not be halted by anything: indeed that it made war between highly developed industrial states impossible. This attractive, but eventually fallacious, proposition was formulated with great brilliance by the British writer Norman Angell in a book first published in 1910, *The Great Illusion*. Capitalists thought that their version of internationalism had made states so dependent on the bond market that they could not afford to give any shocks to business confidence. Socialists believed that the existence of a self-consciously international proletariat could frustrate the plans of the militarists.

Inter-connectedness meant a development of complex forms of social organization, as governments and companies responded to the problem of control across distance. The rise of the large corporation was both a response to, and a facilitator of, the economic expansion and growth of the pre-1914 world. The company involved the substitution of mechanisms of control for the market. Instead of a company trying to assess whether the many products it bought from suppliers were reliable or not, it moved to own those suppliers, to enforce controls. Thus companies moved toward *vertical concentration*: controlling both the suppliers and the purchasers of their products. In this way, especially in the United States and Germany, gigantic trusts were created. By 1907, the German firm Krupp (steel, engineering, and munitions) had 64,300 employees. Countries such as France and Britain, where social circumstances favoured the family firm, which generally limited the scope for expansion, found that their industries were losing competitiveness relative to the newer rivals.

There was one precedent for the existence of such an institution, in which the actions of thousands of individuals needed to be controlled and coordinated: the state, and in particular the army. The first commercial organization on a scale to rival the army was the railroad. Railroads remained unique in their complexity and size and in the management problems they posed: the German railroad was the largest employer in the world by the end of the First World War. Firms recognized their debt to the state when they started to term their white collar workers *Beamte* or *Privatbeamte*: the *Beamte* was the civil servant, whose organizational pyramid had made possible the miracle of social organization that constituted the modern state.

The large corporation had a double debt to the state: it borrowed its structure, but also developed an economic symbiosis with it. In Imperial Germany, the formation of price and quantity cartels was facilitated by the existence of tariffs, which opened a possibility of a cooperative strategy of double-pricing between enterprises: higher domestic prices, protected by the tariff regime, and lower world prices, to fight for market share. In Germany, there had been 143 cartels in 1895; by 1910 there were 673, with the Pig Iron Association of 1897 and the Steel Works Association of 1904 dominating the market for the central products of industrial activity. The newer industries of the turn of the century—chemical, pharmaceutical, electro-technical industries—had been built on the basis of substantial public investment in education: in technical high schools, and commercial and engineering schools.

The result of the rise of the large firm behind the protective carapace of the large state convinced many observers that organization was replacing the market, or that the age of bureaucracy was succeeding the era of the merchant or dealer. In 1915, the socialist economist Rudolf Hilferding formulated a new theory to describe this new phase of 'organized capitalism'.

# The First World War

The First World War reinforced this lesson. One of the great and terrible ironies of the century is that a conflict that was started by traditional élites at least in part as a measure of social defence (on the argument that a 'short victorious war' would defuse political opposition) in the end demonstrated the feasibility of socialism. The model for the successful application of 'war socialism' was Germany, even though Germany lost the war. Almost immediately after the outbreak of the conflict, the German Government created a War Raw Materials Administration, which under the leadership of Walther Rathenau and Wichard von Moellendorff started economic planning. Systematic observations of the labour market, of prices and wages, and of foreign trade and credit allowed a more rational allocation of resources than was possible in the uncoordinated and anarchic market.

The other belligerents quickly saw the necessity of such German-style measures for building a war economy. The British Prime Minister, David Lloyd George, swept away the commitment to old-fashioned liberalism of his predecessors in 1916 with a pledge to introduce a 'new collectivism'. One of the ministers responsible for economic warfare, Sir E. H. Carson, warned that 'British industry would be beaten in a stand-up fight against the organized state-aided efforts of Germany' if the government continued to adhere 'rigidly to the old system of laissez-faire and refused to learn the lesson that in modern commerce, as in war, the power of organized combinations pursuing a steady policy will speedily drive out of the field the unregulated competition of private enterprise'. The French Minister of Commerce, Etienne Clémentel, wanted German style economic councils that would allocate raw materials and fix prices.

The war created expectations about redistribution and social justice. Rathenau argued that the sacrifice of the trenches could not be rewarded with postwar wage reductions. Since, however, such expectations in every country far surpassed what could be paid out of national resources, the longer the war went on, the greater the demand for peace terms that would—through reparations, indemnities, territorial cessions, or the transfer of patents—compensate for the losses of the war. The legacy of the war included the creation of new states and new frontiers. Expenditures on social provisions increased. For many belligerents, the postwar consequence was the continuation of inflationary wartime finance. Britain and the United States had enough social cohesion to allow a stabilization of the budget, at the cost of a major depression, in 1920. Alone in Central Europe, Czechoslovakia followed the same strategy, which was massively unpopular—especially as the neighbouring countries were rapidly depreciating their currencies and engaging on an export offensive. The Czech Finance Minister, Alois Rasin, who had scored this 'success', was assassinated. Elsewhere, in Austria, Germany, Hungary, and Poland, inflation moved ahead at ever higher rates, as businesses persuaded the government to allow higher administered prices and labour interests pressed for higher wages. Inflation became hyper-inflation, and the currencies were only stabilized in the mid-1920s at great cost (again of depressions), and with the help of external assistance from international committees, international loans, and the newly established League of Nations. Even for countries which had no hyper-inflation, and stabilized at under-valued exchange rates (as did France between 1926 and 1928), the transition to stability was a political shock.

Countries stabilized primarily because they hoped that they might have access to the newly invigorated capital markets. But those markets were over-burdened by the international complexity of the question of the retrospective financing of the War—the complex of war debts and reparations. Eventually these problems played at least some part in the complete breakdown of capital flows at the beginning of the 1930s. However, it is too simple to argue, as some such as Peter Temin do, that the Great Depression was simply the product of the First World War.

The Great Depression is the central event in the economic history of the twentieth century, and much of the rest of the century was spent attempting to draw the appropriate lessons from an economic collapse of unprecedented magnitude. In part the Depression followed from strategies of protection against the forces of international integration that had already been formulated, with substantial success, in the later nineteenth century: tariff and labour protection, a welfare state, and intervention in the capital markets. But the magnitude of the problems that such protective legislation and policies were supposed to solve had grown immeasurably with the legacy of the First World War.

# The fragile basis of 1920s prosperity

Had the guns of August 1914 exploded belief in the inevitability of economic and moral advance? It was certainly harder to be optimistic. But after the horrors of the war it was also hard not to have a nostalgic yearning for the internationalism and the security of the prewar world. The hope of the peacemakers was a 'return to normalcy': the old certainties should be restored. But at the same time they should be secured and institutionalized through international institutions—the Covenant and the League of Nations—and treaties, such as the permanent pact of peace concluded in 1926 at the initiative of the US Secretary of State Frank Kellogg and the French Foreign Minister Aristide Briand. Such a framework would allow the markets to operate: and indeed international capital resumed its flow. The German artist George Grosz, in a memorable caricature, saw the dollar as the sun that warmed the European continent. Migrations resumed. And markets, it was assumed, would make peace: observers of the 1920s were struck, for instance, by how dependence on foreign capital imports made even eccentric, destructive, and belligerent figures such as the Italian leader Benito Mussolini into responsible and even pacific statesmen.

Many observers were also impressed by the vigour of the European revival (except in Britain, where the 1920s were very sluggish). American production and management techniques, notably Fordism (assembly line production) and Taylorism (time–motion studies of individual industrial processes) were adopted as best practice by some European businesses. Coal mining and automobile production in particular were 'rationalized'. By 1929 83% of Ruhr coal was mined by mechanical means. Much of this rationalization reflected the international diffusion of technology, some of it by trans-national corporations. Thus the models for European automobile production of the future were provided by Ford plants in Cologne and General Motors' purchase of the Adam Opel works in Rüsselheim.

Eventually, the search for new means of securing integration ended in the late 1920s with a series of shocks. The international political situation in Europe was burdened by an impossible conflict over war debts and reparations. Impossible, because the more credits flowed, the more inextricable the situation became. Germany was supposed to pay a substantial part of the burden of the war through the reparations imposed under the Versailles Treaty. France needed reparations not only to reconstruct, but also to pay the wartime debt to Britain and the United States. Germany—that is German corporations and the German public sector—borrowed substantial sums largely on the American market; this borrowing financed at least indirectly the reparations payments. But as the payments were made through the second half of the 1920s, it became increasingly apparent that this was not a game that could be played for ever: that at one moment, there would come a choice when either the United States could continue to receive repayments of war-debt financed by means of German reparation payments, or US creditors could have their private loans serviced. At least some German policy makers, notably Hjalmar Schacht, President of the German Reichsbank, made this calculation in all cynicism, in the belief that the resulting debacle would demonstrate the folly of reparations. The reassessment of the reparations burden in 1929 through the Young Plan, in which at last a final term was set for the payment of reparation (payments were to continue until 1988), made clear to more investors the impossible nature of their bet and Germany's chances of external credit deteriorated dramatically.

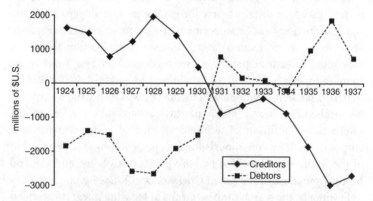

**Figure 3.2** Capital flows, 1924–1937.

Source: Charles H. Feinstein and Catherine Watson, 'Private International Capital Flows in the Inter-War Period', in *Banking, Currency, and Finance in Europe between the Wars*, ed. Charles H. Feinstein (Oxford, 1995).

International markets were further dislocated by the fall in commodity prices. Since the middle of the 1920s, raw material prices were falling, in part as a consequence of the extension of the area of production during the First World War, in part as a result of inept schemes for price manipulation, such as the Stevenson scheme which aimed to keep an artificially high rubber price. This price decline made the situation for many capital-importing countries more difficult. But, from the perspective of the industrial countries, the results appeared beneficial, since raw materials and foods—at that time a much larger component of household budgets than currently—were cheaper. With additional available income, consumers might buy new products. Such calculations sustained the giddy glitter of the jazz age.

A further weakness lay in the tendency of every country to respond to economic problems in the 1920s by trade measures, as had already occurred before 1914. With prices fluctuating more dramatically, the results were much more harmful than in the relatively stable prewar world. Thus in 1925, once the limits placed by the Versailles Treaty on German tariff autonomy came to an end, Germany immediately reapplied the rates of the Bülow tariff of 1902. But with the fall in agricultural prices, these rates rapidly proved inadequate as a response to the pressures of the farm lobby. By the 1920s, many states built into their tariff measures a flexibility which allowed them to raise rates in the light of changing circumstances. The model for this legislation was the US Fordney-McCumber Tariff Act of 1920, which envisaged rapid decisions by an expert and apolitical Tariff Commission. Flexibility, however, in practice meant an upwards ratchet effect. It was not that the level of protection was especially high at the outset (most analysts now see that the overall level of protection was actually lower than before the First World War). But the possibility of such measures being applied in response to other, financial problems, and the increased popularity of non-tariff protection (quotas) made for a greater restriction of trade.

Tariff policy was not the only means with which states responded to rapidly changing market situations. On a national level, many states saw cartellization as a means of stabilizing prices and expectations. Germany, which had had around 700 cartels on the eve of the First World War, in 1925 had 2,500 and in 1930 3,000. This theme also became an international issue: could not cartels help to stabilize prices and production on an international level? Attempts at restoring Franco-German friendship on an economic basis revolved around arrangements such as the International Steel Cartel (1926), which is sometimes viewed as the central diplomatic event of that rather optimistic year. The League of Nations followed the discussion with great interest and in 1927 organized a World Economic Conference, at which cartels were proposed as the best solution to the question of international order.

States also engaged in increased redistribution through the budget in response to greater social expectations of 'protection'. In some part, the new demand simply reflected the human cost of the War, the support of widows, orphans and the permanently disabled. But in part, the demand reflected also the perceived need to buy social peace in the face of a threat of the spread of bolshevism. For France, social services accounted for 4.3% of central government expenditure in 1912, but 21.7% in 1928; the comparable figures for Germany are 5.0% and 34.2%. Correspondingly, total figures for government expenditure rose.

Difficulties in exporting meant that one of the nineteenth-century solutions to the problem of 'surplus population' appeared ever more difficult. Already in the 1890s, the German Reichskanzler Leo von Caprivi had defended his attempts to liberalize trade policy by saying that the alternative would be pauperization and increased emigration. 'We must export: either we export our goods or we export our people.' In this period, one response to trade crises and financial crises in both the countries of mass immigration, and in some industrial countries, was to restrict the movement of people. Citizenship and nationality, and the entitlements they brought with them, now became central elements in political discussions in some countries of immigration.

In Australia and the United States lower growth and the financial crises of the 1890s conjured up mass protests against immigration. Australia began its strict 'white Australia' policy. Americans complained that the new immigrants were replacing skilled native workers. In 1897 the US Congress debated a reading test for immigrants. Ten years later, a commission was established to find a way of restricting the 'new immigrants' who were allegedly coming only for economic reasons and for a short time.

Such resentment against foreign migrant workers also took hold in some European countries. Germany in particular had in the late nineteenth century become a country of immigration, with over a million foreign workers, especially in mining and in eastern agriculture. There was a clear demand: the Prussian Agricultural Ministry had indeed in 1890 commissioned a study on the feasibility of employing Chinese farm labourers in Germany. But simultaneously the efforts to stop such inflows intensified in the 1880s and 1890s. In 1885, the Prussian Interior Minister von Puttkamer had ordered the exclusion of Polish temporary migrants, and immigration was rigorously controlled after 1887. The Oberpräsident of Westphalia ordered 'suitable measures' to secure a 'drastic' reduction in the number of Poles in the Westphalian industrial area. Perhaps the most famous critic of the labour policy implications of late nineteenth-century globalization was Max Weber. He explained his objections to immigration on the basis of different propensities to consume: since Polish workers were satisfied with poorer nutrition, their employment would be a danger to living standards in richer countries. 'There is a particular situation of economies, disorganized in a capitalist fashion, in which the higher culture is not victorious, but is rather defeated, in the struggle for existence.'

After the First World War, in many West European industrial countries alarm at losing out in this Darwininan struggle was exacerbated by the fear of demographic stagnation. Almost everywhere, birth rates had dropped dramatically in the 1890s. Apart from France, where this 'demographic transition' occurred much earlier, at the start of the nineteenth century, the movement was remarkably simultaneous in Western Europe, North America, and a few Latin American states (Argentina and Uruguay). Most European countries experienced a drop in marital fertility between 1890 and 1910: Germany and Hungary in 1890, Sweden in 1892, Austria in 1908 and Italy in 1911. The First World War gave a new shock to fertility (in addition to the losses in Europe of a substantial part of the male adult population). By the 1930s, many observers believed that modern democratic states would become extinct because they had already fallen significantly below net reproduction rates. In France, birth rates had long been a cause for concern, and for comments about national decline or decadence. In the 1930s the economist Alfred Sauvy showed that the age structure meant that the decline would become more rapid in the foreseeable future: that the French population would fall by a quarter between 1955 and 1985. In reaction to widespread concern,

French governments embarked on not very successful attempts to increase the birthrate.

Similar concerns were voiced elsewhere. For Germany, Ernst Kahn predicted a decline from 65 million to 50 million by 1975. For England and Wales, Enid Charles produced an optimistic forecast showing a decline from 40 million to 38.5 million in 1975 and 20 million by 2035, and an analysis on a more pessimistic base of 31.5 million in 1974 and 4.4 million in 2035. These interpretations had political consequences, as fascist and Nazi propagandists began to insist on the desirability of a 'healthy' demographic stock. The progressive Swedish economist Gunnar Myrdal in lectures at Harvard in 1938 stated, on the eve of a new World War, that, 'to my mind no other factor—not even that of peace or war—is so tremendously fatal for the long-term destinies of democracies as the factor of population. Democracy, not only as a political form but with all its content of civic ideals and human life, must either solve this problem or perish.' In February 1937 the British House of Commons debated a motion that 'This House is of the opinion that the tendency of the population to decline may well constitute a danger to the maintenance of the British Empire and the economic well-being of the nation.'

Despite the fears about falling population, and in response to concerns about ethnic dilution, immigration was generally much more restricted than before the war. The most striking legislation was the 1921 US Emergency Quota Act, which used the share of the American population in 1890, in other words before the big waves of Mediterranean and East European immigration, as a basis for setting limits for new immigrants by country of origin. Canada listed 'preferred' countries (Belgium, Denmark, France, Germany, Netherlands, Norway, Sweden, and Switzerland) whose citizens were admitted on the same terms as those of Britain; and then 'non-preferred' European countries, whose peoples could only come as agricultural labourers or domestic servants. South Africa after 1930 virtually halted immigration from 'non-preferred' countries altogether. Australia negotiated limits on the passports issued to immigrants from East European countries and Italy.

The result of the new policies and legislation was a dramatic decline in emigration from those areas with high population increases, and which had figured prominently in the pre-war emigration statistics. The consequence was that large parts of Eastern,

South-Eastern, and Mediterranean Europe, where birth rates remained very high, tried to look for alternative strategies for the employment of 'surplus population'. The development of industry, and a search for export markets was one such approach: but it required an openness of export markets (which was increasingly threatened) and also open capital markets. For Poland, for instance, the growth of the labour force was such that a growth in industrial employment of over three fold (at an annual rate of at least 6.6%) would have been needed to absorb it. Given productivity increases, industrial output would have had to rise even faster. But these are difficult targets at the best of times—and in the interwar climate impossible, because of the instability of the export markets, and of capital markets.

# The failure of the capital markets and the Great Depression

What happened to the capital markets? Why did the revival of confidence of the 1920s prove so short-lived? The gold standard, which had been the basis of credible and stable monetary and financial policies before the war, had been suspended at the outbreak of hostilities, and a decade of monetary chaos followed. In the revived international gold standard, independent central banks were believed to be the key to a restoration of confidence, but they functioned in a quite new way. Their role was seen as running monetary policy in accordance, not with domestic priorities, but rather with the requirements of the international system.

Central banks were to be established before a country stabilized on gold in order to prepare the institutional ground and to give a guarantee of confidence by limiting the options for government policy, and in particular for governments' attempts to buy popularity by monetizing debts. The new institution should be independent of governments. As the Brussels Conference formulated it in 1920: 'Banks and especially Banks of Issue should be free from political pressure and should be conducted only on lines of prudent finance.'

The new central banks of the interwar years included those associated with currency stabilization schemes in Austria, Hungary, and

Germany; but the principle was extended throughout the world. Where there were already central banks, harsh stabilization packages, often with an overvalued currency, were supposed to establish confidence, and thus attract international inflows. Perhaps the most striking example was Italy in 1927. Mussolini went for the prestige of the 'quota novanta', ninety lire to the British pound, although this imposed a substantial cost on Italian business. In the style of the times, the worst affected industries might be helped by protective tariffs and quota arrangements (quantitative limits on imports).

The Central Bank Governors now—in distinct contrast to the pre-1914 world—saw themselves as members of a club, engaging in friendly and intimate relationship with each other. 'You are a dear queer old duck and one of my duties seems to be to lecture you now and then', wrote Benjamin Strong of the Federal Reserve Bank of New York to Montagu Norman of the Bank of England. In particular Strong, Norman, and their German colleague Schacht shared a similarity of outlook and behaviour.

This harmonious relationship, built up on the basis of close personal ties, came under strain because of US payments surpluses which were recycled as capital exports. With newly established confidence, and above all under the impact of US lending, commercial banking systems outside the United States expanded rapidly. In Austria, total bank deposits increased between 1925 and 1929 at an annual rate of 6%; for French deposit banks the comparable figure is 13%, for the German Great Banks 25%, for the principal Italian banks 28%, and for Polish banks 34%. How rapid these expansions were may be judged by a comparison with the United States and with Britain. Over the corresponding period, all bank deposits in the United States rose at an annual rate of 3.2%; and in England and Wales by 1.3% annually.

The expansions created the appearance of inflationary finance. They could not be controlled by orthodox means. If Central Banks attempted to tighten money by raising rates (the classical remedy under the gold standard for the restraint of over-rapid development), they would *increase* the incentives for hot money inflows, and thereby reduce their control of the market. The doctrine of Central Bank control and autonomy as a precondition for confidence and capital flows thus ran into the objection that any step the Central Bank might take on discount rates might be ineffective.

But apart from discount rates, the Central Banks had few weapons in their quest for monetary stability. In the United States, Britain, and Japan they might engage in open market operations—the purchase or sale of securities to increase or decrease respectively liquidity—but elsewhere the statutes forbade such procedures because of the fear that they might be used as a mechanism for launching a new inflation. Even in the United States—where there might have been thought to have existed a much greater room for manoeuvre—the Federal Reserve system in fact was highly cautious in its open market policy until 1933, in other words until after the catastrophe of the Great Depression.

In Central Europe, the conventional way of restraining development was by rationing credit at the Central Bank. 'The Central Bank is trying, primarily, to operate by fixing, not the price of the service which it renders, but the amount of the service which it will render.' But it could only really be effective in this during a period of stringency or crisis: and Central Banks in Central Europe thus needed crisis, institutionally, in order to be able to control the development of their markets. The same institutions that were supposed to minimize crises suddenly had an interest in shocks rather than stability.

Not surprisingly, within a few years of the first stabilizations the central bankers became rather gloomy about the new world they had constructed. In March of the year in which US capital exports peaked, the Governor of the New York Federal Reserve Bank, Benjamin Strong, wrote: '1927 is going to be a barren and disappointing year for Europe ... stabilization and reconstruction, which have been the vogue since the League first dealt with Austria, have for the time being passed out of fashion'. The vigour of the 1920s capital markets effectively paralysed the central banks' capacity to act. But it is important to note that the malaise followed not from short term movements as such (the extent of such movements at the end of the twentieth century was clearly much larger), but from the reactions of markets to inappropriate policies and false signals.

There were plenty of economic problems in the world before the dramatic collapse of Wall Street in October 1929. Australia, highly dependent on wool exports, or Brazil, almost exclusively reliant on coffee exports, were deeply depressed. In Germany cyclical production indicators had already turned round in the autumn of 1927 (the stock market weakness appeared even earlier). The story of what produced 1929 in the United States is still slightly mysterious, at least for believers in the rationality of markets. What did stock market investors know on 'Black Thursday', 24 October 1929, that they had not known on Tuesday or Wednesday? There had been 'bad news' since early September: and the weight of evidence had accumulated to such an extent that there was a panic in the face of the likelihood of the future decline of stock prices. The only plausible answer for those looking for a rational account of the stock market collapse is that American investors were contemplating the likelihood of the implementation of a new piece of legislation, which went under the names of Hawley and Smoot. This tariff bill had begun as a promise in the presidential campaign of 1929 by Herbert Hoover to improve the situation of the American farmer (with the agricultural price collapse, the farmer was the major loser of jazz age prosperity). In the course of congressional debate, however, each representative tried to add on new items (there were 1,253 Senate amendments alone). The result—a tariff with 21,000 tariff positions—was extreme protectionism: but worse, until the final narrow voting in June 1930, there was constant uncertainty about the future of trade policy.

But if the story of the Depression does not begin with the stock market crash and Smoot–Hawley, neither does it end there. There were some signs of recovery in 1930: stock prices in the United States rebounded, and the lower level of the market made foreign issues appear attractive again.

What made the Depression the *Great* Depression rather than a brief-lived stock market problem or a depression for commodity producers was a chain of linkages that operated through the financial markets. The desperate state of the commodity producers along with the reparations-induced problems of Germany set off a chain of domino reactions. In this sense the Depression was a product of disorderly financial markets.

In the events of 1931, which made the Depression 'Great', financial contagion brought the continent into crisis. At the beginning of *Anna Karenina*, Leo Tolstoy famously describes how happy families resemble each other, but each unhappy family is unhappy in its own peculiar way. At the beginning of 1931, all the central European economies had problems, but they were quite special ones.

Hungary was above all a victim of the worldwide collapse of agricultural prices, which declined at first gently between 1925 and 1938 and then plummeted. It had become a budget crisis because of two highly costly and ultimately ineffective schemes to stabilize the price of wheat (a buffer stock and a direct price subsidy). As the wheat price continued to fall, these operations required increased subsidies. Domestic and foreign creditors—who in November 1930 had still been willing to buy Hungarian short term debt at a good price—now worried about the ability of the government to service its debt, and began to anticipate a default. They thus withdrew money from Hungarian banks, and Hungary had a banking problem. The withdrawals took place across the exchanges (creditors converted pengö into foreign exchange) and the crisis thus threatened the maintenance of the gold standard attachment. What started out as a budget issue transformed itself into a banking and foreign exchange crisis.

In Austria, the causation ran the other way round: the largest bank, the Creditanstalt, was unable to produce its accounts on time, and its depositors panicked. It was clear that the government could not allow such a big institution to fail, and the cost of the bank bailout would have to be borne by the state. With every week that passed, the calculation of that cost became ever higher. Depositors, in the Creditanstalt but also in other Austrian banks, also withdrew money across the exchange, and the National Bank lost its reserves. Here a banking crisis became a budget crisis.

In Germany, few people had any idea how bad the loans of institutions such as the Darmstädter Bank in reality were. But there was a widespread fear that the reparations debate might lead to an exchange crisis. Withdrawals weakened the banks, and brought out the latent problems in their portfolios that might otherwise have remained unexposed. The weakness of the exchange position weakened the capital market, so that the government could no longer finance even relatively small short term deficits. Previously it had depended on the banks, but as these lost their deposits they withdrew from such financing. Here a foreign exchange crisis, measurable in terms of the Reichsbank's reserve losses, set off the banking and budget crises.

The sequence of the different aspects of crisis was different in each of the central European crisis economies, but the outcomes were surprisingly similar. In each case, capital movements across frontiers destroyed a banking system that had already been weakened by the effects of war and postwar inflations. And in each case, the concatenation of problems produced a policy paralysis. Years ago, the German economic historian Knut Borchardt analysed the limited room for manoeuvre, and warned against a retrospective optimism about the solubility of problems. The astonishing feature of the world depression was how rapidly this paralysis was transferred across national frontiers. A similar contagion mechanism operated in Latin America.

A crisis in the creditor countries followed the problems of the debtors. In Britain, there were no fundamental problems with banks. But many investment houses suffered from the freezing of their credits in central Europe, and their depositors feared possible insolvencies. The German bank closures of July 1931 set off a run on sterling: rumours of an impending Latin American default provided the final straw that broke the back of Britain's gold standard. The Bank of England refused to use all the instruments at its disposal—interest rate increases, or the use of its reserves—in defence of the parity, as it feared that allowing further transfers over the exchange would bring down at least some of the weaker London banks. The devaluation stabilized the British financial system because of the skill with which it was managed. The pound fell sharply on the exchange, creating expectations that the next movement would be up rather than down, and thus discouraging depositors from realizing their losses. It is important to note—particularly for those who suggest that this British style solution might have been appropriate for central Europe or South America—that in these cases it would have been impossible to find an exchange rate which would have given rise to the expectation of recovery.

The British panic had in common with the preceding debtor crises an abrupt reversal of expectations. Depositors and investors saw a danger of being trapped in a particular engagement, and—as they saw the door closing—rushed to get out. Once this mechanism had operated in one creditor country, it might apply to others. The United States was vulnerable, not because it had an external current account problem, but because it was apparent that US banks were vulnerable to losses elsewhere. The resulting capital movements, which set on quite suddenly after the sterling devaluation of September 1931, changed the possibilities for anti-cyclical measures. Before September 1931, President Hoover had been contemplating quite extensive measures to stimulate the economy through government expenditure.

After the panic, in which as a result of experience elsewhere government deficits were synonymous with failures of confidence, the President started to assert the necessity of balanced budgets. But so,
remarkably, did his Democratic opponent in the 1932 presidential
race Franklin Delano Roosevelt, who made criticism of Hoover's deficits a focal point of his campaign. The withdrawals and the shocks to
confidence only ended when Roosevelt, seeing every other alternative
fail, took the dollar off the gold standard on 20 April 1933, and then
announced (3 July) that he had no intention of stabilizing its external
value since all that concerned Americans was the internal value or
purchasing power of their currency. Again the dollar fell sharply,
encouraging belief that it might be stabilized or even recover. Then
the crises continued in the remaining gold standard countries—
Belgium, France, the Netherlands, and Switzerland—until in the end
they too saw an abandonment of the parity regime as the only way of
ending continual budget strain and bank panics.

Unemployment became the scourge of the age, with over 6 million
registered as out of work in Germany and over 12 million in the
United States at the height of the crisis in 1932. But no one—at least
in the conventional political establishment—seemed to offer any
hope of providing an acceptable or social solution. The British Prime
Minister, Ramsay MacDonald, caught the mood of political passivity
and inaction of the slump years when he noted in his diary at the
beginning of the depression, at Christmas 1929: 'Unemployment is
baffling us. The simple fact is that our population is too great for our
trade . . . I sit in my room in Downing Street alone and in silence. The
cup has been put to my lips—and it is empty.'

There are some general lessons that might be drawn from the
experience of the Depression. First, countries with high foreign debts
and weak banking structures are vulnerable to deflationary shocks.
Secondly, the mechanisms of financial contagion transfer the weakness to creditor countries with sound banking systems. Thirdly, the
most obvious transmission mechanism was the fixed exchange rate
commitment. As soon as Britain or the United States—or Belgium or
Switzerland—abandoned the gold standard link, while preserving fiscal orthodoxy, the banking threat that had been a prime mechanism
for the transmission of depression disappeared.

Most contemporaries, however, drew a much simpler and much
more ideological lesson: first, that the international order had failed;

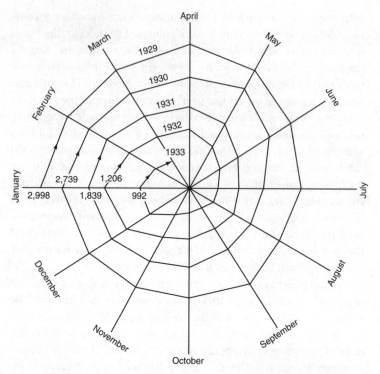

**Figure 3.3** The contracting spiral of world trade, January 1929–March 1933: Total imports of 75 countries (monthly values in terms of old US gold dollars (millions)).

Source: Charles Kindleberger, *The World in Depression* 1929–1939 (Berkeley, 1986).

secondly, that the market mechanism had produced internationalization, and needed to be replaced by a healthier concentration on domestic ordering and planning.

## Economic nationalism: quotas and tariffs

The components of the new economic nationalism involved all the elements that had previously been central to the integrated world economy: control over trade, over the movement of people, and over capital. Now everything was to be national—labour and goods, and capital. John Maynard Keynes brilliantly described this development in his 1933 essay, 'National Self-Sufficiency'. 'We wish', Keynes stated, '—for the time at least and so long as the present transitional, experimental phase endures—to be our own masters, and to be as free as we can make ourselves from the interference of the outside world.'

The most notorious of the mechanisms for managing trade in the 1930s was known as 'Schachtianism', after the central banker of the 1920s who was reappointed by Hitler and then in addition was given the position of Minister of Economics. Schachtianism involved a restriction and a bilateralization of trade. In fact, the bilateralization of trade had begun before the appointment of Hitler as German Chancellor in January 1933: it was a response to the financial crisis of 1931, and Germany had already concluded six bilateral treaties with south-east European countries in 1932. Schacht simply extended these measures, and built up a comprehensive trade control (the 'New Plan' of 1934). Such moves tended to reduce trade. Since in a multi-lateral world, few countries have balanced trade accounts with each other, but have surpluses and deficits that correspond to trade relations with other countries, trying to make each bilateral trade account balance reduced the overall volume.

German policy-makers also took up a theme that was current in contemporary economic discussion. Many contemporary commentators, including Keynes and Werner Sombart, expected the share of international trade to enter a secular decline as previously agricultural and commodity-producing countries industrialized. The international division of labour would decrease as many areas moved away from their dependence on commodity exports, and the preeminence of the industrial countries would be eroded. Hitler took up this theme: in 1933, he commented that 'If this export of the means of production were continued indefinitely, it would simply be the end of the vital prerequisite for European industry. Therefore international agreements on limiting the export of the means of production are necessary.'

The contribution of Nazi policy-makers was to add a highly political element to trade relations: in offering favourable access to German markets to some south-central European producers, Schacht helped to create a political dependence, which sucked these states into the German political orbit.

France and Britain evolved schemes for tariff protection that favoured their colonial possessions ('Imperial Preference'). The departure from free trade principles was most striking in Britain, which in the nineteenth century had been the principal upholder of the idea of open access. It was a response to the acute financial crisis of 1931. After the October 1931 elections, the new Chancellor of the Exchequer was Neville Chamberlain, a man who made many destructive contributions to the politics of the 1930s, and who had inherited from his much greater father, Joseph Chamberlain, a commitment to tariff and Empire. He overrode the objections of the Prime Minister Ramsay MacDonald, who retained a classical left-liberal commitment to the principles of free trade. Tariffs, Chamberlain believed, would not only be a way of saving British industry, but also of increasing British power through a strengthening of Empire. 'There is no article of your food', he told the British people, 'there is no raw material in your trade, there is no necessity of your lives, no luxury of your existence which cannot be produced somewhere or other in the British Empire.' Emergency customs legislation in November and December 1931 imposed higher duties on a range of manufactured goods, and the new approach was consolidated in 1932 in the Imports Duties Act. At the Imperial Conference in Ottawa (July 1932), the member states of the British Commonwealth organized a series of preferential trade treaties.

France too expanded her regime of tariffs and quotas as a response to the financial trauma of 1931. The immediate French response was decree legislation imposing special levies on countries with devalued currencies (12 November 1931); and in the second half of 1931 the system of quotas was extended to cover agricultural products. The French Empire was excepted from the protectionist legislation, with the result that the share of the Empire in French imports rose from 12% in 1931 to 33.6% by the middle of 1936. The combination of French and British measures to protect their imperial possessions in turn worsened the situation of the eastern and Balkan producers, who found themselves consequently locked in ever greater dependence on Germany.

# Economic nationalism: planning and racism

The fight against the misery of the Depression for most countries was a struggle against the ill of unemployment. The most striking and successful application of what became known as 'Keynesian' measures—contra-cyclical fiscal expansion—occurred in Sweden. Finance Minister Ernst Wigforss combined a sensitivity to developments in contemporary economics with a vision of the political coalition—between farmers and industrial workers—that might support reflation and expansion. Such coalitions were probably easiest to achieve in small countries, which felt increasingly threatened by the hostile international environment in the 1930s. In Switzerland, employers and workers reached an agreement in 1937, after the franc devaluation of 1936 had ended the constraints that had previously made fiscal expansion impossible. In France, the Matignon agreements under the Popular Front government of 1936 introduced substantial improvements for French workers—a 40 hour week, paid holiday, binding collective agreements, and 15% wage increases—but did little to recreate the social solidarity and stability that similar measures produced in Sweden or Switzerland.

These modest successes of political consensus and fiscal expansion were overshadowed by the economic performance of two dictatorships, which aimed even more explicitly at the mobilization of 'national labour'. For Germany, the 'battle for work' was also dressed up in civil engineering projects, such as the construction of the divided highways (*Autobahnen*), large dams, and party and prestige buildings. But the aim of recovery policies was increasingly subordinated to military objectives and rearmament. Preparedness for war was an explicit goal of the Four Year Plan launched in 1936.

The title of the German economic project makes it clear how much Germans, and others, were impressed by the scale, and the success, of the Soviet industrialization drive, initiated by the First Five Year Plan (1928–32). In 1921, Lenin had conducted a strategic retreat from the era of 'war communism', and for eight years the Soviet state had a mixed economy, under what became widely known as the NEP (New Economic Policy). Many small and medium-scale enterprises were denationalized, and agriculture was left in the private sector. The results had been disappointing, with very low levels of investment, and increasing food shortages in the cities as peasant farmers hesitated to market their produce. The aim of the planners was to break through the impasse by very high levels of investment in capital goods industries, which would permit a later, postponed, expansion of consumption. There were large prestige projects, such as the Dnepr dam, or whole new industrial complexes (Magnetic City, or Magnitogorsk, in the Urals). In this way, the Soviet Union attempted to fulfill the ultimate aim of the plans: to catch up with, and then overtake, capitalism.

The planning of the 1930s was not very scientific, and relied largely on finding bottlenecks in production that could then be tackled by 'storm' methods. The First Five Year Plan owed its particular brutality to the simultaneous campaign to collectivize agriculture. Millions of peasants left their farms, with the result that Soviet industry had too many rather than too few workers—but too few skilled ones. The original plan had been for the industrial labour force to rise from 11.3 million to 15.8 million; but in fact, by 1932 there were 22.8 million industrial workers in the USSR. As a consequence, the Soviet authorities imposed restrictions on internal movement: most significantly, the December 1932 Passport Law, which aimed at ending the chaotic movement of individuals.

In the end, the Soviet experiment offered the most total example of the mobilization of national labour. Keynes, who deeply disliked Soviet politics, offered a congratulation to the Russian periodical *Za Industrialitsu*: 'It is . . . true that the growth of industrial production is much facilitated in a state which starts from a very low level and is prepared to make great sacrifices to increase industrial production without making a close calculation as to whether it is strictly speaking profitable and advantageous for the existing generation of workers.'

Finally, capital movements across national boundaries were now considered as destructive and destabilizing. To the extent that they aimed explicitly at offering a planned alternative, Keynes approved of the Nazi and Soviet experiments. The central bankers, and others, interpreted the large sums that flowed as a response to the signals they sent as 'capital flight', a term with a strong moral overtone, which implies desertion and national betrayal. Estimates of capital flight for Germany in 1930 amounted to a sum equivalent to an eighth of National Income, in France for 1938 of a quarter. These short-term capital movements were so substantial that they endangered the ability for regulators to control the national economies. Such flows created the basis for a myth that 'mobile international capital' was undermining the national economies.

Because governments and central banks attached so much prestige to the reestablishment of the fixed parities of the gold standard, they opened a window for speculators who did not believe that those policies would succeed. In the nineteenth century there had been few cases of abandonment of the gold standard: once the system had already collapsed in 1914, once governments faced the intractable budgetary difficulties of the postwar era, short term movements began to follow a quick entry, quick exit strategy.

The logic of attaching prestige to a difficult economic objective was that the speculator became a national enemy. Sometimes the attacks were linked with class conflict: the left in France attacked the '*deux cent familles*' who frustrated the reforms of the 1924 centre-left government (the *cartel des gauches*). The British Labour party believed that it had been undermined by a 'Banker's Ramp'. Sometimes the objections were racially based: speculators were identified as cosmopolitan, Jewish, or alien. The stereotypes and the behaviour of the vulnerable minorities reinforced one another. Faced by mounting anti-Semitism, Jews tried to move their capital out of many Central European countries; and as they fell foul of new legislation to control speculation, they reinforced the stereotype of the 'Jewish' speculator (in Hungary, in the year *before* the introduction of anti-Semitic legislation in 1938, 112 out of 187 currency offences were committed by Jews).

After the outbreak of the major financial crises of 1931, central banks transformed themselves once more: no longer apostles of internationalism, they secured a happy bureaucratic *raison d'être* as the implementors and invigilators of increasingly complicated schemes for exchange control. This role was facilitated by a turnaround in economic thinking, not just in Nazi Germany—where autarky became a guideline for policy—but in almost every country.

The collapse of the economy now brought, in general, a turning away from the market. Even moderate and pragmatic analysts, such as the director of the League of Nations' Economic and Financial Section, Sir Arthur Salter, believed that the future lay in regulation and control. With the encyclical *Quadragesimo Anno* in the crisis year

1931, the Catholic church looked for a 'third way' between capitalism and socialism. Increasing regulation and planning encouraged those who saw the function of the state as being to externalize the costs of economic adjustment: to impose those costs on those outside the national community. The state's duty lay in protecting its citizens, and ensuring that the inhabitants of other national communities suffered as much as possible. This was of course quite the opposite of the traditions of classical economic liberalism, in which there is a mutuality of gains.

The path away from the market and toward control was also a path to political dictatorship. The most obvious examples were in Russia and Germany. But the sentiment that democracy had failed in fulfilling a basic social need was widely shared by many democrats. In his diary for February 1940, for instance, André Gide noted: 'We must be prepared for the fact that after the War, even if we are victorious, we will be in such a swamp that only a decisive dictatorship can pull us out.'

At this time, the nation-state and its control mechanisms was supposed to give guarantees against the threats from the world economy. But the protection became more dangerous and destructive than the threat.

# The war and planning for a better world

During the Second World War, a new philosophy was formulated. Only economic internationalism could provide a remedy against the world of political nationalism and war. Even Germans started to speak about the restoration of a multilateral payments system on a European basis, in place of 1930s bilateralism. But such plans— grandiosely announced by Economics Minister Walther Funk in the summer of 1940, when German arms seemed universally victorious— amounted to little more than propaganda, since in the circumstances of the World War Germany could not survive without the credits implied in bilateral clearing accounts.

The trajectory of alternative beliefs about the economy and its management can be contemplated through the eyes of the greatest economist of the age, Keynes. A great internationalist, who exploded with frustration at the form of the peace settlement at the end of the First World War, and who turned to economic nationalism in the 1930s because the world of inter-connectivity had so clearly failed, now shifted once more toward economic internationalism. The British government asked him to formulate plans for a new international economic order in response to Funk's 1940 campaign. Keynes was clear that whatever the response, it could not simply be a return to old-style nineteenth-century economic liberalism ('Manchesterism'). On the other hand, the new order required a measure of international cooperation.

Most of these discussions focused on how 'Schachtianism' might be avoided in the postwar world, and how a liberal trading order might be created. The suspicions of international capital movements were such that even the makers of the postwar economic order, who assembled at the Mount Washington Hotel in Bretton Woods, New Hampshire, in July 1944, believed that capital flows were unlikely to resume, that they were inherently destabilizing, and that they should therefore be regulated and controlled.

The liberal postwar settlement is unthinkable without the massive preponderance of the United States. There, the World War enabled not merely economic recovery from the Great Depression, but also a quite unique degree of economic preponderance. By 1945, the United States produced over half the world's manufactured goods, with the most productive technologies, and accounted for four fifths of the world's exports of manufactured goods. When the American policy-makers set out a view of an inter-connected world economy with unparalleled clarity, they also spoke from a position of enormous strength. Addressing the Bretton Woods conference, Secretary of the Treasury Henry Morgenthau stated: 'I hope that this Conference will focus its attention on two elementary economic axioms. The first of these is this: that prosperity has no fixed limits. It is not a finite substance to be diminished by division. On the contrary, the more of it that other nations enjoy, the more each nation will have for itself . . . The second axiom is a corollary of the first. Prosperity, like peace is indivisible. We cannot afford to have it scattered here or there among the fortunate or to enjoy it at the expense of others.'

In 1945, continental Europe was destroyed physically and politically. Apart from the neutrals, Switzerland and Sweden (which had both played a part in the Nazi war economy), every state had faced invasion and military defeat. Much of the post-1945 history of European recovery, and European integration, involves the export of American ideas, technology, and capital to Europe. In this way the globally integrated world that existed before the Great War and the Great Depression was put together, piece by piece. But that—as the saying goes—is another story.

# 4

# Politics

## Kevin Passmore[1]

If the nineteenth century brought into being most of the 'isms' with
which we are familiar—liberalism, socialism, nationalism, feminism,
and conservatism—the late nineteenth and early twentieth centuries
turned them into institutionalized contenders for state power, and
invented two more—fascism and communism. Parties did not
emerge smoothly. Some liberals feared that party discipline would
compromise free expression of opinion, while some conservatives felt
that politics should be the preserve of the upper classes. Electoral
manipulation was integral to politics in Hungary, southern Italy,
Spain, Bulgaria, and Greece. But by 1914 both left and right viewed
democratization as an historically inevitable process to which all
must adjust or face oblivion. Mass politics seemed, moreover, to be a
necessary consequence of unprecedented social change: advances in
communications by road, rail, print, telephone, and wireless, and the
gradual expansion of education.

Historians have agreed, not unreasonably, that there was a connection between the growth of parties and pressure groups and these
social changes. More debatably, historians at one time assumed a too
simplistic relationship between social change and politics. Liberal
historians held that the existence of a strong bourgeoisie guaranteed
political democratization. They expected that the bourgeoisie would
ultimately triumph over those who resisted 'modernization'—landed
aristocrats, peasants, artisans, and the factory proletariat. These latter
groups were said to have espoused antidemocratic ideologies ranging
from fascism to communism in a vain effort to halt the progress
of the market economy and liberal democracy. Social historians, in

[1] I would like to thank Garthine Walker for her comments on this chapter.

contrast, expected that 'experience' of class struggle in an industrial economy would convince workers that their true 'interest' lay in socialism. In spite of their great differences, liberals and social historians shared the assumption that history ineluctably moved towards a pre-determined end. Both spilled much ink in order to explain away deviations from the expected. If the bourgeoisie failed to head the movement for democratization, then the 'aristocratic spirit' must have corrupted it; if workers did not espouse socialism, they must have occupied an atypical position in the class structure, or their national state must have been 'peculiar'.

Recent studies of early twentieth-century politics have revised the old story in three major ways. First, political projects are now seen as contingently related to social conditions. Thus the predilection of large parts of the industrial proletariat for Marxist socialism would now be regarded as a product of historical *circumstances*, not as a 'normal' response to the concentration of workers in large factories and cities. Secondly, while continuing to emphasize the ways in which political projects are shaped by class, recent histories bring into play other social differences too—gender, religion, ethnicity, and nation, for example. Thirdly, rather than seeing party activists just as reflections of social forces, recent histories stress the role of activists themselves in shaping and defining their constituencies. Generally, activists saw one particular form of social difference, be it religion, nation, class, or gender, as fundamental, and they sought to organize political action around it. Their task was a difficult one, for other forms of identity constantly interfered, and activists themselves tended to define their cause in such a way that many of those they purported to represent were excluded—socialists, for example, spoke for the proletariat, but excluded some workers from their definition of the proletariat. Indeed, the struggle of activists to maintain the primacy, or even purity, of the religion, class, nation, or gender they wished to represent was a major source of political conflict—especially as this was an age in which grandiose schemes for social, eugenic or racial engineering seemed to become realizable.

How do these considerations impact upon our understanding of the titanic political struggles of the early twentieth century? There was clearly a broad movement in favour of democracy in the first years of century. In some countries left-liberal democratic parties were in government. The old élitist conservative regimes of Sweden,

TABLE 4.1: *The enfranchisement of men*

| | |
|---|---|
| France | 1848 |
| Greece | 1864 |
| Germany | 1871 |
| Belgium | 1893 |
| Norway | 1898 |
| Denmark | 1848, 1901 |
| Finland | 1906 |
| Austria | 1907 |
| Sweden | 1907 |
| Russia | 1917 |
| Netherlands | 1917 |
| Britain | 1918 |
| Italy | 1919 |
| Poland | 1919 |
| Czechoslovakia | 1919 |
| Yugoslavia | 1919 |
| Romania | 1919 |
| Spain | 1930 |
| Hungary | 1945 |

central, and eastern Europe were internally divided, lacked broad support, and often relied on coercion to stay in power. In western Europe conservatives themselves had begun in their own way to embrace mass politics, at the price of further internal strife. The Great War enormously weakened the opponents of democracy, shattering the Austrian, German, and Russian Empires, and strengthening the left everywhere else in Europe. Yet unless the old order had been completely destroyed, as it had in Russia, its powers of resistance to liberal democracy remained great. Moreover, the old right was joined by a new fascist right, which perverted democratic ideals, and incorporated them into a mass movement designed to crush the left. Soon, liberal democracy was on the defensive, all the more so as many of its own supporters were disappointed by experience of democracy in practice. The interwar years revealed the prejudices that underlay apparently universalist democracy. Many of those who had hitherto supported democracy sought in the extreme right an alternative way of realizing the promises democracy had once encapsulated.

# The Left, 1900–1914

Before 1914 most nationalist, socialist, and increasingly feminist groups agreed that the realization of their goals was dependent upon the existence of parliamentary democracy. Democracy was conceived in universalist terms, and was held to lead quasi-automatically to liberation and equality. In fact, pre-1914 notions of democracy were implicitly exclusionary, in terms of nation and ethnicity, gender, class, and religion. The chickens came home to roost in the interwar years.

## Nationalism

By 1914 nationalism was a mass force in the major multinational states. The Irish were the most nationalist of the nations in the British Isles. In the Habsburg Empire nationalism was strong amongst Poles, Romanians, Serbs, Croatians, and Slovenes, and in the Russian Empire amongst Poles, Lithuanians, and Finns. Nationalists were usually liberal, and saw self-determination and democracy as synonymous—when the majority gained the right to choose its own fate, the nation would become free. Few were conscious of a contra-diction between the idea that the nation rested on the exercise of the vote by free individuals, and ethnic, cultural, religious, and above all linguistic notions of nationalism. These latter conceptions implied that individuals had no choice regarding the nation to which they belonged, and that some might be excluded or included whatever their desires. The authoritarian potential was underlined by the tendency of many exponents of nationalism to see democracy as a continuous, emotional, quasi-religious affirmation of the nation.

Linguistic nationalism flourished because of the aggressive assimilationism of the Hungarian and Russian Governments—Polish students had to read Polish authors in Russian translation. Austria was more tolerant of linguistic diversity, but linguistic groups were locked into a bitter competition for jobs, education, and political influence. The introduction of universal male suffrage in the Habsburg Empire drew more and more people into this conflict. There was a dark side to linguistic nationalism, for liberal nationalists believed their own languages to be vehicles of enlightenment and others to be carriers of reaction. Displaying a liberal faith in the power of education, nationalists believed that individuals could be assimilated into the progressive nationality by learning its language. A foretaste of what was to come could be seen in Hungary, where a liberal-nationalist movement had won power in 1867, and embarked on a campaign to Magyarize the new state. In 1906 the Hungarian liberal Széll declared 'Every citizen is equal before the law, with the single limitation regarding language'. Romanian, Serb, and Croatian minorities in Hungary were driven to opposition, just as the consolidation of new national states after 1918 would create new oppressed minorities all over Europe.

The apparently universalist claims of liberal nationalism were also tempered by class. Liberal nationalism was usually bourgeois, and the Czechs provided the most successful example. Nationalist movements found it harder to win peasant and working-class support. Polish peasants were suspicious of nationalism as a movement of urban intellectuals and landlords, while Belorussian peasants almost entirely lacked national consciousness. There were some exceptions. In Ireland and the Ukraine, nationalists, with the help of the clergy, mobilized better-off peasants against respectively English landlords and Russian, Jewish, and Polish town-dwellers and landowners. Although working-class parties were far from indifferent to the national question, nationalism and socialism were associated explicitly only in Latvia and Finland—in both cases because opposition to Russification was cross-cut by antipathy to German and Swedish ruling classes respectively.

Women played significant roles in most nationalist movements—in Russian Poland a small number even belonged to terrorist groups. Yet women were confined to 'feminine' areas such as defence of education in minority languages and welfare work. In terrorist squads they carried messages and secreted weapons in their clothing rather than engage in combat. Notions of female passivity and responsibility for the home were as rooted in nationalist movements as in any other part of bourgeois society. National symbols, associated with the idea of sacrifice, were generally female, but it was men who embodied practically the national ideal: in the words of the Norwegian national anthem, 'all that the fathers have fought for, the mothers have wept for'. Nationalists actively fought for women's suffrage only where it seemed to be a useful means of attacking opponents. So in 1912 Czech nationalists sponsored an illegal female candidate to the Bohemian Diet in order to expose Germans as unenlightened reactionaries. Irish Nationalists, however, opposed women's suffrage bills on the grounds that their defeat might bring the anti-nationalist Conservative Party to power in London. It was not that nationalists were hostile in principle to women's suffrage, especially in the Czech lands, where there was a strong liberal tradition. Rather they expected women to subordinate feminist demands to the national cause. Nationalists were prepared to grant women the vote, but they would not allow feminists to win it for women.

## Feminism

Feminism, like nationalism, was a product of the socio-economic developments of the late nineteenth century—a cause and consequence of the expansion in opportunities for women in education and employment. Feminism also resembled nationalism in that it was an 'imagined movement' with disputed boundaries. 'Equality feminists' minimized gender differences; some went as far as Christabel Pankhurst in Britain and Madeleine Pelletier in France, in demanding liberation from childbirth and marriage. Equality feminists were usually liberal individualists. They demanded equal rights and a growing minority prioritized the suffrage. 'Familial' feminists, in contrast, felt that biological specificity entitled women to legislative protection as mothers, wives, and workers. These distinctions were not watertight. Some suffragists claimed that women would bring feminine idealism to politics; some familial feminists held that the vote would permit the enactment of welfare legislation.

Liberal feminism was dominant before 1914 and as such was part of a broader movement for democratic reform. Not surprisingly feminists shared the preconceptions of the movements with which they were associated. In Britain and Germany some liberal feminists endorsed the property franchise. Czech feminists fought against the sole use of German in international women's conferences. Czech and Romanian feminists campaigned for female suffrage, but Austro-Germans and especially Magyar feminists feared that extension of the vote would benefit ethnic minorities. As educators women were at the forefront of efforts to assimilate speakers of 'inferior' dialects,

TABLE 4.2: *The enfranchisement of women*

| | |
|---|---|
| Finland | 1906 |
| Iceland | 1908, 1911 |
| Norway | 1913 |
| Denmark | 1915 |
| Russia | 1917 |
| Britain | 1918, 1928 |
| Austria | 1918 |
| Germany | 1918 |
| Hungary | 1918 |
| Netherlands | 1919 |
| Poland | 1919 |
| Sweden | 1919–1921 |
| Czechoslovakia | 1919–1920 |
| Belgium | 1920, 1948 |
| Spain | 1932 |
| France | 1944 |
| Italy | 1945 |
| Portugal | 1945 |
| Yugoslavia | 1945 |
| Romania | 1946 |

and as welfare workers they tried to convince the proletariat that nationhood would resolve class conflict.

Feminism was not, however, synonymous with liberalism. To the left, as we shall see, there were advocates of women's rights within socialist parties. To the right, although Churches were hostile to feminism, they offered an opportunity for women to organize outside the home. Meanwhile working- and lower-middle-class women joined Catholic trade unions, which were antisocialist, but often favoured protection for women at work and the vote. Some women's organizations, such as the Patriotic League of French Women and the Norwegian Housewife's League—both of which were linked to conservative parties—were frankly antifeminist. Such movements drew upon a positive view of bourgeois domesticity. In the home women regulated children's education, directed domestic servants, and provided the point of departure for a crusade to moralize society through voluntary work. They saw liberal-feminist dismissal of domesticity (often more apparent than real) as a devaluation of their own lives, and regarded efforts to encourage women's non-domestic employment as undermining the supply of servants. At the International Women's Congress of 1900, there were clashes over a proposal to grant servants a weekly rest day. This antifeminism sometimes led to engagement in the new mass parties of the right.

## Socialism

The electoral breakthrough of socialism after 1890 seemed to confirm the correctness of Marx's view that the concentration of workers in towns and cities would lead naturally to the socialization of production. Yet there was no simple correlation between levels of industrialization and the strength of socialism. Britain, the most industrialized country in Europe, had little socialism to speak of, while in semi-industrialized Finland socialism depended upon landless labourers and tenant farmers. Moreover, circumstances determined whether workers identified with fellow proletarians, employers, religious, or national groups. Either side of the Rhine, in Belgium, the Netherlands, and parts of Germany and France, substantial proportions of the working class voted for Catholic parties, while in the Celtic fringes of Britain working-class liberalism remained strong in 1914, not least because of the Liberals' support for 'Home Rule all round'.

Actually, some sense of class was rarely absent from working-class movements whatever their political colour. Catholic parties were usually divided by conflicts between trade union and bourgeois wings. South Wales 'Lib-Labs' combined support for Liberalism with contempt for bourgeois Liberal activists. One Lib-Lab journalist wrote in 1902 that workers had become the true carriers of liberal principles, not the 'floating garbage of political nonentities whose contemptible performances render the name of "Liberal" nauseous to all men and women'. Class consciousness was present in non-socialist workers' movements, but working-class interests were defined differently, and class allegiance was not the sole or primary source of identity.

Socialists did prioritize class (as they defined it), and emphasized the deep chasm that divided bourgeoisie and proletariat. Reformism—the notion that capitalism, could be ameliorated through legislative intervention—was weak except in Britain and Switzerland. The German socialist Edward Bernstein's view that working-class conditions were improving under capitalism, that final collapse was unlikely, and that reformism represented the only way forward, found little favour.

Those, such as Lenin and Luxembourg, who sought to hasten the destruction of capitalism were more numerous than reformists. In any case, neither employers nor the state were willing to countenance significant reform—the German, Russian, and Swedish political systems were predicated on the exclusion of socialists. Left-liberal governments in Italy and Greece lacked the strength and resources to deliver on their promises to the labour movement.

The socialist mainstream rejected both reformism and the violent seizure of power. They regarded democracy as necessary for the construction of a party ready to profit from the end of capitalism—a strategy which rested on the belief that the state could be 'captured' from the bourgeoisie and used for socialist ends. The majority, personified by Karl Kautsky in Germany, saw organizational defence as paramount, and feared that premature action might disorganize the party. Socialists were therefore enthusiastic participants in campaigns for democracy in Belgium, Finland, and Austria. In Russia, Germany, and Sweden socialists held that the weakness of the bourgeoisie made it imperative for socialists to carry out the bourgeois revolution themselves. And when democracy appeared to be under threat from the right, socialists were prepared to defend essential liberties—as in France during the Dreyfus Affair. Even left socialists like Jean Allemane in France and Karl Renner in Austria hoped that universal suffrage would force the bourgeoisie to unite against the proletariat, thereby precipitating revolution.

Most socialists rejected nationalism on the grounds that it was bourgeois. Yet involvement in the struggle for democracy, and the conviction that the state could be used by the proletariat, entailed implicit endorsement of the nation-state. As Jean Jaurès said, nations were the precondition of freedom. So it is not surprising that French and German socialists should have been willing to defend their homelands against Prussian and Russian 'reaction' in July 1914. Socialists assumed that ethnic rivalries would disappear with the progress of democracy and equality. Yet the opposite sometimes appeared to happen. In the Habsburg Empire socialists were drawn into the language conflict. Although the Czech party condemned bourgeois nationalism so vociferously in the 1901 elections that it lost 80% of its seats, relations with the Austro-German socialists—the former accused the latter of dragging their feet in the campaign for universal suffrage—had in 1897 deteriorated to the point that the social democratic party of Austria had to be federalized along ethnic lines.

Socialists agreed with Auguste Bebel there could be 'no emancipation of humanity without the social independence and equality of the sexes'. Women joined the Finnish and German socialist parties in large numbers, and the contributions of women such as Rosa Luxembourg, Clara Zetkin, and Alexandra Kollontai to socialism had no parallel in liberal or conservative movements. Yet socialists dismissed feminism, like nationalism, as bourgeois. And they did little to promote women's suffrage. Behind this paradox lay the insistence that class take precedence over any other form of solidarity. Zetkin condemned feminism as a bourgeois distraction from the class struggle and suggested that since working-class men had no wealth, they could not be sexist. Socialists defined the proletariat in male terms and relegated women workers to a secondary position. Women's paid work was deemed to be temporary; they were said to lack the skill and strength of male workers. Socialists also took from bourgeois liberalism the idea that socialism would permit the full flowering of the rational, autonomous individual, and shared age-old perceptions that women were more emotional than rational, and consequently best suited to domesticity. Female activists were channelled into areas where their 'sensibilities' were most valuable, such as the peace movement.

Just as nationalists assumed that national democracy would overcome class and gender conflict, so socialists convinced themselves that social democracy would resolve gender and national tensions. In fact, the advent of universal male suffrage encouraged socialist parties to concentrate their efforts upon those workers who could vote—i.e. men.

## Left liberalism

In many countries left liberals took the head of the democratic movement. The 1900s were the heyday of the French Radical-Socialists, the Danish Radical Venstre, British new liberalism, Giolitti in Italy, and Venizelos in Greece. Left liberals saw the autonomous individual as the basis of a capitalist and democratic society organized in accordance with the dictates of reason and science. Hence their opposition to established Churches, which were seen as defenders of privilege and purveyors of obscurantist education. Left liberalism therefore appealed to non-conformists in the British Celtic fringe, to the anticlerical bourgeoisie in France and the low countries and to freemasons isolated in the towns of the Catholic Italian South. Whereas more conservative liberals rejected any form of state inter-ference with the free play of individual interest, left liberals permitted workers to defend their interests in trade unions. They also believed that the state should intervene to ensure that the disadvantaged could realize their potential as individuals—hence their support for educational and social reform. Because of their espousal of equality and freedom, left liberals attracted the support of nationalists, socialists, and feminists. But they struggled to reconcile the challenges represented by these movements with their faith in the individual.

Left liberals did not favour socialism. They hoped to incorporate workers into capitalist society through ownership of property, in the form of smallholdings or shares. They disliked the word class, prefer-ring to speak of the people instead. Rights were bestowed on trade unions to encourage class collaboration rather than conflict— Venizelos granted generous rights to unions, but forbade as immoral the use of 'proletariat' in their titles. When trade unions espoused collective interests too forcefully, as in France in 1906, the Radical government of Clemenceau used the full weight of the state against them. In Britain the resistance of Liberal Party caucuses to working-class candidatures pushed trade unionists towards the Labour Party. In Sweden liberals forced constitutional government on the king in 1906, but failed to exploit their victory because some preferred a franchise rigged to exclude urban workers.

Left liberals found the challenge of national minorities equally difficult to deal with. Their belief in self-determination could lead to sympathy for autonomist movements. In Britain, the Liberals favoured home rule for Ireland, partly because they needed the back-ing of Irish nationalists in Parliament, and partly because the notion of the indivisible state was less powerful amongst British liberals than it was among continental counterparts. The French Radicals developed the doctrine of popular sovereignty differently. For them democracy and majority rule implied the unity of the national state. They distrusted Catholics and socialists for their loyalty to an extra-national source of authority. Radical distrust of linguistic particularism was as strong as that of Hungarian liberals. In 1906 a

Radical government forbade teaching of the catechism in 'backward' Breton.

Left liberals were lukewarm towards female enfranchisement. They defined the individual in masculine terms and did not believe women sufficiently rational to exercise the vote. In France, the irrationality of women seemed to be confirmed by their greater religious practice, and so the Radicals were convinced opponents of female suffrage. In Britain Liberals feared that women would vote for the Conservatives. Moreover, left liberals favoured policies designed to 'improve' the population qualitatively through eugenicist projects for healthy reproduction or elimination of the 'unfit', and quantitatively through the encouragement of births. These schemes assumed that the primary duty of women was to bear children.

Nowhere was left liberalism in a position to federate democratic forces. In Britain, labour unrest, suffragist protest, and opposition to Irish Home rule provoked a sense of malaise among the ruling Liberals; in France, conservative liberals were increasingly influential in centrist coalition governments; Giolitti lost power in Italy in 1914, having been squeezed between socialist, Catholic, and conservative opposition. Elsewhere left liberals had never been strong. In the low countries anticlerical left liberals were excluded from power by religious parties; in Scandinavia they were divided by town–country conflicts; in Germany and Sweden the bourgeoisie's antisocialism deprived left liberalism of potential support; in Russia liberal dreams of class collaboration were ruined by the industrial struggles provoked by the Lena Goldfield massacre of 1912; in the Habsburg Empire liberalism was subsumed within nationalist movements.

In spite of the divisions and contradictions of the democratic movement, history seemed to be on its side. Moreover, the right was just as divided by class, religion and ethnicity. And except in Russia, it had been forced to compromise with democracy—at the price of further division.

# The Right, 1900–1914

Politically, the right was divided into two tendencies. Liberal conservatives preached the freedom of the individual to define his/

her own future according to their capacities (assumed to vary according to class, heredity, and gender). For liberal conservatives, individualism underpinned market economics, representative institutions, and government by the most able. Conservatives, in contrast, regarded churches, hereditary landed aristocracies, monarchs, and upper chambers as pillars of hierarchical societies in which the individual was defined by membership of family, profession, and nation.

These two rights had much in common. Both unanimously defended the social and political pre-eminence of the ruling class, and were resolutely opposed to socialism, feminism, and national separatism. Often this drew them together. In Britain the growth of new liberalism pushed many Liberal Party voters towards the Tories. Likewise, French moderate republicans accepted support from ex-royalists in the 1890s. In Italy in 1911 the Gentilone agreement between liberals and Catholics, showed that fear of socialism had moderated clerical opposition to a state founded on the ruins of the Pope's temporal power. In Germany, Conservatives, National Liberals, and the Catholic Centre formed an antisocialist front.

Conservative and liberal-conservative rights were also united by a sense of male honour. There was a mania for decorations (honours) in this period and women were not usually eligible for them. Most strikingly, the political duel (a symbolic proof of virility rather than a battle to the death) remained widespread in Spain, Germany, France, and Austria-Hungary—the Hungarian Prime Minister István Tisza fought three whilst in office. Furthermore, from the 1890s masculinity became more explicit in right-wing politics. At a time when ideas about genetics, race, social health, and national power were being popularized, some right wingers called for a new cold-blooded and warlike masculinity. The other side of the coin was insistence upon the maternal vocation of women. In Britain, France, Germany, and Italy politicians worried about the allegedly greater fertility of hostile neighbours, while in Austria-Hungary ethnic groups feared that rivals might outstrip them in the production of babies. Anxiety was compounded by the attraction of feminism to many upper-class women, for it seemingly diverted women from the vocation of motherhood and challenged the male monopoly on public life.

Alliances between conservative and liberal-conservative rights were reinforced too by the conviction that national separatism, feminism, and socialism were aspects of the same evil—the placing of self-interest above the public good. The right therefore linked the dangers it faced: strikes were dismissed as the work of crowds subject to 'feminine' passion; minority languages were seen as 'unmanly'; socialism and feminism were imagined to issue from a Jewish conspiracy, and so on.

Yet if the right mentally assimilated the dangers it faced, it was uncertain about how to deal with them. It agreed neither on the nature of the threat nor on what had to be defended, and sometimes the more serious the danger, the more conservatives feared that the solutions of rivals would aggravate the situation. They did not even agree on the nature of honour. In Germany, whereas aristocrats paraded decorations as symbols of inherent superiority, liberal conservatives believed that only sobriety and hard work could earn respect. Liberal conservatives condemned duelling as an irrational way to settle disputes. Catholics rejected duelling for the bad example it set to the lower classes: the German Centre Party activist Gröber held that one could not 'wean workers from their rough ways if their betters continued to butcher each other at twenty paces'. Many feminists agreed—even the aristocratic Hungarians campaigned for the suppression of duelling. Thus embedded within the debate about duelling were fundamental differences in the way in which the social order was conceived.

Moreover, conservatives viewed the threats they faced through the lens of pre-existing religious and ethnic identities. The persistence of the religious issue as a source of division among the wealthy in Italy was symbolized by the limited—and secret—nature of the afore-mentioned Gentilone Pact. In Germany the Catholic Centre fought to end the underrepresentation of Catholics in public life, and in 1905 the appointment of Martin Spahn, son of a Catholic politician, to a chair of Catholic history provoked conflict between Protestant and Catholic Germany. In France, monarchist, republican, and Catholic conservatives constituted a united right only in the sense that potatoes in a sack constituted a sack of potatoes.

Although in eastern and southern Europe socialism was weaker, fear of democratization might have brought the élites together. The reality was of complex struggles between administrative factions, bourgeoisie and landowners, conditioned by religious and ethnic cleavages and the predilections of monarchs. Tsar Nicholas II saw Russia as a landed estate owned by himself and managed by the aristocracy. He resented reforming administrators such as Petr

Stolypin (Chief Minister, 1906–11) as barriers between himself and his people. King Carol I of Romania, in contrast, sided with liberal bureaucrats against conservative landowners. Elsewhere in the Balkans the landed aristocracy was not politically important, having been expelled with the end of Ottoman rule, and so bureaucratic and professional factions battled for dominance. In Austria the introduction of universal suffrage (1907) put paid to what remained of aristocratic influence. But because Parliament was paralysed by ethnic quarrels, the enlightened despotism of the bureaucracy still dominated the political system. Albert Gessman, leader of the Christian Social Party, failed to create an antisocialist alliance in Austria because he did not understand that for bourgeois Czechs, Germans and Southern Slavs, rival ethnic groups posed just as great a threat to their interests (as they conceived them) as did the socialists.

In Hungary the aristocracy was dominant. Far from being conservative, it ostentatiously upheld a parliamentarianism forged in a historic struggle for nationhood against Habsburg absolutism. The Magyar élite promoted access to the professions, commerce, and even the aristocracy for all ethnic groups, on condition of assimilation to Magyar culture. Yet Hungarian liberalism was increasingly hard-pressed by the National and Catholic People's parties. The latter parties, which recruited from the lesser gentry, commercial, and administrative classes, condemned the élites for failing to pursue assimilation with sufficient vigour.

The difficulties of the right were compounded by the emergence, from the 1890s, of popular conservatism. The new right was not sharply separated from the old. The German Conservative Party adopted the demagogic antisemitism of peasant radicalism at the Tivoli conference of 1893; in France the liberal-conservative Progressists assimilated nationalism and antisemitism during the Dreyfus Affair, while in 1911 the British Conservative Willoughby de Broke claimed that 'if our present leaders do not take care, a middle party of Tories who mean business will smash them'. New and old rights perceived the same threats to society: in Germany the nationalist right included a League in Struggle against the Emancipation of Women, an Imperial League Against Social Democracy, and a host of organizations designed to defend ethnic Germans against minorities.

Yet this overlap should not obscure the fact that the new right castigated established conservatives in the name of 'the people'. The new right drew upon its own distorted, democratic idealism, and connected it to religious, ethnic, gender, and class antipathies. German peasants denounced Jews and Junkers; Hungarian civil servants and professionals resented Jewish competition for jobs; French nationalists condemned anticlerical bias in state appointments; small traders in Budapest, Paris, and Vienna resented Jewish big business and department stores. The radical right saw successful reaction as conditional upon a remaking of the ruling class. The Black Hundreds in Russia demanded a popular autocracy and the Pan-German League a people's Kaiser.

The mixture of radicalism and reaction in the new right is encapsulated in its attitude to women. Radical rightists wished to restore the virility of the political system. They saw the ruling classes as 'effeminate'—hence the duelling fetish of the French nationalist Paul Déroulède and the Italian futurist Marinetti's 'scorn for women'. Yet the new right was torn between opposition to women's involvement in politics and the desire to use women to fill seats at public meetings. Consequently women were attracted to movements as diverse as the Primrose League in Britain and the Pan-Germans, for their mass character seemed to offer political openings not usually available to them. The Women's Division of the German Colonial Society endeavoured to recruit servants for colonial families, in order to minimize contact of German babies with native nurses. Domesticity, class interest, and racism were harnessed to right-wing mass politics.

Some new right movements, such as the Primrose League, and increasingly the Christian Socials in Austria, were constitutionalist. Others, like the Black Hundreds, the Pan-German League, the Italian Nationalist Association, and Carson's Ulster Volunteers prefigured fascism. Before 1914 most, nevertheless, wanted to revitalize the existing system rather than bring an alternative élite to power at the head of a mass party. Nevertheless, popular conservatism, whatever its form, testifies to the extent to which the notions of popular sovereignty and reform had invaded the right, and demonstrated the malleability of these slogans. Even Kaiser William II felt that military intervention in politics had no relevance in Germany, for legitimacy depended on mass loyalty. When liberal democracy hit the rocks in the interwar years, conservatives were well placed to step in, for the explicit exclusions of far right politicians could be found implicitly in democratic politics too.

# The impact of the Great War

In 1914 Europe was home to a broad movement for democratization and equality, expressed in left liberalism, socialism, nationalism, and increasingly feminism. Yet before 1914 few envisaged immediate transformation. Socialists concentrated on piling up votes, and Lenin famously postponed revolution to beyond his lifetime. Nationalists generally limited their demands to greater autonomy. Feminists mainly sought to improve their position within a patriarchal order. The most significant revolutionary outbreak of the period, in Russia in 1905, was defeated relatively easily once the government succeeded in dividing the opposition. Since it had enough loyal troops it could pick off villages that participated in the massive peasant uprising one by one. Yet the events of 1905 showed what *might* be achieved where a regime had been weakened by military defeat.

The Great War dramatically altered the balance of political and social power. The Tsarist autocracy was forced to draw upon the skills of the liberal bourgeoisie to organize the war effort. Workers were needed to work in armaments factories; in Britain, France, Italy, and Germany socialists were brought into government. Women organized social services and took over male jobs in factories and offices. To bolster fighting spirit governments made extravagant promises of land for peasants, reforms for workers, and independence for nationalists at a time when war had reduced their ability to deliver. The Russian autocracy collapsed completely under the strains of war, revolution broke out in the defeated countries and unrest spared neither victorious nor neutral states. In 1918–19 women gained the vote, land reforms were enacted, trade union rights recognized, socialists participated in government in Germany, Denmark, Sweden, Czechoslovakia, Hungary, Russia, and Austria. Democratic nation-states were created out of the ruins of multinational empires; democratization advanced in Britain and Scandinavia. Only in Spain, did democracy fail to take root.

Yet the victory of liberal democracy depended upon a fragile balance of power. It was seriously weakened by the refusal of America or Britain to back democracy economically or politically. Furthermore, war brutalized politics in a way that worked against the left. To be sure, the Bolshevik victory in Russia owed much to the willingness of leather-jacketed, gun-toting Bolshevik militants to take advantage of the wave of violence against the ruling classes that swept across Russia in 1917, and then to suppress it ruthlessly once the Red Army had defeated the Whites in the Civil War. Where the ruling classes had not been destroyed, however, they proved hard to dislodge. Their armies invariably crushed ill-armed popular insurrections. Not a single communist rising succeeded in interwar Europe, and left-wing resistance to military intervention in politics and fascist violence was largely ineffective. Mussolini succeeded in his desire to 'write history with the fist, not the pen'.

Often the use of violence and compulsion was implicit in the vogue for social engineering. Total war had reinforced the notion that individuals could and should be moulded to the purposes of society and nation, and seemed to offer new means of achieving such ends, through state intervention and scientific techniques of managing everything from factories to housework. Interest in the 'science' of eugenics became widespread in political circles, and elaborate schemes were conceived for raising birth rates and improving the ethnic purity and military fitness of the nation. Socialists were attracted to eugenicism by barely acknowledged doubts about the suitability of the 'rough and violent' proletariat for the historic role allotted to it. Soviet social engineering found its well-spring in disgust at the 'Asiatic barbarism' of the Russian masses. On the extreme right, eugenicism was often married to biological racism, which began to displace liberal assimilationism. Eugenicism came in many varieties—left and right, negative and positive, racist in Britain and Germany, familialist in Italy and France. Many eugenicists and natalists saw parliamentary 'chatterers' as ill suited to the task of hardening the nation for participation in international struggle.

The spread of political violence, the obsession with national power, and interest in social engineering contributed to a general retreat of liberalism in the interwar years. Socialists—the firmest defenders of democracy—lost votes to communists and to the far right. Left-liberal parties like the British Liberals, German People's Party, and to a lesser extent the French Radicals all declined. Liberal-nationalist élites in Hungary and the Balkans abandoned schemes to integrate industrialized nation-states into the world market, and idealized the healthy peasant family instead. Liberal feminism succumbed to political polarization and the weight of familialism. In Hungary the historically liberal women's movement echoed radical-right demands for the exclusion of Jews from the professions. In Britain the Pankhursts threw themselves into patriotic war work, and relations with hitherto friendly Irish suffragists deteriorated. Many of the new states of eastern Europe were pushed towards right-wing authoritarianism as the drive to create homogenous nations engendered conflict with national minorities. Assimilation of minorities relied more upon compulsion, and was combined increasingly with exclusionary biological racism. Ukrainian schools were closed in Poland; Slovenian schools in Austria. The chief victims were the Jews, who by 1938–9 found themselves legally excluded from employment in Germany, Hungary, Italy, and Romania. The Polish nationalist Roman Dmowski spoke of the 'end of the Jewish chapter in history'.

Disillusion with liberal democracy was compounded by its failure to satisfy many of those who had placed so much hope in it. Some countries refused to grant women the vote; where female suffrage was implemented it changed little. Women represented only 3.3% of those elected to the Czechoslovak Parliament in 1930 and in Britain only 36 served in the Commons between the wars. Only in Finland did women make a real impact in Parliament, and in 1924 Denmark's first socialist government appointed a woman as its Minister of Education. Likewise, workers were disappointed. Socialist parties were quickly excluded from coalitions in Sweden, Austria, and Germany. Although most states did implement significant measures of social reform, the coalitions of socialists, left liberals, and reformist Catholics that had made them possible soon broke down. The experience of democracy for many workers was one of actual or potential unemployment. Some east European and Balkan states did make a success of land reform—especially where it was possible to disburse the property of formerly dominant nationalities, such as Hungarians and Germans in Czechoslovakia. In Romania, Poland, and Hungary, in contrast, the failure of land reform poisoned political life.

The conditions of interwar Europe exposed the exclusiveness of apparently universalist democracy. Women, peasants, workers, and ethnic minorities were not granted rights as citizens or as equal human beings, but because they had 'earned' the right to a stake in the land, to 'homes fit for heroes' or to 'protection', by 'proving' their patriotism in war. Given this implicit hierarchization of citizens, it is not surprising that granting of political rights should have been accompanied by renewed insistence upon domesticity for women, or that workers and peasants should have been expected once again to sacrifice their 'selfish interest' to the nation when the economic situation deteriorated. The prevalence of the linguistically and/or ethnically unitary notion of the nation-state made the plight of minorities even worse, for they were often regarded as fifth columns for foreign powers.

The decline of liberalism coincided with reinforcement of right-wing hostility to democracy, which was regarded as too favourable to socialists, feminists, and national minorities. Yet conservative hopes of restoring the *status quo ante bellum* soon faded. Deposed royal families, for example, quickly faded from the political scene. Monarchism was weak amongst the Russian Whites, and was irrelevant in Austria. The élites were forced to negotiate with a mass reaction, composed of all those who felt threatened by the post-war social upheaval. This mass movement was characterized by deep hatred of socialism, communism, feminism, and ethnic minorities, but also by resentments against the élites and indeed an aspiration for change. In fact, interwar politics can be understood as a struggle to attach the reformist promise once embodied in democracy to communism, fascism, or social democracy.

# The failure of the Left, 1919–1933

In spite of the enormous fear of communism in interwar Europe, there was little chance of a repeat of 1917 outside Russia, and by the late 1920s Stalin was cynically proclaiming that the Communist International would not bring about a single revolution in a hundred years. The October Revolution had succeeded because of the fragmentation of the ruling class, the collapse of the army, and Lenin's willingness to back working-class demands for control of the factories, peasant desire for land and village self-government, self-determination for minorities, the aspirations of women, and soldiers' desperation for peace—although the party had serious misgivings on each of these issues. The Bolsheviks were thus able to extend their appeal well beyond the ranks of the proletariat. Peasant support for

Bolshevism quickly declined thanks to requisitioning and conscription but the Whites were even more ruthless towards the peasantry. Thus the support that the Bolsheviks enjoyed in the towns tipped the balance in their favour in the Civil War. Subsequently, like the Tsarist state before them, the Bolsheviks used superior force to overcome peasant resistance village by village. Then in 1921, in order to counter food crises and conciliate the peasantry, Lenin introduced the New Economic Policy.

Lenin's dramatic shifts between proletarian purity and opportunist concession provided the international communist movement with an ambiguous legacy. On the one hand Leninism was guided by an inflexible notion of working-class interest embodied in a movement of professional revolutionaries. In *What is to be done?* (1902) Lenin had doubted the revolutionary capacity of the proletariat, and placed more emphasis upon the role of the intelligentsia (the progressive bourgeoisie)—indeed, he denied that the latter was distinct from the former. The agent of revolution was a party which spoke for an abstract notion of the working-class interest, not the workers themselves. On the other hand, Lenin's low opinion of the proletariat co-existed with a faith in the intrinsically revolutionary potential of national minorities and the poor peasantry. Indeed, communism often seemed more like a sort of revolutionary populism led by an élite defined by doctrinal purity than a class-based movement.

In the Soviet Union the outcome of these tensions—never inevitable—was Stalin's revolution. Although Stalin set forced collectivization and purges in motion, he fed off and aggravated the people's hatred of the rich, the bourgeoisie, engineers, party officials, intellectuals, and wealthier (often only slightly wealthier) peasants. This popular movement was based more on the notion of 'us', the toilers, against 'them', the parasites, often identified with Jews and foreigners, than on class in the Marxist sense. Although this populist hatred proved difficult to control it provided much of the momentum behind Stalin's revolution. This was especially true when Stalin turned against engineers and intellectuals in 1928–9, and during the great purge of the party in 1936–7. During the latter Stalin spoke of the 'enemies of the *people*' rather than the proletariat, and encouraged ordinary people to denounce senior officials and army officers. By freeing up jobs in the bureaucracy, the purges created opportunities for social advancement for workers and peasants, who in turn became targets of popular resentment themselves. Stalin, ironically, used popular dislike of the Bolshevik hierarchy, which often extended to himself, to establish absolute control over the Party, in the name of the ideological purity of the vanguard of the proletarian revolution.

In the international communist movement the tensions of Leninism were never resolved. Béla Kun's Hungarian Soviet Republic failed partly because of a narrowly proletarian interpretation of Leninism. The revolution of March 1919 had resulted from unrest among workers of Budapest coupled with the expectation that Trotsky's Red Army would evict Czech and Romanian armies from Hungary. Yet communist preference for nationalization over workers' control of factories and for state farms over distribution of land to the peasantry, rapidly lost them mass support. They also alienated nationalists by attacking national symbols, and the fate of the revolution was sealed by failure to hold off the Romanians. The ruling élites, which had never been weakened to the extent of their Russian counterparts, returned in the baggage of the Romanian army.

Communists were never unaware of the need for non-proletarian allies, so long as leadership of the party was preserved. In the 1920s the Comintern insisted that any such alliance must be revolutionary in nature, and the results were mixed. Following Lenin, much attention was paid to national minorities. In the USSR itself, the administrations of Soviet Republics like the Ukraine were taken over by Ukrainians, for it was felt (somewhat unrealistically) that the construction of socialism would reduce national loyalty to a secondary phenomenon. Ironically, the USSR inadvertently promoted, or even created national feeling amongst groups such as Belorussians. The Comintern also took up the cause of national minorities outside the USSR, and won some support amongst Slovaks in Czechoslovakia, Ukrainians, Belorussians and Jews in Poland, Jews in Romania, and Italian immigrants in France. The cost was often alienation of the dominant ethnic group in the working class, especially given the Comintern's insistence that border states be incorporated into the USSR. Another danger was that communists would see national struggle as a cause in its own right. In the USSR the Ukrainian party became an object of suspicion. In France, Alsatian communists identified the Alsatian *volk* as the agent of revolution and denounced the twin enemies of capitalism and French imperialism. Alsatian dissidents were expelled from the party in 1929, for having taken to its logical conclusion Lenin's contention that national liberation movements were objectively revolutionary.

Neither did communists have much success in winning the support of women. Again the problem was that the Comintern espoused women's rights, but sought to subordinate gender issues to proletarian revolution as defined by the party. The Soviet Union had accorded unparalleled rights to women, from abortion on demand to quotas for representation in soviets. The visibility of communist activists like Kollontai, Zetkin, the Romanian Anna Pauker and the Spaniard Dolores Ibarruri ('La Pasionara') did much to enhance in bourgeois eyes the image of communism as destructive of the family. Yet women participated in communist organizations only on condition that they subordinate 'bourgeois' feminist concerns to the revolution. Lenin famously admonished Zetkin when he heard that she had been discussing 'sex and marriage' with women at a time when 'the first proletarian state in the world is battling with counter-revolutionaries of the whole world'. Moreover, women were expected to adhere to masculine ideas about how a professional revolutionary should behave. Marxist scientists urged women to become more like proletarian men. Communists concentrated on mobilizing workers in the workplace, and the image of muscle-bound metal workers and miners became central to party propaganda. And whereas stereotypical views of women as bearers of harmony had permitted them to play a significant role in the socialist-led peace movement before 1914, communists had an entirely different attitude to violence. The French communist, Maurice Laporte, boasted in 1921 'We do not moan about war and its horrors as those in the Second International do. Down with snivelling and humanitarian pacifism.'

Within the limits represented by the masculine domination of the party, women often used party ideology creatively. Kollontai rejected both 'bourgeois' feminism and the 'hypocritical' notion that the sexual problem should be relegated to the realm of family affairs. But since joining or voting for the communists involved flouting social conventions, most women were repelled by it. Women constituted only 7.4% of Soviet party members in 1920; nor was the German party successful amongst female voters. In any case communists implicitly distinguished between women within the party, who had subordinated their femininity to politics, and those outside it, to whom more conventional notions of femininity applied. The majority of Bolshevik activists, including Lenin, felt that female equality would strengthen the family.

Whereas communists prioritized revolutionary struggle, socialists remained convinced that parliamentary democracy provided a viable route to power—all the more unanimously since their insurrectionary minorities had been lost to communism. The German socialists identified absolutely with the Weimar constitution. Having been propelled into government, socialist parties were willing to enact measures such as the eight-hour day. But mainstream socialists still remained convinced of the inevitable collapse of capitalism. Their 'all-or-nothing' mentality meant that they had to combine reforms—which the bourgeoisie resented greatly—with conventional financial policies. Major experiments in welfare policy in municipalities such as Avesnes in France and 'red Vienna' were conceived of as 'partial realizations of socialism within the womb of bourgeois society' rather than as reform of capitalism. Even in Britain the Labour Party in office rejected reformist schemes put forward by Keynes and Mosley as mere tinkering, leaving little alternative but to support the Treasury view of financial policy.

Socialism largely failed to broaden its support. Municipal socialism was concerned primarily with the proletariat. German socialists (the SPD) alienated peasants and small business by insisting that 'organized capitalism' would create large economic units amenable to socialist management. Feminism became a dirty word in the British Labour Party, while the SPD placed greater emphasis upon maternalism and its women's sections declined. In Avesnes crèches were introduced into factories not to liberate women, but to improve the health of the population.

The dangers of socialist dogmatism had been cruelly exposed during the Russian Revolution. Moderate socialists refused to endorse Soviet power, sanction peasant claims on the land, end the war, or satisfy the claims of national minorities on the grounds that only a democratically elected assembly could resolve such issues. In Italy, socialists espoused an equally dogmatic 'maximalist' programme, which forbade coalition with bourgeois or Catholic antifascists. This left the way clear for conservatives to combine with Mussolini's Fascists in a parliamentary coalition. Socialist preconceptions made it equally difficult to respond effectively to the Depression and to the rise of Nazism. German socialists noted the appeal of Nazi anticapitalism to many workers, but their conviction that they alone knew the 'real' interests of the proletariat convinced them that pro-Nazi workers would eventually realize that only the SPD offered a genuine alternative to capitalism. The need to prevent loss of their electorate to the communists further encouraged socialists to insist upon the primacy of class, and made it difficult for them to compromise with bourgeois parties in antifascist alliances. Most socialist parties appealed for the defence of constitutional legality, which they saw as the precondition of socialism, and divisions within the movement revolved around how best to do this. German socialists attempted to bolster the semi-authoritarian Brüning government in order to defend the last vestiges of constitutionalism against the Nazis. The Austrians hesitated between backing the lesser evil of the Dollfuss regime against the Austro-Nazis and armed defence of the constitution. Neither strategy was successful.

The communists were just as ineffective. Before 1928 their approach was haphazard. Bordiga insisted that fascism was a necessary stage of capitalism and a precursor of revolution, while Gramsci, Dimitroff, and Zetkin held that it represented a potentially fatal danger to the proletariat. After 1928 the Bordiga line won out as the Comintern announced revolution to be imminent and declared to be fascist anyone, including socialists, who obscured this truth from the proletariat. This 'class against class' policy had some success in Germany, where socialist control over the Prussian government and police made social democracy look like an ally of capitalism. But in France, where there was a tradition of left-wing co-operation, communism was marginalized, and in Greece even the revolutionary wing of the party rejected the Comintern's analysis. Whilst it is doubtful whether communist parties, often with tiny memberships, reliant upon the unemployed in Germany, and faced with near universal antipathy on the part of other movements, could have done much to resist fascism on their own, the sectarianism of 1929 to 1933 did little to facilitate the formation of broad antifascist movements.

# Fascism and conservatism

The extreme right posed a far greater threat to liberal democracy than did the Left. But conservative dictatorship was much more common than fascism, and even in Germany and Italy fascism came to power only with conservative support. Conservatives and fascists shared hostility to communism, socialism, feminism, liberalism, minorities, and parliamentarianism, and both prioritized nation over class. Yet fascists were equally convinced that the old right represented an obstacle to national regeneration, because of its allegedly soft attitude towards subversion, its cosmopolitanism, and unmanliness. Fascism's hostility towards the establishment was manifest in its use of mass mobilization, its recruitment from discontented parts of the conservative rank and file, and its endeavour to create new national communities, often defined racially, which would eradicate class and gender conflict. Authoritarian conservatism, in contrast, represented the non-democratic rule of army, bureaucracy, and sometimes the Church—albeit usually in the name of the people and usually without total destruction of parliamentary institutions. The old right attempted to co-opt fascists, but feared that fascism represented a variant of Bolshevism.

Furthest removed from fascism was the Piłsudski regime in Poland. Initially, it was not clearly right wing, for it had been supported by trade unions, socialists, and national minorities. With time, however, the regime moved to the right and depended increasingly on officers and landowners. In Romania Carol II intervened in 1920 to evict a government perceived as too favourable to national minorities, and again in 1937–8 against the danger represented by the fascist Iron Guard. Carol established a government under the patriarch of the Romanian Orthodox Church, who introduced a corporatist state. Likewise in Hungary, the Regent, Admiral Horthy, ensured the political pre-eminence of the old right until in 1932 social and economic crisis obliged him to appoint the pro-fascist Gömbös to the premiership. Gömbös's power was circumscribed, and subsequently Horthy turned back to the old right. Nevertheless, a sort of dual government developed, as fascistic junior army officers, engineer, and medical associations interfered in administration.

Fascism in eastern Europe was altogether more dynamic than authoritarian conservatism. Its radicalism derived from the efforts of nationalists to construct ethnically homogenous states. In Poland Dmowski's proto-fascist Endeks demanded the creation of Polish commercial and professional classes, largely at the expense of Jews. Likewise the Romanian Iron Guard drew support from students and intellectuals who regarded themselves as the vanguard of the Romanian nation in its battle against Hungarians and Jews. In Hungary doctors and engineers demanded restriction of Jewish influence in the professions. Fascism also drew upon peasant discontent. In both Romania and Hungary peasants had opposed the liberal and conservative governments of the 1920s for their tax policies and their opposition to land reform. The Iron Guard and the Hungarian Arrow Cross promised to regenerate the nation through economic autarky, land reform, and eugenicist strengthening of ethnically Romanian and Hungarian peasant families. Both movements also won considerable working-class support by exploiting opposition to Jewish employers. In Hungary the Arrow Cross bit substantially into the socialist vote and the national miners' strike of 1940 was led by fascists.

This radicalism ensured that fascism could not form the alliances with conservative forces required to win power, even though fear of communism was endemic—in the form of powerful myths related to Russian expansionism and the Jewish quest for world domination. In countries where large proportions of business was in Jewish hands, antisemitism threatened to turn into a general attack on private property. In 1939 the conservative Hungarian Justice Minister resigned, claiming that antisemitic measures represented 'the expropriation of value created by others'.

Mussolini and Hitler were more willing to play down their radicalism. The Italian fascists engaged in a destructive campaign against socialism in the winter of 1920–1, while from 1928 to 1933 the Nazis presented communism as the main danger to the nation. Mussolini endorsed financial rectitude, rejected republicanism, and converted to Catholicism. Hitler did not go as far, but he was prepared to woo business support. Both dictators contracted long-lasting alliances with conservatives. The Italian monarchy remained in place, and the army was loyal to it, while the Church retained privileges. When Mussolini finally broke with parliamentary democracy in 1925 former members of the old Italian Nationalist Association, which sought to popularize the monarchy rather than replace it, were as influential as hard-line fascists. In Germany, conservatives were weaker than in Italy, but remained influential to the end. Nazi racial and expansionist policies could not have been implemented without the help of the army and civil service.

Yet it would be a mistake to see the willingness of the old right to bring Fascists and Nazis into government in Italy and Germany simply as a consequence of the lesser radicalism of Nazism. In fact both Fascists and Nazis combined parliamentary negotiation with extra-parliamentary pressure. The March on Rome has too easily been dismissed as a charade by historians who wish to downplay fascist populism. Nazi radicalism was displayed in the grassroots campaign against the 'undemocratic' governments of Brüning and Papen in 1932. In effect, the Nazis reinserted the symbols of the left—muscular workers and corpulent capitalists—into a discourse founded on the primacy of the biologically-defined nation. Communist voters were largely immune to this populism, and the great majority of Nazi voters were bourgeois or peasant Protestants. Yet in July 1932 around 27% of all workers voted for the Nazis and by then one in six of those who had voted for the SPD in 1930 had deserted to the Nazis. Whereas the SPD rejected in the name of doctrinal purity a public works programme elaborated by the trade unions, the Nazis took it over and attached it to racist nationalism.

In fact, conservatives brought Hitler into the government because, faced with both communist and Nazi subversion, they felt that they had insufficient popular support to establish a right-wing dictatorship. Both the desire to use fascists against the left, *and* fear of the mass fascist movement, shaped the old right's attitudes. It might even be said that the German and Italian rights' conviction that government required popular approval explains why fascism triumphed in those countries rather than in eastern Europe, where there was a weaker tradition of representative government.

Some historians go so far as to see fascism as a form of *revolutionary* nationalism. This is perhaps excessive, since fascism prioritized the interests of the dominant nationality. But fascists were prepared to take on established interests where they seemed to frustrate national interests, and it is impossible to understand the nature of fascism without taking this into account. Radicalism was evident in the efforts of fascist parties to supplant armies and civil services, in the attempt to combine destruction of the left with mobilization of workers within the national community, and in the disregard of economic or military objections to the murder of Jewish war workers by the SS. In Italy socialist and Catholic agricultural workers were forced to join fascist unions. Strikes were called against wage cuts, and one employer was murdered in the name of 'class collaboration'. As a result of a wave of discontent in 1925, in which Fascist unions played a significant role, employers were forced to grant Fascist unions a monopoly on workers' representation. That this victory turned out to be hollow does not detract from the radical ambition of many fascists. In both Germany and Italy fascist regimes failed to convince the great majority of industrial workers of the egalitarianism of the new national community, but innovative leisure and welfare programmes, coupled with repression, might have temporarily depoliticized the proletariat.

Fascist policies towards women displayed similar complexities. One hardly needs to emphasize the aggressive masculinity of movements that emerged partly as a response to the perceived breakdown of orderly gender relations during the Great War. Mosley demanded 'men who are men and women who are women'. Hitler regarded feminism as an invention of the Jews, and ended Weimar's ban on duelling. Mussolini's lieutenant Turati—a fencing champion—settled scores by this means. Francoist soldiers in Spain regarded themselves as ascetic knight-monks and yet were capable of great brutality against republican women—'red whores' in their eyes. The desire for a warlike nation, for a high birth rate, and in Italy the influence of the Catholic Church, all ensured a strict public–private dichotomy in fascist discourse. Both regimes introduced policies designed to remove women from the labour market and to encourage marriage and childbirth for women—so long as they were Aryan women.

Yet the unstructured anti-establishment ethos of grassroots fascism seemed initially to offer women opportunities for political action that were not available in the old right. Fascism brought together right-wing antifeminist women's activism with part of the constituency that had once supported liberal feminism. The former were attracted by fascist emphasis on the family, yet the expectation that mothers promote fascist models of behaviour for their children politicized them, and participation in party-affiliated mass organizations brought them out of the home. By 1940 over three million Italian women held cards in such groups. Particularly important was the space opened up for middle-class Catholic volunteers and social workers—whose efforts had been ignored by the Italian liberal state. Likewise, Italian women teachers, doctors, and lawyers engineered exemption from laws against women's paid work. Inevitably, the advantages of fascist women were gained at the expense of others. Nazi mobilization of women was an integral part of a wider racial vision, and non-Aryan women were held to be incapable of genuine maternal feeling. The pro-fascist Hungarian Women's Union fought against efforts to exclude women from university education, yet demanded a quota for Jews.

In the fascist mind, and indeed the conservative, threats to family, property, nation, and race were barely distinguishable. Perceptions of the precise nature of the danger varied. Catholic conservatives in France, Spain, and Italy saw the atheistic materialism of Freemasons, Protestants, and sometimes Jews as responsible for undermining property, patriarchy, Church, and nation. In Germany and large tracts of eastern Europe conservative fears were brought together in the figure of the Jew. Romanians detected a conspiracy by Bolsheviks, Hungarians, and Jews to undermine their nation, rape their women, and despoil their property. Polish nationalists saw communism as a Jewish conspiracy, and Judaism as a communist conspiracy. Béla Kun's Hungarian Soviet republic was believed to be the work of Jewish doctors and lawyers, so that the cornerstone of the extreme right's programme for national renewal became the removal of the Jews from the professions.

Nowhere was race more central than in Nazism. Even where race was not explicitly referred to it conditioned political discourse. Take Walter Darré's agricultural programme of 1931, elaborated at a time when the Nazis prioritized anticommunism in a bid for conservative sympathy. The only enemies of the peasantry explicitly mentioned by Darré are Marxism and liberalism, and there is no reference to the Jews. Yet the fate of the peasantry is held to depend upon 'a life-and-death struggle with the advancing east', and the peasants are 'to become the source of a blood renewal for the body of the people', to which end Darré demanded a law for the protection of the German peasantry. This is not to say that systematic murder of the Jews was pre-determined in 1933 or even 1938. But the Nazis were always determined upon a radical experiment in racial engineering, which was inseparable from their efforts to eradicate Marxism, and incorporate the proletariat and peasantry into the national community. The Nazis were equally determined upon the acquisition of living space in the east, at the expense of 'Judeo-Bolshevik' Russia. Potential genocide became actual because of closure of the emigration option, the failure of the search for separate peace with Britain and the USA (which required toning down of antisemitic measures), and the launching of the Russian campaign. Yet there is a strong possibility that the Holocaust could have emerged from other circumstances too.

# Antifascism

Not surprisingly, the destructive power of fascism was barely grasped before Hitler came to power. But the Nazis' ruthless destruction of the German left, their drive to break the shackles of Versailles and the consequent stimulation of Mussolini's bellicosity encouraged a rethink. Indeed, the struggle between fascism and antifascism became central to domestic and international politics in those countries that remained democratic after Hitler's accession to power. There is no straightforward explanation as to why democracy proved more resilient in some countries. Britain in 1926 and France in 1936 experienced massive strike waves that *could* have been construed as threatening bourgeois civilization, and especially in France many did see them in this way. Neither is an authoritarian tradition sufficient explanation. Sweden, with a tradition of authoritarianism akin to that of Germany, produced no important movement of the far right, while France, with a long experience of democracy, did. On the one hand, given the ideological permeability of national boundaries, fascism was one of the available options in every country—even where there was little indigenous fascism. On the other hand, the scale of the fascist movement and its chances of coming to power were determined by complex conditions in the individual states.

In eastern Europe, Germany, and Italy, democracy probably had little chance of survival. In Scandinavia and Britain the extreme right's chances were equally slim. In France and Spain, important movements of the far right confronted powerful defenders of democracy, and the outcome depended to a greater extent than elsewhere upon choices and contingencies. Crucial was the ability of antifascists to recapture the leadership of the people that had been seized by the far right in so many countries, and to do this without provoking a major reaction from conservative forces.

One important contingency was the Comintern's change of heart regarding fascism in 1934–5. It was provoked by Stalin's desire to win western military support against Nazi expansionism, the destruction of German communism, the spontaneous movement of communists and socialists in France towards unity following the 'fascist riots' of 6 February 1934, and in the same month the resistance of Viennese socialists and communists to fascist repression. The Comintern now considered bourgeois democracy to be preferable to fascism, and was prepared to ally in 'popular fronts' with just about anyone, socialist or bourgeois, who was prepared to resist fascism. The new policy came too late in much of Europe, and in Germany the mutual hatred of communists and the SPD was so great that agreement was impossible. Yet the French Popular Front did play some part in ensuring the failure of fascism. In June 1936, with communism gaining ground electorally, a left-wing government in power, and millions of workers occupying factories, France looked ripe for a right-wing reaction. Yet when the government dissolved the main fascist organization, the Croix de Feu, there was little resistance.

The reasons for this course of events throw some light upon the survival of democracy in north-western Europe more generally. To start with, whereas the Nazis had managed simultaneously to provoke violence and present themselves as defenders of civilization against communist barbarism, French antifascists managed both to confront fascism on the streets and to convince wide sections of opinion that it was the fascists who threatened law and order. Anti-Nazi demonstrations in Sweden and Denmark in 1933 and clashes between fascists and anti-fascists in London in 1934–6, also permitted the left to present itself as restoring order against fascist subversion. They succeeded partly because the violence that followed the Nazi seizure of power alarmed many conservatives in the democracies, and also because in Britain and France some sections of the middle classes saw fascism as the chief danger anyway.

The French Popular Front also won support outside the male

proletariat. The communists were particularly active in attempting to draw 'the people' into their struggle—on communist terms. The results were ambiguous. The party expanded its support among the indigenous working class, yet the nationalist tone of its calls for resistance to Nazism perplexed many of the immigrants who had hitherto supported the party. Meanwhile the Party forgot antimilitarism and concentrated upon leisure as a means to mobilize young men and women. Jacques Duclos told young women that 'just because you are communists doesn't mean you shouldn't concern yourselves with fashion and the questions of love and psychology that concern your sisters'. Paradoxically this turn to a more traditional view of femininity succeeded in attracting more women. The same was true in Spain, during the Civil War which began in 1936—the Communists restricted the combat roles that had been open to women at first, but also enabled politicization of women in La Pasionara's Association of Antifascist Women, which was largely concerned with support work.

Communists did not see these compromises as merely defensive, and still less did they envisage reform of capitalism. In January 1936 Maurice Thorez declared that the Popular Front 'will be a government that will permit preparation for the seizure of total power by the proletariat'. Rather, where the Nazis had attached reforms to a nationalist programme of racial engineering, the communists combined agitation for defence of democracy and 'immediate demands' with revolution.

In the socialist camp the 1930s witnessed tentative steps towards what we now know as social democracy—a political system based on negotiation and compromise between organized industry, labour, and agriculture. The French Popular Front's introduction of a forty-hour week did not break with traditional socialism. More important was its enactment of price support for wheat. The measure was immensely popular with the peasantry, and right-wing attempts to mobilize the countryside against 'sovietization' failed. In Czechoslovakia and Scandinavia more formal 'red–green' coalitions of workers' and peasants' parties emerged. Regularly in government since 1917, Swedish socialists had gradually abandoned the idea of socialization or even nationalization, and in 1932 they accepted that their task was to manage capitalism. In 1933 the socialists concluded agreements with farmers, parties, granting price support in return for welfare reform and public works. These developments were viewed no more positively by the right than similar gains by the left in Germany or elsewhere, and the Swedish right had long resisted democratization. Yet conservatives lacked mass support, possessed no bastions in the form of a strong monarchy or upper house, and were confronted by a united left with unshakeable support from farmers. The right's only choice was to engage in unconstitutional resistance or to make the best of the new situation. The Saltsjöbaden agreements for collective bargaining (1938), showed that the latter option had been chosen.

It was not, however, enough for antifascists to elaborate 'correct' policies in order to construct a basis for democracy. The Austrian Socialists tried unsuccessfully to win over the supporters of the peasant Landbund in the 1920s. Neither could an alliance of communists, socialists, and agrarians in Greece prevent the Metaxas coup of August 1936. Even where antifascists did win broad support, there was always the danger that the extreme right would resort to extra-constitutional action. The Swedish right did not go down this road, but in Spain, where there was a tradition of military intervention in politics, Franco began a military uprising in July 1936. The balance of forces was favourable to the Spanish right, for the anticlericalism and land reform programme of the Spanish Popular Front had provoked wide opposition amongst the peasantry. The Spanish experience does not, however, undermine the general point that where the left was able to build a broad coalition extending into the bourgeoisie, democracy was considerably stronger. Three years of civil war coupled with military intervention by Italy and Germany were necessary to defeat the Spanish republicans.

## Occupation and resistance

If the Spanish Civil War demonstrated that the political future belonged to those who could bring the most guns to bear, the point was confirmed by fascist conquest of much of Europe. Victory permitted the Nazis to implement an unprecedented programme of political homogenization, ethnic engineering, and ultimately genocide. The Nazis found willing allies in the occupied territories. The Croatian fascists, the Ustaši, took advantage of Nazi occupation to hack to death Serbs and Jews. In the Soviet borderlands militias began to massacre Bolsheviks and above all Jews as soon as German troops arrived. To the south the Romanian Army deported and massacred Jews on a massive scale. The French and Hungarian governments still differentiated (to some extent) between assimilated and foreign Jews, but both were willing to deport the latter at the behest of the Nazis. The Vichy government was, moreover, unique amongst the occupied states in that it used defeat as the pretext for a 'National Revolution', designed to make France a worthy participant in Hitler's New Order.

The Nazis chose not to capitalize on the sympathy they evoked in some quarters. They rejected French overtures for collaboration. In eastern Europe they soon alienated all nationalities by treating them as exploitable and disposable. As the scale and horror of Nazi occupation increased, resistance movements developed in many countries.

In a few countries resistance leaned towards the right, and in such cases the line between collaboration and resistance was somewhat blurred. The Ukrainian resistance fought against both Nazis and communists. The Polish resistance—an alliance of right-centre parties and socialists—and its military wing, the Home Army, proved unable to overcome the prejudice that Jewishness and communism were synonymous. Its refusal to offer more than minimal aid to the Warsaw ghetto rising of February 1943 stemmed from the absurd conviction that support would play into Stalin's hands and endanger the postwar existence of the Polish state. Roman Knoll, an official in the government-in-exile described the 'mass murder' of Jews in Poland as 'monstrous', but argued that 'the non-Jewish population has filled the places vacated by the Jews in towns and cities throughout Poland, and this has brought about fundamental changes which have a final quality about them'. The French Resistance leader Henri Frenay was initially reluctant to condemn the Vichy regime. He declared that 'Jews will serve in our ranks only if they have really fought in one of the two wars'.

In other cases, the conservative rank and file rejected the collaborationism and antisemitism of their former leaders, and were attracted to Christian Democracy, the heir to a democratic version of the populist and reformist strand within the European right that can be traced back to the new-right of 1890–1914. In the 1930s, some disaffected Catholic conservatives had turned to fascism, and indeed, in France, Belgium, Holland, and Croatia, some had initially seen the occupation as an opportunity to find a third way between capitalism and communism. Subsequently, many such Catholics rallied to Christian democracy, which became a major force after the war in France, Holland, and Italy. In 1945 Christian democrats were willing to participate in coalitions with socialists and communists, but in the longer term anticommunist elements became dominant.

Initially, elements of the left too had been tempted by the possibilities opened up by Hitler's victory. Some socialists had participated in pro-Axis regimes in Belgium and France, while the Danish socialists unenthusiastically joined a national unity government that ruled under German protection. In Finland the socialist administration backed the Nazi invasion of USSR. Socialists were insignificant in the resistance in Austria and Czechoslovakia. In France, they were more numerous, while in Italy they were an integral part of the Committees of National Liberation.

Usually, Communist parties dominated left-wing resistance movements. In France, following the Nazi–Soviet Pact the communists had criticized the Nazis only obliquely. But rather than 'collaborating' as some historians have suggested, the Comintern fell back upon the ultrasectarian line of 1928–33, denouncing the war as a struggle between imperialist blocks, and hoping that as in 1917 revolution would flow from war. The invasion of the Soviet Union in June 1941 brought about a repeat of 1934, and a return to popular frontism. The idea was, however, conceived differently now. Rather than defend democracy simply to preserve the possibility of future revolution, Stalin called for the creation of 'popular democracy', which would provide the maximum degree of equality possible in a capitalist society.

Popular democracy did not mean the same thing to all communists, and success depended on local conditions. In Poland Gomulka's attempt to create an antifascist front failed completely, for the Home Army rejected all contact with communism, not least because the USSR refused to give up its claims on Polish territory. Some communists therefore looked to the Red Army. One militant criticized those comrades who had not appreciated that it was a 'revolutionary liberating force'. In Yugoslavia Tito's partisans combined a revolutionary strategy of immediate socialization with a federalist solution to the nationalities problem. In France and Italy, communists were part of broader alliances. In France they profited from the fact that the conservative leader of the resistance, Charles de Gaulle, needed Soviet support to fight off Allied threats to his leadership. In Italy, where Togliatti was a long-standing supporter of popular front-ism, the communists joined Committees of National Liberation along with socialists, liberals, monarchists, and Christian democrats.

The prioritization of national liberation and the need to attract a broad spectrum of support came at a price. The resistance was rarely an exact replica of the nation it claimed to represent. In Yugoslavia, for example, communists pressed Croatian and Slovenian claims on Italian territory in order to buttress their own multinational state. As usual, political and social upheaval brought women into political action. The Greek Resistance, EAM–ELAS, set about the political education of women who had traditionally been forbidden to engage in any public activity. In France and Italy, the unstructured nature of resistance at first permitted some women to participate in combat units, and sometimes to occupy positions of responsibility. But as resistance became more military, women were gradually confined to support roles. Women also confronted the familiar fear that any form of women's organization would promote feminism. In Croatia, in spite of the enormous role played by the communist women's anti-fascist organization, the AFZ, in the resistance, male communists regarded it as unimportant and did nothing to encourage women to join the party itself. When signs of feminism appeared in the AFZ, the party quickly reorganized the movement in order to ensure subordination to male-dominated National Liberation Committees.

# Conclusion

Before 1914 outright resistance to democratization was increasingly rare, and the struggle between right and left revolved around attempts to capture and define the democratic idea. After the Great War liberal democracy came to be associated in the minds of con-servatives with the perceived advances of national minorities, women, workers, and peasants. The subsequent right-wing reaction did not, however, seek to dispose of the notion of popular sover-eignty. Most conservatives were now convinced (rightly or wrongly) that political stability required some form of popular sanction, and mass expectation of change remained high. Those conservatives who turned to fascism saw old-style élitist politics as partly responsible for the threats they faced. Fascism also gained support from the many people who were disillusioned with liberal democracy. In fact the inability of democrats to satisfy the aspirations they had fomented merely exposed the limited conception of democracy they espoused—democrats spoke in universalist terms, yet often denied rights to many. Liberal democracy was further weakened by the attraction of communism for some workers, peasants, and ethnic minorities. Like fascists, communists struggled to incorporate a broad constituency into a disciplined movement, but they prioritized class rather than nation. Swedish socialists meanwhile sought the incorporation of farmers and workers into a revitalized parliamentary democracy. Thus the interwar years were characterized by a struggle to attach the ideals of democracy, popular sovereignty, and social justice, previously monopolized by liberals, democrats, and socialists, to communism, fascism, or social democracy.

Just as the First World War had resulted in a shift in social and political power so did the Second. Except in the Baltic, national states reappeared in eastern Europe and the Balkans, socialist and communist parties massively increased their votes, and by 1946 women in every country except Switzerland had the vote. Now that the hollowness of the fascist claim to embody national sovereignty and aspirations for reform had been exposed, the centre of political gravity shifted to the left. Yet 1945 did not represent a clean break with the past. Democracy remained as problematic a concept as ever: now social democracy, Christian democracy, and communist popular democracy struggled for possession of the field, and as always military, political, and economic might played a considerable part in determining the outcome. Although humanist, tolerant, and pluralist values had made some headway during the war—notably in the Italian Action Party and in Blum's plea for 'socialism on a human scale', democracy remained for many a unitary absolute. Eastern European states were ethnically homogenized by population transfers—the Nazi government, amazingly, appealed to the Red Cross and the Vatican in the hope of halting deportation of Germans from Romania to the USSR. Having been in the forefront of the resistance, socialist parties gained some of what they wanted, but women were less fortunate. Many more women gained the vote, but their social and political position hardly changed at all. In Communist eastern Europe feminism continued to be dismissed as bourgeois, while in the west eugenicist social welfare programmes, with their emphasis on motherhood, were taken over by the re-established democracies. In Italy, for example, the impressive, but unenforced, body of legislation produced by the Fascist state served as the basis for the postwar welfare state. In Italy, as elsewhere, overtly discriminatory practices were removed from welfare provision, but more subtle inequalities remained. The dividing line between democracy and fascism had never been watertight.

# Society

## Richard Bessel

On 22 April 1945, as the Second World War was nearing its end in Europe, the city of Cottbus was captured by the Red Army. An important site of armaments production a little over one hundred kilometres south-east from Berlin, Cottbus had been the target of severe bombing which had killed or severely injured thousands of its inhabitants and made thousands more homeless. Declared a 'fortress' city by the Germans, it became a battlefield when the Soviet Army made its final, successful attack. When the fighting was over, fewer than 8,000 civilians were left in a city which before the war had numbered over 50,000 inhabitants. One of the survivors, the 70-year-old blacksmith Robert Niebatz, wrote to his daughter at the end of September:

Arnold shot his entire family on the Wednesday before the Russians marched in, and I am living above the forge as caretaker. Lotte has been with me since the 5th of May, as her flat has been confiscated. My old flat and the entire neighbourhood was burnt down on Sunday, the 22nd of April. There was a real drama on the day the Russians marched in. Your flat is half occupied . . . There are no more pensions. 10 Marks per month support is sufficient to buy what no longer is available . . . Although I will do everything possible to protect you from hunger, except for fresh eggs there is little in the way of fats. I have, thank God I stayed here, saved 4 of Arnold's hens, from which I have 2 layers which have 18 chicks.

What Robert Niebatz beheld in the remnants of Cottbus was typical of Europe in 1945: settlements reduced to rubble, societies scarred by violence and death. When the Second World War ended, 'European society' was, literally, in ruins. Millions of people had been killed—on the battlefields of a devastated continent, in the cities and towns which had been bombed, in the extermination camps of the criminal

Nazi empire. Millions more had been uprooted from their homes, the objects of what we now call 'ethnic cleansing'. Families had been torn apart, communities destroyed, institutions shattered, governments and states liquidated. Peacetime societies had been displaced by societies in uniform. The economies of much of the European continent were exhausted; industries were smashed and agricultural production stood at a fraction of pre-war levels; large proportions of the continent's inhabitants were hungry, destitute, homeless; the great majority of its Jewish population had been murdered. A continent whose people once had prided themselves on their standards of civilized behaviour and culture had become the site of the great slaughterhouses of the twentieth century.

In so far as one can speak of 'European society' in 1945, therefore, it was society in ruins. By 1945 Europe's populations had experienced the worst inflations and worst depressions, the most vicious dictatorships and the most destructive wars in modern history. Europe's peoples had suffered—and had committed—the most terrible crimes in recorded history; its landscape was a charred ruin. The story of 'European Society' between 1900 and 1945 appears in large measure to have been a story of destruction.

# Europe in 1900

It is difficult to imagine a greater contrast than that between the shattered landscape of 1945 and the picture presented by the European continent at the beginning of the twentieth century, a continent which in 1900 had appeared increasingly prosperous, orderly, and civilized. Since the Napoleonic Wars at the beginning of the nineteenth century, Europe had been remarkably peaceful on the whole, at least relative to what had come before and what was to come afterwards; millions of its inhabitants had enjoyed degrees of prosperity and security hitherto unknown, as industrialization and technical progress helped raise living standards for millions of people. Despite the high levels of emigration especially from the south and east of the continent, the populations of most European countries were growing rapidly—something which was taken as a sign of national health and virility. European societies had become safer and more orderly; European states had grown in power and apparent stability; European economies were, with the exception of that of the United States of America, the richest on earth; European cities provided the model for urban civilization around the world. Not only in hindsight, the pre-1914 world appeared to many Europeans as a world intact—peaceful, stable, and secure. Looking back in the late 1980s at his childhood before the First World War, Werner Wachsmuth (born in 1900, and from 1946 to 1969 Director of the University Hospital in Würzburg) observed:

The word that best characterizes life in the [German] Empire until the assassination in Sarajevo in 1914 is I dare say the word 'tranquillity'. It was neither the calm before the storm nor the calm of idleness, rather it was the feeling of security. Fear like we know today and have known for years and like that which has gripped the majority of humanity was unknown to us back then. All the more so the news from Sarajevo hit us unexpectedly, like a bolt of lightning from the sky, and at a stroke altered our carefree world.

Of course, it would be misleading to imply that the European continent had been paradise on earth when the twentieth century began. European societies were deeply and often bitterly divided; millions of Europeans, particularly those on the land, endured terrible poverty; in many areas—southern Italy, Ireland, the Russian countryside, or Andalucia—many peasants lived lives hardly different from those which their ancestors had lived hundreds of years before. Enormous social and economic inequality characterized all European societies. Even in the most prosperous, such as in Britain and Germany, where some workers could expect reasonable if not luxurious standards of living, the incomes of unskilled or even skilled labourers were only a tiny fraction of the incomes enjoyed by professional and white-collar employees. Life expectancy was, by present-day standards, low, childbirth dangerous, infant mortality high. In Germany, which was hardly among Europe's most poverty-stricken countries, at the turn of the century roughly one fifth of new-born babies did not survive their first year and average life expectancy during the first decade of the century was a mere 46.5 years (44.8 for men, 48.3 for women). The spectre of tuberculosis, the scourge of societies characterized by poverty, poor housing, and crass inequalities, haunted Europeans from the Atlantic to the Urals. Even at the end of the First World War, tuberculosis was responsible for a sixth of natural deaths in France, for example. However, European living standards were considerably better than they had been fifty or one hundred years before, and they were getting better. Europeans looked optimistically to the new century.

## The impact of war

If Europe's nineteenth century had been regarded as a century of progress, this optimistic perspective was smashed by the guns of August 1914. The enormous achievements of European civilizations— the unparalleled economic and industrial expansion, the growth of the state and its organization of society, the unprecedented scientific and technological progress—were mobilized to enable Europeans to cause death and destruction on a scale never before imagined. From the very beginning, when the lights went out in Europe in the summer of 1914, social structures and people's daily lives were turned upside down. Tens of millions of men were mobilized and sent to the battlefield, of whom nine million were never to return and tens of millions more came back disabled and with their health destroyed. In the weeks immediately after war was declared millions of people were thrown out of work, as economies shifted abruptly to satisfy the needs of the armed forces at war; millions more found new employment in war industries during the years which followed. The fields of northern France were turned into a wasteland, often resembling a moonscape, as were wide areas across a huge and fluctuating eastern front stretching from the Ukraine to East Prussia and Galicia. The wartime destruction and the peace settlements which followed caused millions of people to lose their homes. After the greatest voluntary human migration which the world had ever seen, from Europe to the Americas in the century before the outbreak of the First World War, the Great War ushered in the era of forced migrations, the century of the uprooted—something which demolished traditional societies in much of Europe more effectively than economic and social 'progress' ever could have done.

The First World War cast its shadow over Europe for virtually the entire twentieth century. The carnage on the battlefield left behind roughly three million widows and perhaps six million children without a father, left to face a future often marked by poverty and insecurity. The scars that the war left in families and communities across the European continent did not heal for decades, and the landscape of northern France is dotted with war cemeteries containing the remains of hundreds of thousands of soldiers of the Great War. The commemorative monuments dedicated after the First World War—the tomb of the unknown soldier at the Arc de Triomphe, the Cenotaph in Whitehall—remain places of public ceremony. It has only been in the last decades of the twentieth century that the immediate demographic effects of the First World War—the millions of casualties, the steep wartime declines in births among the main combatant powers—have faded away with the passing of time. When tracing the development of European society during the first half of the twentieth century, it appears that war indeed has been 'the father of all things'. The First World War has been seen with some justification as the great 'civilisation break', the fundamental rupture which destroyed nineteenth-century European civilization and thrust Europeans into the 'colder world of modernity', the catastrophe which sent the continent spiralling down into its 'age of extremes'.

Violence, more than perhaps anything else, is both a cause and consequence of social breakdown. Probably the most important and terrible consequence of the Great War was the spread of violence in politics and public life during and after the conflict. After a century in which the European continent had generally become a safer place, life in Europe became considerably more dangerous. This cannot be explained simply by asserting that men who were somehow brutalized by their experience in the trenches subsequently ran amok in civilian societies after the war was over. There certainly were those who found it difficult to return to a peaceful existence, for example those finding a temporary outlet for their skills in Italian Fascist squads and German Freikorps units during the immediate aftermath of the First World War. Most veterans of the trenches, however, wanted nothing more than to return home and to normal, peaceful civilian life, and most were successful in doing so. The problem was a broader and deeper one—of a fundamental shift in culture and behaviour as the First World War unleashed an era of European civil war and political and social violence affecting broad areas of the continent. In the east, after the victory of the Bolsheviks in the autumn of 1917, Russia was plunged into a vicious civil war which led to mass starvation, a virtual collapse of the economy, the depopulation of the cities, and millions of dead, widowed, and orphaned people. In Germany, following the remarkably peaceful collapse of the old Imperial order in November 1918, a new era characterized by political violence, assassination, and brutality in everyday life followed during the 'great disorder' of the immediate post-war years. In Italy post-war public life was marked by a rising tide of violence, which formed the climate of fear and hatred in which Mussolini succeeded in seizing power. Across Europe, the upsurge in violence not only lent politics a new and disturbing character; it also profoundly disturbed societies which before 1914 had generally seemed secure.

Those who suffered particularly from the violence unleashed were Europe's Jews. Throughout Europe, the First World War and its violent aftermath was accompanied by an upsurge in antisemitism, and the revolutionary threat posed by the Bolsheviks was regarded widely as Jewish-inspired. The virulent antisemitism was most threatening in the areas of Jewish settlement in the former Russian Empire, which at the beginning of the century had housed roughly two thirds of the world's Jews and where pogroms became epidemic during the Civil War. This orgy of pillage, destruction, rape, and murder cost tens of thousands of Jews their lives, and terrorized many times more. As one observer put it at the time: 'Hatred of Jews is one of the most prominent features of contemporary Russian life; possibly even the most prominent. Jews are hated everywhere, in the north, in the south, in the east and in the west. They are detested by all social orders, by all political parties, by all nationalities and by persons of all ages.' Yet these horrors attracted little popular notice, something which testifies to the brutalization of European society which occurred in the first half of the twentieth century: the killing in 1903 of forty-nine Jews in a pogrom in Kishinev (in Bessarabia, in the Russian Empire) provoked international attention and international (official) protest; twenty years later, when more than a thousand times that number were killed in the pogroms, this received little notice. Soon to be overshadowed by even greater horrors, this upsurge in violent antisemitism provided a grisly prelude to the Nazi campaign of mass murder two decades later which would claim the lives of the vast majority of Europe's Jewish population and largely destroy Jewish society across central and eastern Europe.

The most terrible social disintegration suffered in Europe after the First World War was that experienced as a consequence of the Russian Civil War. When speaking of 'European Society 1900–1945', one should remember that at roughly the mid-point of this period 'society' in Russia was virtually destroyed: economic life had been brought to a virtual halt, the old social structure was largely destroyed, whole classes (landowners, the bourgeoisie) had been liquidated or driven into exile. The Civil War, the political terror, and the famine of 1921–2 cost millions of lives. Between 1917 and 1922 the population of the lands which became the Soviet Union fell by roughly 12.7 million; war, epidemics and emigration accounted for about two million each, famine for more than five million. In the famine which accompanied political chaos people turned to cannibalism; by 1922 there were over seven million orphaned or abandoned street children begging, stealing, and prostituting themselves in order to stay alive. As Orlando Figes observes in his history of the Russian Revolution, 'even the family had been destroyed'.

In central and western Europe conditions did not sink to quite such abysmal levels, but the hardship suffered there by millions of people was considerable. The Allied blockade of Germany, which continued well into 1919 in order to pressure the Germans to agree to peace terms, caused severe problems of malnutrition. Conditions in post-war Austria were perhaps even worse. Inflation, unemployment, and social dislocation and an acute lack of decent housing—a consequence of the temporary cessation of home-building during the conflict, the already chronic housing shortages across Europe and, in some places, wartime destruction—combined to cause sharp drops in living standards and quality of life. Furthermore, Europe witnessed a phenomenon which became a depressing hallmark of the social history of the twentieth century: the creation of masses of refugees. Whether Greeks fleeing the Turks in the eastern Aegean after the collapse of the Ottoman Empire, Germans fleeing Poland or expelled from Alsace-Lorraine after the First World War, or Russian émigrés fleeing the Bolshevik revolution and Civil War, these uprooted people were the harbingers of a new dark age of homelessness. The triumph of popular and national sovereignty, which was an outcome of the First World War, left millions on the wrong side of new national borders, creating human tragedies which darkened Europe's history for the entire century. While these problems were dwarfed by what arose as a consequence of the Second World War, when almost the whole of the continent became home to societies of the homeless and refugees, they created hundreds of thousands of human tragedies and loosened social bonds built up in the course of the long nineteenth century.

At least the defeated countries of central Europe, Germany, and Austria were largely spared physical devastation, except that caused by the Russian invasion of East Prussia in 1914 and its repulsion. Elsewhere in Europe the First World War left devastated landscapes the like of which the world had never seen before. Affected most intensely were the battlefields of northern France, described by the French Senator Paul Doumer in the late spring of 1919 as 'a desert, a zone of death, assassination and devastation . . . There are corpses of horses, corpses of trees covering corpses of men.' An area which had contained much of France's best agricultural land and most important industrial centres had, in the words of the geographer Albert Demangeon 'been transformed into a desert, a wild steppe'. In November 1918 the ten northern départements contained a civilian population only a little over half that recorded in the census of March 1911 (by 1931, however, their population had nearly recovered to match the 1911 figures—testimony to human resilience and the determination of the French to restore a sense of normality to what had been no-man's land). In the most extreme cases, European society, such as it was, had to be reconstructed in a landscape completely disordered by war. Phrases like 'desert', 'wild steppe', 'lunar landscape' suggest that people regarded what had happened to their society during the Great War as not really of this world.

Perhaps because the destruction visited upon the European continent between 1939 and 1945 was even greater, we tend to have lost sight of the tremendous effort and length of time required to recover from the human consequences of the First World War. In addition to the millions of war dead there were the millions who were permanently disabled. Of the men who served in the British armed forces during the war, roughly 1.2 million subsequently were entitled to a disability pension; in France over a million ex-soldiers were receiving disability pensions during the 1930s. In Germany the comparable numbers were even greater: about 2.7 million men returned from their military service in the First World War with a permanent disability; in 1928 over three quarters of a million people were receiving invalidity pensions; and in 1929 nearly one fifth of the entire budget of the Reich government was swallowed up by war-related payments to the disabled and dependants of the casualties of war. War widows, of whom there were over a half a million in post-war Germany alone, were often left to face severe hardship: those unable to find second husbands—they numbered perhaps 300,000 in Germany—and dependent on limited pensions and meagre earnings from low-paid work, saw their living standards and those of their families decline sharply. Millions of children across Europe were left to grow up without fathers, and without the earnings that their fathers might have brought to the household budget. The human costs of the First World War were paid in instalments for decades.

# Economic crisis

The interwar years are remembered as a period of hardship and economic crisis. Photographs of Germans pushing wheelbarrows piled high with worthless currency during the hyperinflation of 1922 and 1923, of endless dole queues or of forlorn figures waiting for meagre nourishment at soup kitchens during the depression of the early 1930s are among the most frequently reproduced images of interwar Europe. One can hardly overestimate the shock of these economic catastrophes upon contemporaries and their effects on popular mentalities. After a long period of relative economic stability and growth before the First World War, the convulsion of the war and interwar years turned the private worlds of many Europeans upside down. The worst inflations and the worst depression in the history of the modern world took an enormous human toll.

The first great economic shock was inflation. Following decades of relative price stability, the relative value of labour and material goods were suddenly thrown into question. No longer did a given effort bring a given reward, as inflation eroded the relationship between work and reward. At the height of the 'great disorder' of the German inflation, in 1923, prices were changing daily and some items (such as rents, which were subject to government controls) became ridiculously cheap while others (such as clothing) became prohibitively expensive. Money ceased to have almost any value at all and people were driven to barter; eggs replaced Marks as units of account in everyday transactions. Germany was not alone in suffering hyper-inflation. The currencies of post-war Austria, Poland, and revolution-ary Russia were also completely debauched. Other countries escaped more lightly, but all European societies were affected by inflation to some extent. Even in the United Kingdom, which enjoyed relative monetary stability, prices were roughly twice as high in 1920 as they had been a decade before; even those countries which had remained neutral during the First World War, such as the Netherlands, Sweden, and Spain, were not spared the effects of the inflationary climate unleashed by the conflict. Everywhere the meaning of money was undermined to a greater or lesser degree.

The post-war inflations caused not just economic hardship but also profound uncertainty and fear. Violent swings in the labour market, wildly gyrating prices, and sudden disappearances of goods from the shops brought new anxieties; and many people sought ref-uge in 'real goods' by stealing them, as the inflation was accompanied by a massive increase in crime, largely property crime. In Germany, for example, the number of criminal convictions at the height of the inflation in 1923 was nearly twice what it had been in 1914. Particu-larly alarming to contemporaries were increases in convictions among women and adolescents, apparent evidence that society was falling apart. Life appeared more threatening; concern was expressed that young people, corrupted by war and inflation, lived only for the pleasures of the moment; the apparent peace and stability of Euro-pean society before the summer of 1914 seemed a world away; and for those millions of people whose lives were blighted by the Great War (or by Russia's Civil War)—people who had lost fathers, husbands, sons, limbs, homes—the insecurity and uncertainty of daily life became all the greater.

The insecurity created by inflation was matched by the deeply damaging social consequences of the other great economic scourge of interwar Europe: unemployment. Mass unemployment was a feature of societies across the continent after the First World War, beginning with the post-war depression which affected most developed economies on the continent in 1921, and returning during the early 1930s on a scale which had never been witnessed before. The crude statistics are dreadful enough: at the end of 1932 roughly 22% of the British labour force (including over 36% of the Welsh), 17% of the Belgian, 34% of the Dutch and 31% of the Swedish labour force were unemployed, as were at least six million Germans. Yet such figures hardly convey the deeply damaging effects of long-term unemployment upon societies, communities, families, and individuals.

Among the most revealing pictures of what the unemployment of the early 1930s meant in human terms comes from the evidence gathered in 1930 by a team of young sociologists who made a detailed study of the 'unemployed of Marienthal'. Marienthal was an industrial village not far from Vienna, where the local economy was devastated by the closure of the textile factory which had been the main source of employment. The Marienthal study, the first use of modern survey techniques to investigate a community, depicted the disintegration of community and family life due to widespread long-term unemployment. One life story amply demonstrates how tragic could be the lot of Europeans born at around the beginning of the twentieth century:

F.W. was born in 1897 in Marienthal. His father was a bricklayer. The son went to school from the age of six to fourteen . . . At fourteen he entered the factory to learn his trade in the print works and stayed there two years. Then his father moved to Neufeld because of a quarrel with his colleagues in the shop . . .

In Neufeld, the whole family again went to work in the factory; in the beginning F.W. did unskilled labour, then rose to be a machine operator, not paid any longer by the hour but by the week. He was very happy, fitted in very well, and gave up his free time to catch up on his education. In 1915 he was drafted. He could have gotten an exemption but turned it down and went. He regretted it after a few weeks. First he went to Vienna for training and then to the Italian front, where he caught malaria which he never got rid of; he is still somewhat an invalid. In 1917 he was put into a hospital and stayed there until the collapse of the [Habsburg] Empire.

Then he returned to Neufeld for two years. His parents supported him, refusing to let him go back to the factory because he was too weak; his elder brother had been killed in the war. From 1920 to 1925 he worked on a construction job in Zwillingsdorf. When the job finished, he returned to Marienthal, doing some unskilled work in the factory. He soon managed to get an office job in the print works. He was very satisfied with it, except that it did not pay much.

In 1922 he married. His wife, who was a year older, came from Ebenfurth. They have two sons, aged two and seven. The whole family is undernourished. Even during the war things were better than they are now. His aim had always been to work his way up, wherever he started. He always put all his efforts behind his work and could turn his hand to anything. If he was given the chance to start, he was sure to work his way up. He is the man who during the first year of unemployment sent off 130 applications for jobs without receiving a single answer. He has not yet earned a single groschen to supplement his unemployment relief.

Now all hope is gone. He wishes so very much to live by his own earning. His wife, who had never been out of work, is now a complete wreck, especially her nerves; she is always ill and moody. He has no hope left and just lives from one day to the next without knowing why. The will to resist is lost.

Particularly dispiriting was the fear that conditions might never improve, that hope for a better future had disappeared. As one local man observed of the young unemployed on Teesside during the slump: 'Some young lads hardly worked . . . it was soul destroying for them. And you see they'd accept almost anything, take things lying down because they'd never known any better.' With the benefit of hindsight, we know that the Depression did come to an end, and that the next war and then the postwar boom would bring something like full employment and unprecedented prosperity to much of Europe. But to many working people of Europe during the early 1930s, it appeared that a hole had been dug from which they might never emerge.

Widespread though unemployment was in the 1930s, it was not all-embracing. Before the astounding economic development which occurred in the second half of the twentieth century, a large proportion of the European population was neither dependent upon industry for a living nor resident in large cities. In Poland, for example, more than 60% of the working population were engaged in agriculture after the First World War, and in Bulgaria, Romania, and Yugoslavia the figure was over 70%; even in Czechoslovakia, with its well-developed economy and comparatively high levels of industrialization, two fifths of the population were dependent upon agriculture. Many Europeans remained tied to subsistence farming and a poverty-stricken existence characteristic more of the sixteenth century than what we imagine to be the twentieth. In Poland, according to the 1921 census, two-thirds of dwellings in the countryside consisted of a single room, whose average number of occupants was five people. Even in a more economically developed country like

Germany, where roughly one third of the population was dependent upon agriculture, the living conditions of rural labourers after the war were hardly better.

With so many Europeans living (in often dreadful conditions) on the land, many if not most people were not affected directly by the mass unemployment which afflicted industrial societies during the 1930s. However, they were hit hard by the world-wide slump in the prices of agricultural produce, which sent the rural economies of many countries into a tailspin. What was worse, opportunities for escaping the crisis on the land had been removed by the disappearance of employment opportunities in Europe's urban and industrial centres, combined with the new immigration restrictions imposed during the 1920s by the United States (during the years before the First World War the United States had accepted millions of immigrants mainly from southern and eastern Europe—precisely those countries most adversely affected by the new immigration quotas— and thus had served as an escape route for the surplus population of the poorer European societies). The 'price scissors', consisting of low prices for farm produce and high production costs, together with rural overpopulation and the cutting off of avenues for emigration, created enormous hardship. What this meant in poor peasant communities was described graphically by one Polish observer, Jan Michalowski, in 1935:

Sugar no longer exists in the villages. The majority of children—in the Rzeszów district—have seen it only in the form of sugar-cakes at the Kermis. At present, the grey type of salt is used and sometimes even the red type intended for cattle; in spring, before the harvest, because of the lack of ready cash, even this worst variety is used over and over again, salted water being saved from one meal to cook the next meal's potatoes.

The medium peasant goes about today shod in the same boots, patched and repatched many times, in his one shirt, which is laundered at night. From his others, clothes were long ago made for the children . . . They have one garment apiece, and feel most painfully their lack of clothes. It is easier in summer, but in winter in the northern part of the district one can meet in huts children who are bundled up to the neck in bags filled with chaff, since without clothing they would freeze in the cold, unheated dwelling.

This was a far cry from the happy community described in romantic terms by those searching for the rural roots of alleged national characteristics or lamenting the changes wrought by industrialization. Rural European communities became gripped by fear and anxiety no less than their urban counterparts. It is hardly surprising that this poverty and anxiety, and the agricultural crisis which exacerbated it, gave rise to political radicalism—to strikes by peasants who refused to sell their produce (such as occurred in Polish Galicia in early 1932, and in the Warsaw region later that year), and to violent protest. In France peasant anger was whipped up by the 'Green Shirts' of the demagogue Henri Dorgères. Perhaps the gravest political consequences arose from the difficulties faced by German farmers, squeezed as they were by a combination of falling prices and rising costs and taxation, during the late 1920s and early 1930s. Extreme rural protest erupted most notably in Schleswig-Holstein, where 140,000 farmers took to the streets in demonstrations in January 1928 and where in the spring of 1929 sections of the 'Landvolk' movement called for a boycott of capitalist 'bloodsucking concerns, big department stores and consumer co-operatives' and engaged in terrorist bombings of local-government and tax offices. Not surprisingly, in the years which followed it was the Hitler movement which was the ultimate beneficiary of their anxiety and protest, as the Nazi Party chalked up its most impressive election results in the Protestant rural regions of northern and eastern Germany.

Insecurity became a hallmark of the lives of Europeans not only in the capitalist world but also in the first socialist state, both in the cities and in the countryside. While the population of the USSR, once it was subjected to Stalin's collectivization campaigns and the centralized economic planning which aimed at the rapid development of a state-run industrial economy, did not face mass unemployment, it nevertheless suffered in the extreme. As we have seen, the Civil War and the famine which accompanied it were paralleled by the collapse of Russia's industrial economy and, with that, terrible hardships and the destruction of urban industrial society in the lands under Soviet control. Extreme shortages of raw materials and the consequent closure of factories led to a drastic reduction in the urban population of what had been Russia's industrial centres: in Moscow's factories, which had employed 170,000 workers in 1917, only 81,000 were working in 1921 (of whom 40% were women), and the city's total population was only about half what it had been four years previously. The Russian proletariat largely disappeared under the 'Dictatorship of the Proletariat', and had to be re-created during the next two decades.

This occurred in the most dreadful of circumstances: widespread unemployment during the 1920s and forced industrialization during the 1930s, in conditions which were often unspeakably harsh for the new workers who streamed into the cities. To give just one example: already in 1926 there were roughly 100,000 homeless people in Moscow alone, as thousands of (often unemployed) workers searched in vain for a bed in an 'overnight barracks'. The cities of the Soviet Union, like the Soviet countryside, presented an environment far removed from that of a settled, orderly society.

In the years which followed, with the collectivization and industrialization campaigns, conditions for the hapless Soviet peoples, dragooned into building 'socialism in one country' became even worse. Thanks to the imposition of a planned economy, Soviet citizens may have avoided the capitalist plagues of mass urban unemployment and catastrophic declines in farm prices on world markets, but the hardships they faced and the impact of these hardships upon social structures and people's daily lives were, if anything, even more severe than what confronted people in the capitalist world. In the countryside, the forced collectivization campaign and expropriation of peasant cattle led (as the secret police chief of the Krasnyi region near Smolensk described in February 1932) to a 'mass destruction and slaughter of livestock, both in the individual sector and in the socialized sector', as peasants chose to destroy (and eat) their animals rather than surrender them to the state. With collectivization, the fabric of rural society—and in the late 1920s that encompassed most of the population under Soviet rule—was largely destroyed, as established village structures were demolished and the means of production—farm animals—were slaughtered. In the cities forced industrialization led to the creation of a new urban population and what Moshe Lewin has described as a 'ruralization of the cities': between 1926 and 1939 the urban population of the Soviet Union grew by 30 million; in 1931 alone, more than four million peasants became urban dwellers, and between 1929 and 1935 the total was 17.7 million. Millions more became itinerant workers, labouring on the vast building sites around the country. Altogether the size of the industrial labour force grew roughly two and a half times between the introduction of the planned economy and the German attack on the USSR. The result was a terrible housing shortage with, as Lewin describes, 'consequent attrition of human relations, strained family life, destruction of privacy and personal life, and various forms of psychological strain'. This amounted to a social revolution of incalculable dimensions and brutality: it recast 'society' under 'socialism'.

From the valleys of South Wales to the Urals, from Andalucia to Berlin, insecurity, anxiety, and upheaval characterized European society after the First World War. Yet the profoundly disturbing developments of the interwar years in Europe, terrible though they were for the millions of Europeans who suffered from the effects of inflation, depression, collectivization, and forced industrialization, pale alongside the effects of the events of 1939–1945. By 1945 the dead of the Second World War numbered tens of millions, slaughtered on battlefields from Stalingrad to Normandy, in bombed cities from Coventry to Dresden, and in the ghettos and extermination camps of the short-lived Nazi empire. Tens of millions more had been uprooted from their homes: the 'displaced persons' who had slaved in the Nazi empire and survived, the refugees who had fled conquering armies or were expelled from their homes after the re-drawing of Europe's frontiers in 1945. Europe, which a few decades earlier had been regarded (at least by Europeans) as the centre of world civilization, had been turned into a bombed-out landscape, a mass graveyard.

# Long-term trends

When viewed from Stalingrad, Dresden, or Auschwitz in 1945, it appears apt to describe the history of the first half of Europe's twentieth century as a history of catastrophe. Nevertheless, when focusing on the terrible and disruptive effects of wars, economic crises, and political repression upon Europeans and their societies, we should not lose sight of longer-term changes which were shaping and transforming these societies at the same time, changes which generally are seen in a positive light. The history of 'European society 1900–1945' is, as is all history, profoundly contradictory. Short-term disaster occurred against a background of long-term positive change. Catastrophes, which blighted the lives of millions of Europeans, took place in societies simultaneously being transformed by long-term developments which led subsequently to unparalleled prosperity.

Neither catastrophe nor progress alone characterized the history of Europe during the first half of the twentieth century, but the Janus face of modernity.

Among the most important of the long-term trends transforming European society was the decline in family size. This was a trend which continued, even accelerated during the interwar period in many countries. For example, in England and Wales, the birth rate nearly halved between the beginning of the century and the early 1930s, and the proportion of households containing six or more people declined from 26.7% in 1911 to 15.5% in 1931 (and in 1951 it stood at merely 7.7%). In Germany the decline had been even more precipitous: whereas nearly half of marriages at the beginning of the century produced four or more children, forty years later this had declined to only 13%. Combined with the short-term demographic consequences of the Great War, this led to, among other things, a reduction in the proportion of the population comprised by the young in the developed industrial societies of Europe. Families and households became smaller, with all the implications this had for living standards, as the era of the nuclear family began—an era which, with hindsight, can be seen as a relatively short period which began in the years discussed here and ended in the late twentieth century.

At the same time, a growing proportion of the young were remaining in full-time education, as nineteenth-century trends towards restricting child labour and extending compulsory schooling continued in the twentieth. With the exception of France, which retained a school-leaving age of 13 (as set down by Jules Ferry in the law of 28 March 1888) until 1936, when change finally was instituted under the Popular Front, during the 1920s the major Western European industrial states (Belgium, Britain, Germany, Italy) set the school-leaving age at 14. Increasingly, child labour was replaced by formal education, and during a period when unemployment was on the rise and children and adolescents comprised a smaller proportion of the population. Expectations of childhood and education were changing and, although these trends were interrupted by war and social upheaval, they were continued, indeed accelerated, during the second half of the century.

The changes in birth rates, family size and the extension of schooling were instrumental in transforming the place of women in European societies. Of all the revolutionary social transformations which have occurred in twentieth-century Europe, the shift in the roles of women in the public sphere may prove ultimately most important. Of course, the facts that European women were bearing fewer children and that those children were spending more of their childhood and, increasingly, their adolescence in school were not the sole causes of the transformation in women's place in society; nor can one claim that European women had achieved anything like social equality by mid-century. However, the changes which unfolded during the crisis-ridden first half of the twentieth century should not be under-estimated. The First World War played a part, propelling hundreds of thousands of women (temporarily) into employment outside the home (on the railways, in heavy industry, in offices) of a sort which would have been inconceivable a few years before. So too did the changes in the job market which saw a steep decline in what at the turn of the century had been the chief source of employment for young unmarried women—domestic service—a continued decline of agriculture (where women had helped on family farms) as a source of employment, and a rapid rise in jobs available in offices and in the service sectors. Nor should one overlook the bringing of women into the political sphere: the extension, in many countries, of the vote to women (in Britain in 1918—at least for women over the age of 30—in Germany in 1919, but in France not until 1944). European women were increasingly emerging from the private sphere into the public arena.

One may view these changes, as Victoria de Grazia has done, as representing a 'nationalization of women' in the twentieth century which in some ways may be compared with the nationalization of men in the nineteenth. Socialization increasingly took place outside the home and family—in schools, in (often state-run) mass organizations, in the armed forces (and their auxiliaries). Women were brought into the public sphere—as citizens who voted, as employees who worked outside the confines of the home, and increasingly as mothers who gave birth not just for themselves, their husbands or their children but for the 'nation'. As Alfred Grotjahn, Social Democrat and Professor of Social Hygiene in Berlin, put it amidst concern about the steep wartime decline in births in Germany in 1915: pregnancy was the 'only female contribution to war and military power which equals . . . men's wartime national service'. The most private matters had become public concerns.

At the opposite end of the age scale, the number and proportion of elderly Europeans grew substantially during the first half of the twentieth century. Between 1900 and 1930, the proportion of people aged 65 years or over increased from 8.2 to 9.3% in France, from 4.9 to 7.4% in Germany, and from 4.7 to 7.4% in Britain. Despite the temporary setbacks during and immediately after the First World War, life expectancy in Europe increased considerably: whereas in 1910 men's life expectancy stood at only 46.7 years and women's at 49.7, by 1930 the figures had risen to 53.6 and 57.0 respectively. Consequently, the place of the elderly in European societies began to alter markedly, and—despite the severe economic and political crises which marked the first half of the century—significant steps were taken to provide pensions and a measure of state-financed security for (the growing numbers of) the elderly. Following the German lead under Bismarck during the 1880s, European states began to provide support for the elderly and to create what was in effect a new class of people: pensioners. At the outset of the century, relatively few people could have expected to reach what we now refer to as 'retirement age', and for those who did, life could be hard. Few were able to enjoy pensions; for example, as Paul Thompson observes, in Edwardian England 'they were only normal among civil service and railway office staff: altogether, only one man in twenty was covered'. More typical was the fate of workers who, Thompson notes, 'kept on as long as they had strength, typically shifting to worse-paid jobs as watchmen, roadmen or carrying out minor repairs. Once past this, the ageing couple would slip helplessly towards extreme poverty.' By the middle of the century, however, eventual 'retirement' and receipt of a pension had become the realistic expectation of many Europeans. Poverty and death were no longer necessarily the immediate fate of most Europeans at the end of their working lives.

The growing provision of pensions for the elderly, of which the developments which occurred in interwar Europe were only a part, may be seen as one element of a profound shift from dependence upon other individuals—in the main family members—to dependence upon the state. This indeed is one of the major underlying themes of the social history of Europe's twentieth century. The First World War was a major catalyst for this change, as huge numbers of people became dependent upon state support in its wake. As we have seen, millions of men returned home disabled; millions of women were widowed and children orphaned. These millions of individual human tragedies had occurred in the service of states which, in order to maintain wartime morale and underpin their fragile legitimacy (in the case of the Russian, German, and Habsburg Empires, unsuccessfully), reassured those who sacrificed themselves that—as for example was repeated ceaselessly in wartime Germany—'you can be sure of the thanks of the Fatherland'. The vast extension of the state in wartime, the growing numbers of old people, the pressure to create something of a welfare state, the idea that the state had a responsibility to intervene in the labour and housing markets, the extension of educational provision, economic crises which appeared to demonstrate that laissez-faire capitalism and the 'night-watchman state' were inadequate to meet the needs of people in modern nation-states, the establishment of dictatorships (most notably in Italy, Russia, and Germany) which sought to extend their control over all aspects of the lives of their subjects—all these factors led to a huge increase in the size of the state and in people's reliance upon it for their material welfare. Correspondingly, they redefined the boundaries between state and society, and profoundly changed the nature of European society.

The boundaries of European society were transformed in other ways as well during the first half of the twentieth century. Among these was the speeding up of communications. When the First World War broke out, the citizens of Europe read about the unfolding conflict in newspapers which reported the events of the previous days; when the Second World War broke out, the citizens of respective countries could hear their political leaders on the radio (the exception to this was Stalin, who was so taken aback by the German attack on the USSR in June 1941 that he did not address the Soviet people until the beginning of July). Indeed, radios were one of the few items of consumer expenditure that increased during the dark years of the 1930s depression. It was not just wireless broadcasting—the instant dissemination of messages to wide numbers of people—which grew rapidly during the interwar years, but personal telephony as well. Telephones, which had appeared in offices before the First World War, increasingly came to be found in people's homes, at least among the more prosperous strata of northern and western European countries, during the interwar years. As in so many other spheres, North America took the lead: in 1920, 60% of all the telephones in the world were to be found in the United States. In Europe personal telephony advanced most rapidly in the Scandinavian countries, which had the largest number of telephones relative to population, followed by Germany and Great Britain. Automatic telephone exchanges were established (London's first automatic exchange opened in November 1927), greatly increasing the capacity of the network. For a substantial and growing proportion of Europeans, communication had become instantaneous, and no longer dependent upon distance.

Where distance still mattered, it was shrinking. Speed was in the news. Land, sea, and air speed and endurance records captured the popular imagination, and reduced the distance between the continents. Lindbergh's solo crossing of the Atlantic in May 1927 made him an international media sensation. When the British 'Cheltenham Flyer' established itself as the 'world's fastest train' in September 1931, with a recorded speed of 78 miles per hour, this was a major event. When the purges in the USSR were at their height in 1936 and 1937, Soviet newspapers were filled with accounts of the exploits of Soviet pilots—'Stalin's falcons'. The purple prose of a celebratory volume marking the silver jubilee of King George V in 1935 was characteristic of the obsession of the age. Speculating on what would astound 'a Rip Van Winkle of those distant Edwardian days of 1910 were [he] to wake today', it asserted that 'changes in style and speed would surely amaze him most':

It is in our modes of travel that the almost miraculous changes of these years are most obvious . . . From the time when a car ride meant dressing up with fearsome goggles and flowing veils, we have moved to a new age of silent, almost incredible swiftness.

On the straight, new broad highways, our traffic problems are but growing pains. Our Rip Van Winkle staring aghast at a great passenger 'plane zooming high in the skies down to a perfect landing at Croydon or reading amazed of over 400 m.p.h. speed bids, might realize that more clearly than we do ourselves.

No doubt similar comments could be made today. Viewed from the beginning of the twenty-first century, the technological achievements of the first half of the twentieth century have been overshadowed by the even more astounding technological achievements of the second half, achievements which have profoundly altered the nature of European society. In the same way, the increases in life expectancy, changes in family structures, and the development of rudimentary welfare states, as well as the dawn of the era of mass leisure (not only in its fascist versions—the Italian 'Dopolavoro' or the German 'Strength through Joy'—but also in its democratic manifestations under the French Popular Front or Britain's Butlins), during the first half of the century both foreshadowed and created the preconditions for the acceleration of these developments in the decades after the Second World War. The two halves of the century thus not only provide stark contrasts but also present important continuities, particularly in the social sphere. Demographic trends, the increasing involvement of the state in the provision of welfare and the shaping of society, the effects of scientific and technological progress upon people's daily lives are long-term affairs. Terrible though they were for millions of people, the catastrophes and the violence of the first half of the twentieth century, and the breakdown of the seemingly stable order which had formed in Europe before 1914, did not reverse developments shaping European society over the longer term.

Although it may be obvious, it nevertheless bears stating explicitly that the crisis-ridden and destructive first half of Europe's twentieth century provided the preconditions for the remarkably successful second half. If the European landscape of 1945 was one of rubble, it also provided the foundation for the amazing success story of the subsequent half century. For millions of (western) Europeans, catastrophe provided the pre-history of prosperity and security. The terrible failure of (fascist and communist) collectivist ideologies to order European societies and economies provided the pre-history of the triumph of individualist political and economic programmes; the terrible violence of the first half of Europe's twentieth century provided the pre-history of the strange normality of the early post-war years and of the relatively peaceful fifty years which followed the end of the Second World War. Life went on, even after 1945. To return to the letter of Robert Niebatz with which this essay began: in the midst of death and destruction there were survivors, layers of eggs and chicks. The history of a continent which during the first half of the twentieth century gave the world its great slaughterhouses and whose societies were battered to a degree not previously seen in modern times has demonstrated that there is, indeed, life after death.

6

# Imperialism and the European empires[1]

Rajnarayan Chandavarkar

In 1900, European dominance of the world seemed complete. Most 'western' powers were now implicated in empire. Few regions of the world had evaded their hegemony. The sun, it seemed, could not set on the celebrations of Queen Victoria's jubilee or, shortly thereafter, on the mourners of her death. The French empire, having slowly recovered from Napoleonic defeat and disinterest, now revived and expanded. The European powers scrambled to partition Africa and marked out their spheres of interest along the frontiers of the Ottoman empire and the coast of China. Meanwhile, India, for so long the burning ghat of so many imperial ambitions, became, in Curzon's phrase, 'the pivot of the Queen's dominions'. Before he left Calcutta, Curzon erected a memorial to Queen Victoria hoping to match the Taj Mahal, which the Mughal Emperor, Shahjahan, had built for his wife.

Half a century forward, European dominance appeared to lie in ruins. If the Allies had gone to war to defend civilization, Britain and France appeared to have sacrificed their empires for the cause. The costs of reconstruction in the metropole and the empire, the forward march of demos, and the revival of a western liberal conscience seemed to suggest that the future of the European empires lay behind them. After 1945, the centre of financial and political power lurched across the Atlantic. Britain and most of western Europe now

5

[1] For their comments, criticisms, and corrections, I am grateful to Chris Bayly, John Iliffe, Julian Jackson, Gordon Johnson, John Lonsdale, Anil Seal, Tom Tomlinson, and David Washbrook.

depended upon American aid and passed into the orbit of its informal empire. Imperial rivalries intensified to Europe's disadvantage. American statesmen recalled the myths of liberation upon which their united states had been built and offered their European dependencies a dose of anti-colonialism. Across the bleak plains of central Europe, the distinctly menacing shape of another superpower began to haunt the official mind. Indeed, the European empires began to unravel. Once Britain divided and quit India in 1947, it did not take long for the rest of the British empire to be dismantled. In the following year, Britain abandoned its mandate in Palestine in some confusion. The French had already been eased out of Syria, when they attempted to return with muskets and discipline. The Indian Army re-occupied Indochina for the French, Indonesia for the Dutch and Malaya for the British. But the French never fully established themselves in Indochina and the Dutch found that their grip on Indonesia was quickly loosened.

On closer scrutiny, however, Europe's world system seems rather more fragile in 1900 than an initial glance would suggest. As European rivalries intensified, it became clear that Britain was no longer ascendant. Seemingly at the zenith of its power, Britain's share of the world's industrial output declined while its old staple industries, which had underpinned its imperial system, lost their competitive edge. As France, Russia, and Germany began to develop their navies, it could no longer be taken for granted that Britannia ruled the waves. The European powers had been driven to partition Africa by their own rivalries and weaknesses, especially their inability to make local structures of power serve their interests adequately. Moreover, the new territories which the European powers had acquired were often peripheral to their most vital economic interests. They had generally gained more from these regions before they began to rule them and often less than they profited from their informal interests elsewhere. The imperial commitments of both Britain and France were so extended and dispersed, and their rule stretched so thinly over highly turbulent territories, that they could not be sure of their ability to secure their homelands. By 1902, the rise of Japan called for at least a treaty to secure the East. The Boer War confirmed Britain's vulnerability in the empire. Military weakness in the empire drew attention to the physical and moral infirmities of the nation and especially, its casual poor. Within London's 'darkest Africa', in Shoreditch and

Spitalfields, cultural missionaries sought to teach mothers how to raise a generation with the moral and muscular fibre to defend and rule the empire.

Nor did appearances match the reality in 1945. European weakness in 1945 did not signify the end of empire. In 1945, the recently vanquished European powers showed no diffidence in claiming their right to rule in Southeast Asia. The votaries of Europe's liberal conscience recognized the value of retaining colonies in order to demonstrate how they could be governed ethically. The Labour Cabinet of 1945 had certainly not come to power to preside over the dissolution of the British Empire. Nor had Europe lost the will to be brutal to the subject races. European statesmen showed their determination to defend their empires with blood in Kenya, Malaysia, and Cyprus and fought wars of attrition in Vietnam and Algeria. The anti-colonial rhetoric of the United States receded as the State Department discovered colonial responsibilities of its own. Once the freedom fighters of Pennsylvania Avenue understood that self-determination was more laudable in principle than in practice, their subventions became indispensable to the defence of the British empire in Malaya and the French in Vietnam. European empires, sagaciously governed and selectively repressive, could serve as important bulwarks against communism. The winds of change which briefly threatened to blow in 1945 were swiftly stilled. Nonetheless, by the early 1960s, the great nineteenth century colonial empires were being rapidly dismantled. Yet imperialism lived on after the end of empire.

# Conditions for empire

The systems of formal rule and informal influence which had constituted the European empires in the early twentieth century had evolved as a set of primarily political techniques for managing their international economic and strategic interests. As Gallagher and Robinson argued long ago, imperialism had no territorial imperative. It was only when the European powers failed to secure their interests through existing social and political relationships in the regions pulled into the wake of their expansion that they intervened to create conditions more conducive to the realization of their aims. Formal empire provided a means of underwriting the process of expansion and integration of the capitalist world economy. This was, of course, at best a complex, difficult, and contradictory process. The acquisition of territorial control did not always help expansion, just as the abandonment of formal rule sometimes developed the integration of the international capitalist economy. Where the European powers undertook territorial commitments, their purpose was to take resources out of these regions and to deploy them in their own global economic and strategic interests. Formal empire thus underpinned the foundations upon which their international power was built and their global interests pursued.

Formal empire, and the orbits of informal influence around it, depended upon a number of pre-conditions to serve its larger purposes satisfactorily. It required a measure of collusion between the European powers to ensure that they did not meddle in each other's sphere of influence. It required colonial agents and pro-consuls to ensure that formal rule was cheap and preferably free of cost to the metropole. Above all, it necessitated the development of effective systems of local collaboration. What drew local bosses into these accommodations was precisely the knowledge that, if they refused, their rivals would step forward and in so doing, undermine them. To secure these accommodations, colonial agents gave away large areas of local control to their collaborators and accepted limitations on their own freedom to mobilize and direct local resources in their wider imperial interests. Necessarily these bargains often proved unstable. Their conditions were often violated on either side, as collaborators moved into opposition or colonial agents failed to satisfy their clients. Changes in the conditions of local collaboration could swiftly render formal rule too expensive to be viable. Deepening imperial rivalries, for instance, could force colonial rulers to raise taxes and meddle in local domains of power and thus not only provoke resistance but also place their systems of collaboration under terminal strain. For this reason, the fate of the European empires turned upon the conditions of politics in the regions which came under their influence and control rather than upon the flowering of liberal sentiments at home, their domestic prosperity or decline, or even the 'fancy footwork' of European statesmen. The resilient habit of perceiving imperialism as a simple function of western impulses and motives has allowed little scope for the agency of colonial subjects.

The European imperial systems were neither monolithic nor did they work in the same way everywhere. There were fundamental differences within the British empire in the principles by, and purposes for, which its various colonies were ruled. The 'white dominions', increasingly autonomous, were more easily soldered to imperial purposes and yielded collaborators more readily primarily because their external trade was so closely integrated with Britain's. India merited its own cabinet minister. While the India Office super-intended its affairs from London, the Colonial Office was responsible for the rest of the empire. In the late nineteenth century, India came to serve more readily a wider range of Britain's international inter-ests. Between 1870 and 1914, India's exports, produced largely by the initiative and enterprise of small peasant households, paid for two-fifths of Britain's balance of payments deficits. Its revenues, extracted largely from the land, met the costs of running the Indian empire, guaranteed generations of British rentiers returns on their invest-ments in government bonds and railway stocks and paid for the maintenance and deployment of the Indian Army for imperial pur-poses throughout the East. British policy in the Middle East was shaped by the defence of India and in particular by a concern to safeguard the route to the East. The immediate returns from sub-Saharan Africa in terms of trade, and investment were meagre but its benefits measured in relation to strategy and the protection of the whole imperial system weighed in the official mind. The differences between colonies were shaped by the social and political balances within them. Since production conditions and the hierarchies of power varied within them, it followed that shifting imperial strategies affected them differentially.

The French empire was, if anything, more dispersed, various and fragmented than the British. Its development suffered periodic rup-tures, for instance, in 1789, or more significantly, after the Haitian revolt of 1792 and in the years of Napoleonic neglect and defeat which followed. Its late nineteenth-century revival remained largely reactive, until it was severely interrupted by the devastation of the First World War and the collapse and divisions of the empire in the Second. Whereas Britain's restless, expansive economy in the nineteenth and early twentieth century spewed out capital, trade, and migrants across the world, France remained more self-sufficient and more focused upon the European continent and the Mediterranean. Russia was its major field of investment. Its pattern of industrialization did little to disrupt, and remained more closely integrated with, its smallholding agrarian economy. By expropriating peasants and driving them off the land in the Scottish Highlands, Ireland and, following enclosures, in England, British landlords generated an army of economic migrants and colonists, especially for the 'white dominions'. French peasants held on more tenaciously to their land. The task of turning peasants into Frenchmen represented at least as urgent a task of colonization as expansion abroad. The agents of French colonial expansion were drawn not from merchants and peasants but from soldiers and bourgeois professionals. In France, those who sought refuge from 1789 in the army and the empire strove to restore aristocratic glory and rule peasants abroad. Perhaps this social difference may explain the significance of cultural assimilation, civilizing missions, and national honour in French imperialist discourse.

But these differences can be pushed too far. British expansion was scarcely devoid of similar impulses. However, while the French held out before their colonial subjects the remote possibility that they too could become citizens, the British identified themselves by marking out those who could never join their ranks. More significantly, French expansion could be just as discriminating and calculating as the British. Some priorities of French colonial policy are readily identified. It focused on the Mediterranean, which they hoped to turn into a French lake. Like the British, they were concerned about 'the route to the East', in their case to retain access to the 'model colony' of Indochina. In the African scramble, they recognized the value of a contiguous empire in West Africa to secure their position in North Africa and the Mediterranean. It was prudent to ensure, as the Ministry of Marine warned in 1890, 'that we shall never be taken in the rear in Algeria'.

The differences between British and French imperial policies arose from two conditions of their expansion, quite different from an emphasis on civilizing missions and cultural assimilation. The fact that the French economy had been less expansive committed it to a more weakly integrated view of its global interests. The 'fancy footwork' of British colonial policy-makers moved to a rhythm which enabled it, in the last resort, to define its priorities. It often moved to a

distinctly Indian beat. French policy-makers found it harder to identify the vital and minimal interests that it had to protect and thus also
those which it could, if necessary, concede. Secondly, the French
empire, subject to ruptures in the nineteenth century, now seemed in
the twentieth to be especially vulnerable to the competition of its
imperial rivals. In particular the two world wars damaged France's
imperial fabric in deeper and more lasting ways than Britain's.

There were significant differences in the nature and vicissitudes of
the various European empires. The Dutch scarcely participated in the
great European expansion in the nineteenth century. The Dutch
empire was focused upon Indonesia, its prize colony, which yielded
significant, if diminishing, returns in the early twentieth century.
Leopold, King of the Belgians, acquired the Congo as a private estate
but had to surrender it to the Belgian state in 1908 following the
international outrage expressed at his brutally exploitative labour
practices. Belgium's only colony proved to be perhaps the most
profitable in Africa, at first with its rubber and ivory trade and later
its copper and diamond mines, and by the 1930s attracted a considerable inflow of Belgian capital. Despite its metropolitan weakness and
poverty, Portugal acquired substantial territories in the late nineteenth century, largely in the wake of more powerful imperial rivalries in Africa, and retained them longer than most, even as it gained
relatively little from them. Portugal claimed to integrate its colonies
with the homeland while the Dutch relied on experts, whose skill lay
in deciphering the peculiarities of the East, to supervise colonial government. These European powers were not exceptional in their
exploitation of labour. Empires at one level remained at heart a
method of extracting labour and setting it to work in the larger
interests of metropolitan capitalism. Germany acquired an empire,
largely as the outcome of diplomatic intrigues in Africa. Its aim had
often been simply to protect its position in Europe. Germany's short-
lived empire yielded few commercial or strategic benefits and proved
more a liability than an asset. While its colonial administration was
increasingly admired for its efficiency, it proved brutal and ferocious
in its suppression of the Hereros revolt and the Maji Maji rebellion.
By 1919, the German Empire was disbanded and distributed as the
spoils of war among the Allies. Germany's defeat in the First World
War ensured that Europe's most dynamic and efficient industrial
economy played no direct role in managing its global interests. For its

weaker economies, the task of securing their imperial systems, as successive crises engulfed them, would prove extremely demanding. That the core of the European imperial systems had begun to decay was already discernible in 1900. But the weaknesses which had characterized their apogee were brought more fully to the surface by the two world wars and the intervening years of economic crisis.

# Imperial revival and retreat, 1914–1929

In Asia and Africa, the First World War looked more like a European civil war. However, its impact necessarily disturbed delicately balanced imperial systems. Most obviously, the pact between the great powers not to meddle in each other's spheres of influence was buried in the killing fields of Europe and Mesopotamia. In addition, the European powers drew men and materials on a massive scale from their colonies for their military campaigns. This unprecedented degree of intervention in their colonies distorted local economies, violated the ground-rules of collaboration, built upon 'salutary neglect', and provoked widespread resistance. Under pressure from imperial rivalries as well as colonial resistance, the imperial systems could not indent upon dwindling and already over-committed metropolitan resources.

Of course, the European powers drew differentially upon their colonies and with varying effects. About 2,500,000 colonial subjects fought, and about 200,000 died, for Britain during the war. The French conscripted about 600,000 colonial subjects, of whom nearly 80,000 died, and recruited a further 200,000 as non-combatants. Behind the front lines, massed ranks of Arabs, Africans, and Indians were pressed into service as labourers, porters, and camp followers. In East Africa, alone, their numbers were estimated at one million. Britain and France sought to mobilize not only troops but also essential supplies from their colonies and where possible to offset the costs of warfare. India's value as 'the second base of the British Empire' was now affirmed. The 'English barrack in the Oriental seas' had become an ordnance base as well. India absorbed and subsidized Britain's military costs while gifts from its revenues and its national debt, raised by subscription from monied interests contributed substantially to the conduct of the war. Cloth, food supplies, and manufactured goods for the Mesopotamian and East African campaigns were produced in and exported from India. War procurement led to scarcities, hoarding, and inflation. Frequent famines and food scarcities followed in India as elsewhere. Deaths from famines in East Africa exceeded war casualties. In French Equatorial Africa, famines arising from the drive to procure food and labour continued after the war. The French recruitment drive in West Africa in 1915–16 resulted in widespread resistance, from flight and evasion to conscription riots and open revolts in Dahomey, Upper Volta, and the western Soudan and the breakdown of local administration in parts of Senegal, Guinea, and the Ivory Coast. Not surprisingly, colonial intervention and social disruption stirred up conflicts and resentments. The mobilization of colonial resources on this scale could scarcely leave existing social and political balances within them untouched.

Not only were imperial rivalries revived by the war, but they were also heightened when it ended. The war, and the experience of victory, quickened and expanded the imperial ambitions of Britain and France. The collapse of the Austro-Hungarian, Russian, German, and Ottoman empires left vast tracts, spheres of influence and unstable borderlands open to contestation between the Allies. During the war, the impending partition of the Ottoman Empire led the Allies to stake out conflicting claims in the Middle East. Indeed one aim of the Sykes–Picot treaty, hammered out in secret between Britain and France, was to prevent the Allies falling out during the war. When the Bolsheviks leaked its contents in 1917, it upset all their allies and multiplied Britain's embarrassments in the Middle East. As the Allies set out to re-partition the world, Britain's priority was to guarantee the security of India. To this end, the British sought to strengthen their grip on the Suez Canal, assume the mandate of Palestine, assert their hegemony over Mesopotamia, and consolidate their influence on the Arabian Coast, in the Persian Gulf, and in Asia Minor. The rise of Japanese power in the east forced the British to put their faith in lawyers and diplomats, and in case paper defences did not suffice, they hoped to build up fortress Singapore. Japanese ascendancy quickened the imperative to secure the route to India and focused the attention of strategists more closely on the Middle East. It was the defence of India that prompted them to consider imposing order upon the Central Asian borderlands by striking out for the Caspian

Sea or even the Caucasus. It also led them to strengthen the hand of the recalcitrant European settlers through the spine of Africa, in Rhodesia, Nyasaland, through East Africa to Kenya. But such a guarantee could only be secured by screwing up the demands on Indian resources. If these resources were available, they could only be secured at a price. In any case, it would be harder to maintain order in India, if its external defences demanded such massive investments. Maintaining the outer perimeters of the Indian Empire, so expansively imagined, could mobilize local antagonisms as the Iraq rebellion in 1920 demonstrated. It might, as indeed it did, provoke a competitive response, even intervention, by their imperial rivals. The pressure of imperial rivalries was relieved for the moment for Britain because the USA was preoccupied with its own hemisphere, Japan's ambitions were not aggressively manifested, and most European powers had scarcely recovered from the ravages of war. When France, Turkey, and the Soviet Union began to stir once more and Japan re-asserted itself, imperial planners had to hastily reconfigure their dreams.

At the end of the war, France witnessed not so much the revival of the empire as its re-birth. After the battering which it took during the war, its relationship with its empire had, in some measure, to be reconstructed. Indeed, the war drew attention to the economic and political potential of empire. Certainly, projections of imperial glory provided a refuge from the harsh realities at home. French imperial strategy focused upon the Mediterranean, reinforced by its acquisition of mandates over Syria and Lebanon and by a renewed sense of the significance of the Maghreb. By strengthening its position in the Mediterranean, it might improve its access to the east and especially to Indochina. French policy-makers also hoped that colonial development might dispel domestic weakness. By exploiting the colonies more effectively, France might recover its position in the world. Albert Sarraut's plan for 'la mise en valeur des colonies françaises' suggested that colonial development driven by metropolitan capital would enable France to optimize the vast agricultural, mineral, and social resources of her empire and deploy them to restore her own great power status. However, the Sarraut Plan broke against the domestic realities which it was expected to transform. The claims of post-war reconstruction relegated colonial development in the imperial order of priorities. The purpose of imperialism was to expropriate resources from, rather than invest them in, the colonies.

Necessarily, the economic disruptions of war and the intensity of colonial intervention exacerbated social tensions and provoked widespread resistance. During the war, it became clear that Britain would have to offer major political concessions to ensure co-operation. Between 1916 and 1922, Indian politicians, especially in the provinces, adopted a posture of agitation to wring more concessions out of the impending political reforms and to seize the moment to expand their following. These agitations culminated in the non-cooperation movement, led by Gandhi, between 1920 and 1922. The Gandhian satyagraha frightened colonial rulers but elicited patchy and uneven popular support. It comprised disparate local struggles which found in the Congress campaign a national platform for their grievances. Frequently, these local conflicts had begun before non-cooperation was initiated and often continued long after it was called off. They were not driven simply or even primarily by a concern with national issues. While they provided the substance of the Congress campaign, they were so various that they could rarely be conducted in harmony by the nationalist leadership and always seemed liable to run swiftly beyond its control. By 1922, this marriage of convenience between politicians in search of constituents and followers striving to recruit leaders had begun to disintegrate. Its effect was to show that, even in India, resistance did not need to assume massive proportions before the imperial powers began to doubt whether the benefits of formal rule outweighed its costs and burdens.

In Egypt, too, the British intervened on an unprecedented scale, recruiting for the Labour Corps with more zest than wisdom and requisitioning corn, cotton, and camels with abandon. Their actions inspired the prolific composition of fellahin dirges and provoked increasing resentment which culminated in widespread and violent protest in March 1919. Colonial pro-consuls and their military advisers briskly assumed that the causes lay no deeper than the instigation of trouble-makers and deported Saad Zaghlul, the leader of the Wafd Party, together with three associates. But Zaghlul's support was by no means confined to the coffee-house intellectuals in Cairo. The Wafdists had attracted the support of village élites and, indeed, a wider popular following, as the often violent protests which followed Zaghlul's deportation revealed. Resistance on this scale led to the imposition of martial law and resulted in massive repression, facilitated by the troop ships passing through the Canal on their way back to Britain. The rapid collapse of the revolt, however, only confirmed the British in their belief that Egyptians were inherently volatile.

But the natives seemed restless everywhere. In 1920, rebellion in Iraq cost the British £50 million and some 400 soldiers' lives to suppress. It was far from clear that the gains from holding Mesopotamia offset such losses. Similar problems of control proliferated across the empire. In May 1919, the Indian Army was drawn into yet another futile and expensive Afghan adventure. Soon after, Palestine was wracked by the first of several violent conflicts between Arabs and Jews. Persian nationalists increasingly resented the presence of British military and financial advisors, and as the Russians began to stir once more in the Caspian, it seemed prudent to cut back on British commitments rather than to attempt to hold positions which they could not defend.

Similar pressures mounted on French colonial rulers. The Destour Party in Tunisia called for the establishment of a representative assembly, led strikes and protests and demanded independence in 1920. Abdel-Karim's explicitly anti-colonial revolt in Spanish Morocco gradually drew the French into a long repressive campaign. In Algeria, the Islamic reformers, led by Sheikh Abdelhamid Ben Badis, asserted the religious and linguistic unity of the nation, defined its distinctive culture, and rejected notions of assimilation. At the same time, Algerian workers in France formed the Étoile-Nord Africaine in 1926. Led by Messali Hadj, the Étoile rejected the blandishments of assimilation in favour of independence.

Perhaps the most significant movement of resistance which the French encountered was the Druze peasant revolt in Syria between 1925 and 1927. It arose partly from the deprivation and disruptions of war. However, French statecraft exacerbated the tensions thus generated. First, French anxiety that the influence of Arab nationalism would reach the shores of the Maghreb led them to an unduly stiff-necked response in Syria. They lumped the nationalists together and thus missed the opportunity of dividing them by attaching the moderates and isolating the radicals. Secondly, their propensity to play the various minorities against the Sunni Muslim majority, or urban notables against rural magnates, undermined their legitimacy, which deriving from the League of Nations was already rather weak. Thirdly, the French failure to attach significant urban notables to their rule often pushed them into opposition. Having once supplied the Ottomans with collaborators, they now sought to develop a wider following in order to compel the colonial regime to deal with them. Yet these urban notables had always been wary of unleashing popular forces which they could not control. However, as the peasant movement developed, these notables had little alternative but to associate with it, sometimes even to assume its leadership. French military repression eventually broke the back of peasant resistance. In its aftermath, the French conceded a greater measure of self-government. Its effect was to shore up the old political leadership of urban notables and large landowners, already considerably weakened by the Druze revolt.

As colonial crises proliferated, imperial policy-makers found little relief in domestic politics from their encircling burdens in the empire. *La mise en valeur*, far from facilitating post-war reconstruction in France, had been quickly crushed by its demands. Similarly, British statesmen had to accommodate their own huddled masses. Politicians competed to buy the votes of a wider electorate with welfare and evinced a reluctance to spend on defence. The search for collaborators at home ruled out the possibility that London could offer subventions to its colonial agents to buy off discontent in the empire.

Colonial resistance forced pro-consuls in region after region to effect significant adjustments to their rule and to reward their collaborators by transferring more power to them. By thus cutting themselves out of significant domains of power, colonial rulers sometimes had to accept growing limitations on their ability to determine the outcome of colonial politics. In the process, they were forced to consider whether formal empire was, indeed, an obsolescent method for perpetuating and advancing metropolitan capitalist interests.

In the 1920s, the British revived informal influence as a method of perpetuating and developing their world system. Necessarily, it took different forms in different regions. It had long seemed safe for Britain to dismantle formal controls in the 'white dominions' in the expectation that they would remain within its imperial system. In the 1920s, however, collaborating élites in the dominions sought greater autonomy in foreign policy, refused to be dragged into war by Britain and in South Africa even dumped its prize collaborator, Smuts, at the polls. Mother country, it seemed, did not always know best. The place of the dominions within the empire had to be re-defined in 1931 as 'equal' and 'freely associated' members of 'the British Commonwealth of Nations'.

In India, the British attempted to extend informal influence within the framework of formal rule. To this end, they sought to retain firm control in those areas deemed vital for their imperial interests, while devolving power where it seemed to matter less. The real benefits of the Indian Empire were weighed primarily in terms of its ability to serve Britain's global interests. To extract Indian resources and to deploy them for their larger imperial purposes, the British needed to establish a unified and centralized structure of rule, even as it proved vital for them to devolve power to secure collaboration. This contradiction between the imperative to centralize power and to diffuse it through the political system to maintain control lay at the heart of their technique of formal rule. By providing greater power to Indian politicians in the provinces and denying them much influence at the centre, the British hoped to avoid compromising their position as sole arbiters of Indian politics. In the 1920s, the Montagu–Chelmsford reforms seemed to offer a shrewd blueprint for colonial control. Local bosses and their political agents recognized that the real prizes lay in provincial politics, where they could control budgets, hold office, make policy, and through the disbursement of patronage build up factions and parties. Conversely, there was little need to organize at the all-India level where officials remained firmly entrenched. Political parties, like the Congress and the Muslim League, themselves loosely constructed supra-regional alliances, atrophied. So it appeared that the Montagu–Chelmsford reforms had worked their magic. But they could not provide a lasting solution. For the Montford plan to work, the British had to allow provincial politicians larger budgets to spend. Yet this could only be achieved by reducing their imperial commitments.

In Egypt, the British attempted to consolidate their influence by conceding sovereignty in 1922. But they took care to retain control over their core imperial interests in the region: the security of the Suez Canal, defence and foreign affairs, and the administration of the Sudan. This offer of independence, as Lord Milner explained, was 'calculated to strengthen and not weaken our Imperial position'. The Wafdist revolt had demonstrated that Egypt could no more than India be held down by force. Shrewdly devised concessions to the nationalists might defuse their challenge and win over its 'saner elements'. In the event, the Wafdists continued to triumph at the polls. But their own internal divisions, together with their differences with the Court, ensured that the new arrangements satisfied imperial needs until the late 1930s.

In some regions, less central to their global interests, the British pulled back and relied upon old opponents who already seemed firmly in power: Mustafa Kemal in Turkey, Reza Khan in Persia, or even Amanullah in Afghanistan, who might serve as a counter-weight against the revival of Russian power in Central Asia. Elsewhere, the British felt compelled to hold on against the odds. In Iraq, even after the rebellion of 1920, the British were reluctant to pull out, lest Feisal fall. They had, after all, already abandoned him once, in Syria. Iraq's value for the defence of India and for safeguarding oil interests was substantial and they feared that it would be difficult to identify reliable collaborators. However, if Feisal had to be propped up, he would have to pay the costs of maintaining order. Similarly, in Palestine, the apprehension that if they pulled out some other malign power would creep in and cast its shadow over the Suez Canal, and the suspicion that Arabs and Jews were too volatile to safeguard imperial interests, ensured that the British retained the mandate.

In the 1920s, colonial resistance had exposed the limitations of formal rule. If collaboration could not easily be secured, formal empire would quickly become unviable. Conversely, political changes in the Middle East and South Asia suggested that it would be increasingly difficult to hold on to formal empire by informal means. To expand informal influence, imperial rulers had to develop colonial economies. Good book-keeping and prudent management was no longer enough. But the European powers could neither raise colonial resources nor dredge up metropolitan capital to invest in colonial development. In any case, colonial rulers always feared that capitalist development would undermine the institutions and power structures upon which they depended. The attempt to revive techniques of informal influence only deepened doubts about whether they could be made to work much longer.

In the 1920s, the French Empire appeared more vulnerable to reviving imperial rivalries and perhaps more constrained by domestic crises. As pressures mounted on their rule in various regions, the French appeared to respond to each case discretely. They were less favourably placed than, for instance, Britain, to take a global view of their disparate interests and to define their imperial priorities accordingly. There is little sign here of an overview which would enable them to make concessions in one sphere in order to tighten their control over another which mattered more. The main priority was to hold on. Forty years later, Amilcar Cabral was to point out that the Portuguese held on to their colonies because they could not afford 'neo-colonialism'. In the 1920s, the French could rarely afford informal influence or invest any expectations in its exercise. Their attempts to incorporate favoured colonial élites appeared feeble. Political reform foundered on the opposition of the colonial settlers (*colons*) often joined for example, in Indochina by some indigenous élites. It was certainly complicated in the French empire by the connection between the franchise and citizenship. Colonial subjects had to naturalize as French citizens in order to vote. The argument that the best way of keeping Algeria French was to enfranchise and assimilate did little to temper the hostility of the settlers, who promptly undermined the Jonnart reforms of 1919. Since military service was an important prerequisite for naturalization, indigenous élites were disturbed, in the aftermath of the war, by the prospect that their labourers and tenants, rickshaw boys, and cooks would get the vote ahead of them.

# Economic crises and imperial solutions

In the 1930s, the Depression and the stormy revival of imperial rivalries once more tested the viability of formal empire as a technique for advancing metropolitan interests and exposed the limitations of informal influence. By the 1930s, the growing disengagement between the economies of the West and its colonies had become increasingly apparent. Since the late nineteenth century, the opening out of vast tracts of the prairies, the pampas, and the outbacks accompanied by mechanization and large-scale agricultural production ensured that raw materials and food from the colonies supplied a small proportion of European needs. On the other hand, the 'new' industries which provided the dynamic sectors of the 'developed' economies had no need for colonial raw materials or markets, while the traditional export-oriented staple industries ran up against saturated markets in

Asia. As their international competitiveness declined, both Britain and France became increasingly dependent on the empire. The growing dependence of Britain and France on their colonial outlets proved to be a reminder of the industrial debility of the metropole.

As Jacques Marseille has shown, the French colonies served the interests of the metropolitan economy rather better in the late nineteenth century and early twentieth than it has been assumed and rather worse after 1930. For industries which were expanding in the early twentieth century found in colonial markets a refuge from both demand constraints at home and the competition of better established rivals in third markets. But, after 1930, declining or uncompetitive industries placed a larger proportion of their output in colonial markets. Similarly, France purchased colonial products, largely raw materials for the expanding staple industries, at competitive prices before 1930, which in turn boosted demand in captive colonial markets. By 1930, imported raw materials from the colonies, however, had decreasing importance for France and other developed economies and they competed more directly with domestic output. After 1930, therefore, the colonies shored up declining French industries by buying their products expensively in return for the privilege of exporting products which undermined French producers. At a time when Frenchmen regarded their colonies as a symbol of their natural greatness, the colonial relationship reinforced the structural weaknesses of the French economy.

In South and Southeast Asia, slow agrarian expansion, population growth, and rising prices had characterized the late nineteenth and early twentieth century. Widening flows of migration, trade, and production yielded new patterns of regional inter-dependence. In 1930, when the bottom fell out of the market for primary products, linkages of credit, which had underpinned the slow and uneven integration of the international economy, were ruptured. In South and Southeast Asia, creditors who had lent money in return for a share of the harvest saw their assets turn to dust on the threshing floor. The shock of this collapse led to the rapid withdrawal of credit from the countryside.

Similarly, the Depression destroyed the developing interdependence of the regional economies in South and Southeast Asia. As western demand for plantation crops and minerals declined, the European robber barons who had often invested in them began to squeeze costs, retrench labour, and repatriate capital. The repatriation of capital further reduced liquidity and squeezed the supply of credit. Migration flows through the region were checked and even reversed. The cash cropping tracts found declining demand for their products and for food grains in the industrial areas. Rising exports sustained by falling prices often signified declining food availability and a deepening crisis of subsistence. As employment in the mines and plantations contracted, migrant workers returned to their shrinking holdings in the densely settled tracts and the flow of remittances dried up. The social and regional reciprocities on which the agrarian expansion of the preceding half-century had been predicated were ruptured, resulting in deepening social tensions, peasant unrest, and ethnic conflicts. In Vietnam, the violation of what James Scott characterized as 'the moral economy of the peasant' provoked widespread protests against corvee, high taxes, and rental exactions, culminating in 1930 in the mutiny of the Yen-Bai garrison in February, the May Day strikes, and the establishment of the Nghe-Tinh soviets. Large-scale and brutal repression by the French which included search and destroy operations and the bombing, and sometimes the burning, of villages believed to harbour 'ringleaders' eventually broke the movement. But, as the dust settled, it slowly became clear that neither peasant resistance nor the Indochinese communist party could simply be blown away. Similarly, agrarian struggles were witnessed elsewhere: notably in the cocoa 'hold-ups' in the Gold Coast in 1930–1 and again in 1937–8, and in the many localized struggles over rent, credit, and common resources which were fought under the umbrella of the nationalist civil disobedience campaigns in India in the early 1930s.

In the early 1930s, agrarian capital, in full flight from the countryside, sought new outlets for investment in the towns. Subsistence peasants who needed credit for survival now set off for the towns as wage hunters and gatherers. Small pools of capital looking feverishly for new opportunities encountered cheap labour. In some regions, notably in India and Latin America, these conditions provided a stimulus to industrial growth and facilitated import substitution. The growth of import substitution had major implications for European imperialism. It provided increased competition on worse terms for metropolitan capitalists in their captive colonial markets. In the case of the old staple industries, this occurred precisely when their wage costs had weakened their competitiveness in a situation of stagnant demand and had driven them to seek refuge in their colonial markets.

Since colonial economies had little in common with each other, it is neither surprising that they were affected differently by the Depression nor that the timing, pace, and character of their recovery varied. As the French drowned their sorrows in Algerian and Tunisian wine, believed to have a higher alcoholic content, the buoyant metropolitan demand cushioned the impact of the Depression in these regions, especially for the wine-growing *colons*. The dynamism of peasant production in Kenya in the 1920s, with some retraction into subsistence during the Depression, ensured that they were affected less than the sybaritic settlers of the happy valley. The discovery of new minerals in Kenya, however modest, and, more substantially, in Northern Rhodesia helped in some measure to counter the crisis. On the whole, regions which were less fully integrated into the world economy withstood the crisis better than those which had long been drawn into international trade. However, the gold mines on the Rand proved extremely profitable as the dollar and sterling were devalued. Oil strikes in Iraq and the Persian Gulf brought in their wake large construction projects and capital outlays which provided the conventional cure for the Depression in the Middle East before the European statesmen were prepared to prescribe it for themselves.

As Britain's own position in the world economy declined, its statesmen considered the remedy of imperial preference. However, the Imperial Economic Conference, held at Ottawa in 1932, demonstrated that the complementarities of trade within the empire bloc were sufficiently weak to leave each country with too many specific interests to protect. Britain sought preferential access to the dominions, who remained anxious to protect their 'infant' industries, which in South Africa, for instance, was deemed vital for generating the jobs which would keep poor whites from turning black. Similarly, the British government was loathe to sacrifice its yeomanry simply to grant the dominions' primary producers unhindered access to the British market.

Moreover, it soon became clear that empire trade alone could not possibly revive Britain's position in the world economy. For primary producers in the colonies, British demand was insufficient to pull up their falling prices adequately. For the staple industries in Britain, colonial markets lacked the purchasing power to revive their fortunes. Economic recovery required Britain to strengthen its ties with the advanced capitalist economies of the West as well as with the primary producers outside the empire. The Dominions realized after Ottawa that their eggs were too fragile to be placed in Britain's basket alone. France, whose recovery was slower in the 1930s, found greater comfort in soft colonial markets for its decreasingly competitive staple industries, while its own demand for particular products from Indochina and Algeria helped to temper the worst effects of the Depression in its most prized colonies. Nonetheless, the empire could not bale out the metropolitan economy.

Where the Depression facilitated import substitution in colonial markets, it also stimulated the demand for protection. Yet tariff barriers could restrict the access of metropolitan capitalists to vital markets at a time when they needed all the help they could get. Metropolitan capitalists found not only that the empire was insufficient to secure their fortunes, but also that their interests might, if necessary, be subordinated to, even sacrificed for, the preservation of the empire as a whole. Of course, European capitalists, whether 'gentlemanly' or merely aspirational, could see that empire underwrote and perpetuated their interests in the international economy. However, formal empire did not necessarily or invariably offer an optimal technique for the expansion of Western capitalism.

The future of formal empire as a technique for developing European economic and political interests turned upon how far and at what cost its systems of collaboration would release the power and profit necessary to render it viable. Formal rule depended upon scarce colonial resources, which had to be mobilized largely from the land. To extract these resources too ruthlessly entailed the risk of large-scale revolt or simply agrarian collapse. The development of colonial politics further constrained the freedom of imperial rulers to mobilize colonial resources. By the 1930s, deeper adjustments had to be effected to the structure of colonial rule. Nowhere did this prove more pressing than in India.

Many of the assets of the Indian empire which had so conveniently served a wide range of Britain's international interests before 1914 had begun to atrophy between the wars. India's exports no longer generated a sufficient surplus to settle Britain's balance of payments deficits. The Indian market for British manufacturers, especially for Lancashire's cottons, slumped. The Indian army, seemingly the last of the great imperial assets, enabled nearly half of Britain's fighting forces world-wide to be stationed in India free of charge. This was vital at a time when Britain had frozen its own defence expenditure for an infinitely extensible decade. But, in the 1920s, the Indian army already consumed two-fifths of government expenditure and its use for imperial purposes now opened up fierce disputes about who would foot the bill.

More revenues would have to be raised if the Indian Empire was to fulfil its imperial obligations or indeed if it was to serve a wider range of metropolitan interests. To extract more revenues in India, the British would have to give away greater powers to their collaborators. But the more securely their collaborators were lodged within the structure of the colonial state, the harder it would be for the British to freely direct Indian resources for their imperial purposes. The problem before imperial strategists was how to concede enough power to a wide range of Indian interests in order to attach them and at the same time satisfy imperial aspirations and significant metropolitan élites. In the negotiations that followed, the British sought to tighten their grip over central government and especially over those matters which bore directly upon their imperial interests while devolving substantial powers to the provinces. In the event, the reforms enabled elected Indian politicians to form provincial ministries on the basis of a legislative majority. Historians have sometimes concluded prematurely that these reforms represented the first sign that the British had begun to wind up their empire. In fact, as the Viceroy, Lord Linlithgow, explained in 1939, they had 'framed the constitution as it stands in the Act of 1935, because we thought that way the best way . . . of maintaining British influence in India'. On the eve of the Second World War, it seemed that Britain had effectively secured control over those areas of governance in India which remained vital to its global imperial interests. Nothing demonstrated this more clearly than Britain's ability to mobilize Indian resources on an unprecedented scale for the Second World War.

Similarly, colonial resistance elsewhere sometimes narrowed British options in the 1930s, but it did not threaten to undermine the basis of their rule. In Egypt, political developments appeared unexpectedly to consolidate Britain's position. Since 1922, the British had failed to persuade the Court, the Wafdists, or any other party to sign the Anglo-Egyptian treaty, even if they largely observed its terms.

In 1936, when Italy marched into Abyssinia, having already expanded in Libya, a Wafdist government in Cairo at last formally accepted the British garrison at Suez and its administration of the Sudan. Bakr Sidky's coup ended the long period of successful collaboration in Iraq but it did not, on its own account, undermine British influence. In Palestine, the sudden acceleration of Jewish immigration from Nazi Germany heightened Arab fears and provoked the revolt of 1936. The growing threat of another world war quickened the urgency for finding a solution. But the British found it hard to take a steady view of the problem or of their own immediate priorities in the region. The Peel Commission recommended partition. It held out the prospect of a colony of settlers obliged to Britain and well placed to defend the Mediterranean outlet of the Iraqi oil pipeline at Haifa. But the Generals favoured a construction of strategic interests which placed particular value on Arab goodwill in the region as a whole, to protect both their route to the east and British interests in oil. In any case, some were convinced that a garrison of Jewish settlers would be insufficient to guard the pipeline, which could be threatened along its length by the Saudis or in Kuwait or even in the Gulf. With the aim of defusing the Arab revolt, and allaying their fears, another 'white paper' in 1939 offered, in place of partition, quotas on Jewish immigration and restrictions on the sale of Arab lands, precisely at the moment when the need to accommodate Jewish refugees from Nazi Germany was becoming most acute. In Kenya and Rhodesia, the settlers who had long threatened, rather more severely than Africans, to disturb colonial rulers now consolidated their power in the local state and leaned towards the British.

For the French, too, after the Rif wars, the Vietnamese peasant actions, and the Baya revolts, the challenges to colonial rule had been largely sporadic and localized. In North Africa, as in Indochina, Syria, and Senegal, the French authorities had often appeared intransigent and draconian in their response to colonial resistance. The Neo-Destour movement in Tunisia, led by Habib Bourguiba, generated some momentum behind constitutional reforms until the French silenced it in the mid-1930s and then firmly repressed it, when it revived with more radical purpose in 1937–8. In Algeria, Maurice Viollette's bill to enfranchise about 25,000 évolués, presented to the French senate in the early 1930s, was returned to the agenda by the Popular Front ministry after it had rejected a petition from the

Premier Congrès Musselman to be allowed to assimilate as French citizens without having to renounce their faith. In the event, the bill was squeezed to extinction between the opposition of *colons* and their allies in the Chamber and of Messali Hadj and the Étiole Nord-Africaine, who argued that it foreclosed on the possibility of independence and who urged Algerians to hold out for nothing less. Messali Hadj was incarcerated and the Étoile banned. Viollette had warned that France would lose Algeria within twenty years if selected Muslims were not given a stake in the Third Republic. Twenty years later, France was on the verge of losing Algeria and commentators looked back upon Viollette's bill as a lost opportunity. For the moment, however, whatever the price they would later be forced to pay for their intransigence, the challenges to their rule seemed readily contained.

As the great powers stirred once more in the 1930s, Japanese expansion posed the most significant challenge to Britain and France. Japan's rapid commercial expansion in the early twentieth century, especially in the inter-Asian trade, threatened to carve out spheres of informal influence within the European empires in South and South-east Asia. Neither Britain nor France could look complacently upon the political implications of Japan's economic growth. Moreover, Japanese territorial expansion placed the eastern defences of India under threat and menaced Britain's grip on Malaya, while it exposed French interests in Indochina and the Pacific. To both France and Britain, it seemed that the Americans held the key to the containment of Japan. Indeed, after the Japanese invasion of Manchuria in 1931, the British acknowledged that they would have to 'eventually swallow any and every humiliation in the Far East' unless the Americans rode to their rescue. By the end of the decade, both Britain and France were, if anything, in a weaker position.

As tensions mounted in Europe, familiar questions about whether Britain could defend its global interests simultaneously in each sector yielded largely pessimistic answers. The Italian invasion of Ethiopia, Mussolini's pact with Hitler, and the outbreak of the Spanish Civil War threatened the Main Fleet's highways to the naval base at Singapore, which alone stood between Japan and the eastern defences of India. The anti-comintern pact between Germany and Japan in November 1936 revived the dilemma about whether the priorities of imperial defence for Britain lay to the east or the west. To prepare for an impending war in Europe would greatly weaken Britain's position in Asia. To focus on the empire and weaken defences in Europe could encourage German expansion. To prepare to fight on all fronts would make impossible demands on scarce resources and would in the long run undermine the empire.

Appeasement offered a way forward. It arose less from the calculation that a strong Germany might serve as a bulwark against Soviet Russia, than from the British expectation that another world war would raze their tottering empire to the ground. The British had hoped that appeasement would protect their imperial system from the pressure of their rivals. If appeasement relieved the pressure in Europe, Britain could pursue its interests outside. But in the 1930s, Britain's imperial commitments appeared to put its European defences at risk. Far from offering Britain a means of exercising its influence in the world, formal empire threatened to limit its options and hollow out its defences in Europe. Far from facilitating the projection of Britain's power in the world, its formal empire now appeared to force upon it a growing sense of its own fragility.

For France, too, 'the dangers for our possessions which a hostile attitude towards Japan would entail' meant that the rising power in the East would also have to be appeased. For Britain, appeasement in Europe might enable a more aggressive policy in Asia. Both saw the wisdom of striking a balance between cautious resistance to Japanese expansionism and discrete support for China. Both entertained the hope that if Japan could be tied down by war in China, the pressure on their Asian and Pacific interests would ease. The French, like the British, were reluctant to take on the Japanese. As Admiral Petit pointed out in 1938, if by provoking Japanese military action, 'we are obliged to retreat . . . our moral situation in the Far East, especially in the eyes of our Indochinese, will suffer greatly'.

In 1939, it slowly became apparent that not even diplomacy in Europe could remedy Britain's infirmities. Once appeasement lay in shreds, Britain had to reinvigorate its imperial system and build on its strengths. In particular, the empire offered Britain the potential to mobilize dispersed resources on a gigantic scale. Of course, such mobilization would entail large political costs. As the prospect of world war grew more imminent, so it became clear that Britain would have to find more troops quickly. Inevitably they turned to India. The Indian Army doubled in size with each year of war and by 1945 had

expanded by a factor of ten. But customary solutions dragged familiar problems in their wake. In the 1930s, the Indian Army was capable
of doing little more than cuffing non-violent Gandhian satyagrahis
into obedience or jail. In 1938, the Auchinleck Committee declared
that it was incapable of fighting a modern war. It had to be modern-
ized and equipped. To preserve their pacts of collaboration, the British exchequer would simply have to pay for imperial defence. In 1939,
the cost of using the Indian Army for imperial purposes was estimated to amount to £34 million. By 1945, its cost exceeded £1,500
million, or about 17% of Britain's gross domestic product.

## Imperial revival: the Second World War

The apprehension of imperial decline before 1939, military defeat and
colonial resistance did nothing to diminish the British, or, more
remarkably, the French, appetite for empire. If anything, it was whet-
ted by the war. Indeed, the war inaugurated another period of
imperial revival for Britain. Manpower, food supplies, and materials
were again mobilized on a massive scale from the colonies. Metropolitan decline was not an insuperable impediment to the maintenance and even expansion of empire. After all, the viability of empire
had depended upon the power and profit which imperial rulers could
generate from their colonies. Just as Britain had expanded its empire
vastly when its domestic base was beleaguered after 1918, so when it
could barely defend itself in Europe in 1940, it mobilized the
resources of the empire above seemingly inescapable constraints. The
imperial revival of the 1940s showed that the decline of empire was
not a steady, inexorable process. It was not determined simply by
metropolitan fortunes or colonial resistance. Neither was it a
function of changes in the world economy nor of international politics alone. Least of all, did its fate hinge on the effulgence of liberal
sentiment in the West.

France fell in 1940 but it did not thereby lose its imperial ambitions. Whatever Admiral Petit's concerns in 1938 about 'our moral
situation . . . in the eyes of our Indochinese', French colonial administrators negotiated with the Japanese to serve as the agents of their
conquerors in return for maintaining a mottled façade of their rule.

Colonial administrators and *colons* in Algeria embraced Vichy. In Syria, their alignment with Vichy led to their ejection by Britain. Nonetheless, in 1944, at the Brazzaville Conference, the Free French resolved that the colonies must remain captive. For their colonies, after the war, they would 'preclude any idea of autonomy, any possibility of evolution outside the French bloc of the empire' and warned that self-government 'even in the distant future' was 'to be avoided'.

British policy did not preclude self-government for the colonies. But it claimed to lay particular emphasis upon the timing of withdrawal. Certain circumstances could therefore compel the British to extend their rule indefinitely. As a cabinet committee explained in May 1943, 'Many parts of the Colonial Empire are so little removed from their primitive state that it must be a matter of many generations before they are ready for anything like full self-government. There are other parts inhabited by people of two or more different races and it is impossible to say how long it will take to weld together these so-called plural communities into an entity capable of exercising self-government.'

When the United States forcefully enunciated the right to self-determination in 1941, the British quickly asserted their 'unquestioned right to administer our own colonies including those which we have temporarily lost to the Japanese'. Indeed, the war affirmed for Britain the importance, even the indispensability, of its empire. The Suez Canal and the oil fields focused strategic concerns once again on the Middle East. India's significance as the second base of power in Britain's imperial system was re-iterated. Swept aside at first by the Japanese in Southeast Asia, the Indian Army played a vital role in the Allied recovery in the eastern theatre as well as in Europe through the North African and Italian campaigns. By 1943, India supplied more war goods than Australia, New Zealand, and South Africa taken together. By 1944, the anti-colonial rhetoric of the United States was pitched in a lower key. The Americans would have colonies of their own with a strategic value which they might wish to protect. The British empire, about to emerge from the war as a much reduced force, posed no threat as an imperial rival. If the British empire was propped up, it could help to secure an international order dominated by the United States.

More powerful forces, however, were already at work within Britain's empire. They were prodded into movement by the scale of colonial intervention. Through the thickets of regional variations in the consequences of colonial mobilization, some broad themes may be discerned. First, agrarian tensions deepened as colonial states were forced to grow more food. In the period of slow agrarian expansion between 1860–1930, colonial rulers strove to prevent capitalism from working its magic on the countryside. Its consequence was to discourage investment in agriculture and conserve existing production relations. As a result, in parts of South and Southeast Asia, the agrarian base had long slipped into structural stagnation. During the war, colonial regimes attempted in Asia and Africa to suddenly render agrarian economies highly productive. In parts of Africa, especially in Kenya, this may have been facilitated by the colonial state's attempts to protect and encourage peasant agriculture during the Depression, in the hope that it might yield more revenues. In the 1940s, settler agriculture in Kenya revived with the military demand for their output, in particular for pyrethrum which offered the troops a prophylactic against malaria.

Moreover, the war brought in its wake inflation, hoarding, and shortages. The procurement, sometimes commandeering, of grain, food crops, cloth, and supplies for the war created scarcities and pushed up prices. The presence and activities of the armed forces in particular regions aggravated inflationary pressures locally. In the agrarian crisis of the 1930s, ties of debt had been turned into bonds of labour in South and Southeast Asia. This process was further developed and spread during the war, partly because military needs sometimes increased employment opportunities. In Africa, the demand for rubber, palm oil, tin, and sisal, which expanded rapidly once the Japanese swept through Southeast Asia, led to various forms of forced labour in the plantations and mines. As debtors became labourers, the poor in South and Southeast Asia, often lacked entitlements which they might exchange for food. Starvation and disease increased. With the continued procurement of grain and food for war needs, widespread famines occurred in Bengal, Tonkin, and Hunan. In each case, it was estimated that at least two million people died. In Vietnam, when the Japanese attempted to procure half the rice crop, at low prices in 1942–3, landlords ejected their tenants and left their lands fallow, which necessarily worst affected the poorest rural strata who had to buy their food. The disruption of transport by Allied air attacks and the subsequent failure of the rice harvest in

Tonkin and northern Annam in 1944 resulted in starvation and rising famine mortality. In addition, local systems of exchange were ruptured in ways made familiar by the Depression of the 1930s. For instance, the fall of France cut Algerians off from employment opportunities on the mainland while those who remained behind were deprived of the remittances of migrant workers, upon which they depended. Poor harvests and epidemics, inflation and shortages, combined with the drying-up of remittances to significantly widen the disparity in living conditions between the settlers and the bulk of the Algerian people.

Further, in several regions, scarcities and subsistence crises accentuated rural migration to the cities, which in South and Southeast Asia had already begun during the slump. Most major African cities emerged and expanded in the 1940s: Nairobi, Mombasa, Leopoldville, Salisbury, Bulawayo, Accra, and Lagos. This migration was the outcome of rural scarcities and expectations of urban opportunities. Those who sought refuge from the former were usually disappointed in the latter. The rural poor were held on the margins of the informal sector and in the burgeoning squatter settlements which came to characterize 'third world' cities after the war. Entrepreneurs who gained access to a substantial supply of cheap labour discovered opportunities for profit especially in markets guaranteed by war needs. As landlords and rich peasants invested in urban assets and enterprises on a larger scale, they helped to create the conditions in which rural and urban bourgeois interests could combine to provide a social underpinning for nationalism.

Finally, colonial states intervened heavily in the lives of their subjects to mobilize resources for the war. Yet intervention on this scale built up resentments among collaborators. If colonial rulers broke their pacts by intervening in domains which they had customarily left alone, their collaborators moved more readily into opposition and extracted a higher price for their acquiescence. By calling upon the resources of their world system to restore the balance in Europe, the British served to undermine the formal empire, which had facilitated such mobilization in the first place.

To restore the foundations of formal rule, the British would inevitably have to draw upon the power of their collaborators. This had to be effected with some urgency in India, in view of their importance to British strategy in the war. But in India it posed intractable problems.

Political reform would have to go beyond the provincial level to sat-isfy Indian politicians. Yet by devolving power at the centre, the Brit-ish would severely circumscribe their ability to direct Indian affairs in their larger interests. Moreover, the British could scarcely hope to conduct the war from this vital base, if their own future role in the governance of India was thrown open to debate in prolonged consti-tutional negotiations. Having promised reform, the British would have preferred to postpone its implementation until after the war.

Gandhi and the Congress objected to being dragged into war by Britain without being consulted and demanded 'independence here and now' as their price for co-operation. In 1942, they launched the 'Quit India' campaign and elicited greater popular support than the other major Congress agitations. The 'Quit India' campaign, like its predecessors, comprised a wide range of diverse local struggles which the nationalists appropriated and projected onto a wider arena. Yet again, many of these continued after the movement was repressed; some persisted after the British had quit. In 1942, however, the British had greater military force at their command than ever before and they repressed the movement with speed and ferocity. At the same time, attempts by Jinnah and the Muslim League to define a Muslim position in Indian politics foundered because it alienated those whose support they most needed. With the Congress in jail and Mus-lim politics caught in a web of contradictions, constitutional negoti-ations effectively ground to a halt. More by good luck than good judgement, the British had secured an outcome beyond their greatest expectations.

When the war ended, the British perceived their position in India, in a radically changed light. Their post-dated cheques for political reform had come up for payment just as the bank was about to crash. It was far less clear now that formal rule in India was the best means of advancing Britain's global interests. More political reform could decisively weaken British influence over the Indian political system. At the same time, the colonial state had become more and more Indian. Even the officer corps of the Indian Army had during the war been rapidly Indianized. Doubts proliferated about whether such an administration could be relied upon to safeguard Britain's inter-national interests, repel non-violent Gandhians, or maintain its neu-trality in a communal riot. Imperial strategists became increasingly concerned that they might easily get into a situation in which they would not be able to rule India if they stayed, but could not leave for the chaos that this would cause. This prospect propelled them to a quick settlement. Conversely, the British calculated that having transferred power, they might more readily secure collaboration. As Wavell, the Viceroy, told Churchill in 1944, if India remained 'a friendly partner in the British Commonwealth', Britain's influence in the East would be assured. But 'with a lost and hostile India, we are likely to be reduced . . . to the position of commercial bag-men'. In this light, Britain would not necessarily damage its interests by withdrawing from India. In fact, it might even expand its informal influence. The transfer of power in India did not constitute an imperial retreat but rather a means of maximizing Britain's influence in the world.

As the Union Jack came down, the British re-assessed their position. They were now increasingly dependent upon the United States. However, a friendly India within the 'commonwealth of nations' might enable them to emerge as a third force. India's resources and trade, harnessed by its own government, might facilitate the deeper penetration of Africa, the Middle East, and Southeast Asia. 'If we only pushed on and developed Africa,' Ernest Bevin told Dalton wistfully in October, 1948, 'we could have the United States dependent on us, and eating out of our hand in four or five years.' But Britain's position was weakened by the partition of India. In any case, such calculations were quickly unravelled by political developments in Asia, imperial rivalries, and the changing character of the world economy.

In the Middle East, the British soon found that the reluctance of collaborators to treat with them took matters out of their hands. Their principal interests lay in oil, defence, and the route to India. Developments in India cast into some doubt the rationale of their position in the Middle East. But, more fundamentally, the British could offer no blandishments with which to secure collaboration. They had nothing to give, except the repayment of their large war debts to Egypt and Iraq. Their attempts to sign treaties throughout the region to assure them of a basis for protecting their interests failed successively, nowhere more ignominiously than in Egypt and Palestine. As the Russians threatened the oil fields once more, Britain's role was subordinated to the United States. Differences now arose over Palestine. Here, too, the British were squeezed between American pressure and Zionist resistance. The British remained apprehensive about allowing Zionist leaders complete control over immigration to Palestine and especially about the consequences for their oil supplies of thus alienating Arab opinion. Egyptian recalcitrance had led the British to begin building their garrison in Palestine instead. Now as they prepared to abandon the Palestine mandate, they had to evacuate their base. Frozen by each of these contradictory pressures, they supervised the transfer of the Mandate lightly and effected another scuttle.

In the late 1940s, Britain recognized only too well the significance of those parts of the empire whose export surpluses earned them dollars. Africa's potential for raw material and mineral exports now had to be mustered and mined. After all, upon its accomplishment largely depended the post-war revival of Britain's influence. During the Second World War, the scarcity of raw materials and the disruption of international trade provided a stimulus for economic and commercial development. After 1945, colonial development provided a means of taking the edge off anti-colonial rhetoric in Hampstead as well as in Washington. However, the scale of intervention to mobilize and regulate production necessitated greater meddling in African society. Sometimes, it had disastrous consequences, notably in the attempt to convert Tanganyika into a haven for ground nuts. Often, it breached the ground rules for collaboration. In West Africa, the British assumed that educated élites would constitute more effective agents of modernization than the chiefs who had propped them up for decades through indirect rule. By offering educated élites 'representative' government, the British stimulated political organization. Educated élites did not simply seek representation but the transfer of power and hastened processes which even the most perceptive colonial rulers had expected to unfold more slowly. In East and Central Africa, colonial rulers depended on the unreliable collaboration of white settlers for economic development and discovered that their allies greatly complicated the task of accommodating African demands and managing their discontents.

'In Malaya and Singapore', as Jack Gallagher observed, 'the British entered in 1945 like a bridegroom coming into his chamber.' But this was a bridegroom with a taste for polygamy. The attempt to create a Malayan Union that would acknowledge its plurality forced the British to re-write their constitution to accept the precedence of the Malays while trying to exclude none. The French in Indochina and the Dutch in Indonesia were stretchered into their chambers under the protection of the Indian Army. They found even less enthusiasm in the zenana. Like the British in Malaya, both the French in Indochina and the Dutch in Indonesia failed to firmly establish colonial rule when they returned after 1945. Perhaps, this reflected how lightly their rule had been tethered within existing structures of power before the Japanese invasion. Certainly, the failure of the Dutch to recruit collaborators who could deliver their bargains condemned them to inflexibility and misjudgements in dealing with Sukarno. By December 1948, when the Dutch launched a large-scale offensive against Sukarno, the United States decided to eject them. Indonesia might contribute usefully to Dutch, indeed European, recovery. But the inflexibility of the Dutch response could open the door to radical nationalists and especially communists. Sukarno had already shown his anti-communist credentials at Madiun and could be trusted to catch the falling dominoes. The United States suspended a tranche of aid under the Marshall Plan to the Netherlands and threatened to cut its programme of assistance altogether. Indonesia became independent.

The French needed imperial cures for their domestic infirmities even more urgently. The structure of their empire had been taken apart by military defeat. Not only had the continuity of their colonial rule been ruptured once more, but its conduct during the war now appeared reprehensible. The French Union had survived by bowing before whoever threatened its existence. French colonial officials had accommodated the Japanese in Indochina, the Germans in Syria, and Vichy in Algeria and West Africa. At Brazzaville, they declared that they would brook no colonial resistance. In 1945, as they began to reclaim their colonies, they were swift to respond to opposition with canon and grapeshot. The British and the Americans eased them out of Syria quickly and quietly. In Algeria, the power of the *colons* and the instability of Fourth Republic coalitions made it difficult to assuage grievances and manage discontent. The French combined concessions, which usually offered too little too late, with fierce repression. At Sétif, on VE Day, they responded to the violence of the riots with a ferociously brutal repressive campaign and initiated the slide into the even greater violence of the 1950s.

In Indochina, the French embarked quickly on a war to restore their model colony but never recovered their authority in Tonkin and parts of Annam. At first, they sought to create a network of collaborators and to restore the Bao Dai. But for these men their moment had passed in the 1930s. Nor were the French effectively able to detach parts of the Viet Minh coalition. In 1946, French ships bombarded Haiphong in the hope that they would force the Viet Minh to negotiate. By February 1947, they had occupied Hanoi. But these military actions had unexpected consequences for the French. It committed them to a prolonged war and set them on the road to Dien Bien Phu. The Chinese revolution induced the United States to subsidize this French colonial war and then to take it on. In the 1940s, the Americans had no taste for French colonialism. But they liked Ho Chi Minh less. In their calculations, the future of Malaya, Thailand, and Indonesia turned upon whether Vietnam could halt the forward march of communism. For the Americans, this line of reasoning led eventually to the roof of their embassy in Saigon. In Africa, Southeast Asia, and the Middle East, the future of European, especially British, imperial interests could only be secured within the framework of an alliance with the United States. Washington's freedom fighters of 1941 were to shore up the crumbling European empires in the 1950s and 1960s.

# Perspectives

The success of formal empires as a technique for European expansion depended largely upon the efficacy of systems of collaboration within them. In 1900, it was difficult enough for colonial rulers to secure collaboration by giving away substantial power to their local allies and also fulfil their imperial commitments. By 1950, it often proved impossible. The successive crises of the early twentieth century suggested that formal empire was becoming an obsolescent method for maintaining imperial systems. During the two world wars, the European powers intervened heavily in their colonies and discovered that colonial resistance quickly narrowed their options. Of course, colonial rulers sometimes restored the balance where they could by repressive force—indeed, historians have perhaps insufficiently explored the nature of the violence which characterized and sustained Europe's civilizing missions—but they often found it more effective to secure colonial rule by accommodating a wider range of local interests. By allowing local power-brokers a larger stake within the colonial state, imperial rulers increasingly limited their role as the sole arbiters of the politics in the regions which they ruled. During the depression of the 1930s, it became clear that there were no imperial solutions for domestic crises, even if their colonies provided an important refuge for their declining industries. As imperial rivalries developed into belligerence, imperial commitments appeared to weaken the defences of Britain and France in Europe when it might have been expected that formal empire would enable them to project their power across the globe.

If the difficulties of securing collaboration suggested the obsolescence of formal rule, technological and institutional changes after the Second World War accentuated the process. Thus, changes in the methods of warfare slowly rendered redundant military garrisons secured by vast territorial commitments. Advances in aircraft technology made it possible to police and threaten vast expanses of territory more cheaply from the air, as indeed the British had first attempted in Iraq in the 1920s. Nuclear arsenals irreversibly altered the methods by which military superiority might be projected in the world. Increasingly, imperial powers did better with remote air strips and missile bases than by fortifying massive garrison-states.

Similarly, the development of multi-national business organization indicated the limitations of formal empire as a means of expanding Europe's world systems. In the nineteenth and early twentieth century, formal empire had offered a measure of security for trade and enterprise, preferably for its own nationals. Sometimes, if the needs of strategy or the implications for informal influence or political control, or occasionally, the significance of particular commodities warranted it, the imperial powers intervened to protect the stakes of merchants and speculators. As business organization changed, European powers began to find themselves investing in the maintenance of systems of security which capitalists in rival states could use free of cost. Moreover, some multi-national enterprises showed that while they welcomed the security which empires offered, they did not need colonial powers to negotiate their way around local structures of power. On the contrary, they could sometimes make themselves indispensable to local states. The oil industry was perhaps the first to demonstrate, as the British discovered in relation to Standard Oil in the Middle East in the 1920s, how international capital could burrow beneath existing systems of colonial control.

As the great powers re-partitioned the world after 1945, formal empire played a decreasingly significant role in the process. Indeed as formal rule was dismantled, the western powers greatly expanded their informal influence. Military aid, technical and financial advice, and large loans enabled western powers to extract trading concessions from, negotiate favourable terms for capital investment in, and establish political alliances with post-colonial states. Decolonization became an integral part of the dynamic of a fresh scramble for spheres of influence. By the end of the twentieth century, the collapse of the Soviet Union took the edge off imperial rivalries and permitted a wider American concert. Oil price-hikes, third world debts, and developments in banking practices, the spiralling costs of armaments and technological changes which facilitated dispersed and flexible production and assembly appeared to create improved conditions for western dominance. But it became increasingly apparent that western capitalist interests could not be readily or adequately secured, especially in the face of local resistance, without local agents, collaborators, and foot soldiers.

7

# Culture

Modris Eksteins

## Century's end

Whether the twentieth century would begin in 1900 or 1901 was a question that exercised many minds at the *fin-de-siècle*. Most European states bowed to the arithmetical and historical argument and ushered in the new century on 1 January 1901. A few, however, could not wait, Germany among them. The Kaiser simply announced that the new century would begin with the arrival of the new year 1900. This debate symbolized a growing tension between those who cherished continuity and causality, and those, in turn, who preferred spontaneity and singularity. A fixed sense of time and history confronted the unpredictability of impulse and instinct: authority confronted will. In the 'battle of the centuries', Britain sided with authority, Germany with will. The respective monarchs, Queen Victoria and Kaiser Wilhelm, represented this divide in character and demeanour.

The divisions were not always straightforward. A tide of rebellion and innovation had mounted since the early 1890s, crossing national, class, generational, and gender lines. Political radicalism, feminism, and youth organizations jostled for attention alongside proponents of 'life reform' who advocated drastic changes in diet, sexual behaviour, dress, and education. By the turn of the century 'new' was an epithet applied readily to any contemporary idea or manifestation—the new era, the new woman, the new drama, the *New Statesman*—deemed different but also meritorious. Newness was poised to change from attribute to value.

That said, most end-of-century commentary, in Germany as well as Britain, was celebratory, applauding the past rather than invoking the future. The British scientist Alfred Wallace entitled his book-length summary of the last hundred years *The Wonderful Century*. In its accomplishments the nineteenth century, said Wallace, outdid not only all preceding centuries, but all history since the Stone Age. For him, as for most Europeans, the nineteenth century represented climactic achievement. 'One doubts', wrote a contributor to the *London Magazine* in January 1900, 'whether any future century will equal it in wonder'.

This comparative and historical perspective was the product of a century of stunning European expansion—territorial, commercial, and intellectual. The imperial urge was fuelled not just by notions of easy profit or political prestige but by moral, religious, and, in the broadest sense, cultural responsibility. That responsibility entailed confidence. The confidence, in turn, was rooted in an awareness of history. Replacing theology and philosophy as the *magistra vitae*, history had become in the course of the nineteenth century the principal intellectual tool for interpreting existence. Thomas Carlyle called it 'the Divine Scripture'. For Karl Marx history had replaced God. Benedetto Croce went so far as to assert that history had 'annihilated' philosophy, the discipline to which it had been subservient for so long. The world had meaning only through history. In an attempt formally to record the state of historical knowledge, the *Cambridge Modern History* was published in fourteen volumes between 1902 and 1912. By 1914, at Oxford, more students were enrolled in the History school than in Greats, or classical studies. Indeed, the nineteenth century had been the *saeculum historicum*.

But if the departing century had upon it the stamp of history, indications were accumulating that the next century might challenge this perspective on existence. The inventions and discoveries that had caused the naturalist Wallace to marvel were accelerating instead of abating. Life itself seemed to be brightening and speeding up immeasurably: the electric light bulb, bicycle, X-ray, cinematograph, wireless, and automobile all appeared within a few years of each other around the turn of the century. These strikingly visible achievements rested on a corpus of scientific discovery that seemed to be growing exponentially in the wake of burgeoning public interest in science in the last half century. Marie Curie, Wilhelm Röntgen, Ernst Mach, Max Planck, J. J. Thomson, Ernest Rutherford, and Albert Einstein were hardly household names but their propositions and conclusions, leading eventually to the dissolution of the hitherto supposedly indestructible atom, shattered the Newtonian view of the world that had been in place since the seventeenth century. Matter, these scientists seemed to be saying, was anything but permanent; it consisted largely of empty space. Time was not an absolute either, its measurement being dependent on perspective. Einstein, whose theories of relativity, published in two stages, in 1905 and 1915, were to stand at the forefront of this modern scientific revolution, described the development as the decline of the 'mechanical' view of the physical world. The hallmark of these scientists as a group was that they set out to defy common—or mechanical—sense. Such defiance would become the hallmark of the new century as a whole.

If theoretical science was becoming increasingly abstract and incomprehensible to the layman, the technology that emerged from it was replete with public drama. The automobile was stunning enough, but on 17 December 1903 at Kitty Hawk, in North Carolina, two American bicycle repairmen, Orville and Wilbur Wright, took a power-driven machine into the air for the first time. Flight, more than any other single achievement, made people realize that a new age had dawned. By 1908 the Wright brothers could keep an aeroplane aloft for an hour and a quarter, and in 1909 the French adventurer Louis Blériot crossed the English Channel in one of these new devices. Since antiquity the soaring bird had been a symbol of freedom, and men had been obsessed with replicating the bird's prowess. Now that capability, with its potential for liberation from earthly cares, was at hand. Man could fly; velocity dissolved distance, landscape, fixity.

The excitement was palpable. Pablo Picasso, who considered himself the incarnation of Charles Baudelaire's *peintre de la vie moderne*, insisted on calling his fellow cubist painter Georges Braque 'Wilbourg' after Wilbur Wright. 'Our future is in the air', proclaimed the Spaniard with a painting in 1912. The geometric shapes that formed the basis of cubist composition—its critics derided it as decomposition—hinted at a fourth dimension beyond time, space, and matter related to the new ability to escape existing laws, be they gravitational, moral, or artistic. At an aerial exhibition at the Grand Palais in Paris in 1912 the artist Marcel Duchamp turned to his companions, Fernand Léger and Constantin Brancusi, and said: 'Painting is finished. Who could do better than that propeller? Could *you* make

that?' In an automobile en route to Marseille, the young French novelist André Gide reflected on the links between technology and art.
He saw in both a staggering potential for incitement: 'Locating the
idea of perfection, not in equilibrium and the middle path, but in the
extreme and exaggeration', he wrote in his diary, 'is perhaps what will
most set off our period and distinguish it most annoyingly.'

The premonition, indeed the invitation, of scandal in Gide's thinking was unmistakable. He personally fulminated against convention
and revelled in his own provocations, sexual and artistic. In 1902 he
had published a novel, *L'Immoraliste*, whose principal character,
Michel, is a historian. Michel falls gravely ill, coughs blood, and on
the edge of death embraces less a desire for health than for experience, sensuous, spiritual, total. Gide was to describe himself as 'the
advocate of whatever voice society ordinarily seeks to stifle'. At the
beginning of the century, the rules of proper behaviour, of 'civilization', stifled life. History, the rebel argued, suffocated experience.
Gide sought to reverse that sequence. In the course of his life, as
experience did indeed threaten to overwhelm history, Gide, the out-
sider, became the insider. In 1947, a few years before his death, he
received the Nobel Prize for literature.

Among those whose influence is readily evident in Gide's life and
work are Friedrich Nietzsche and Oscar Wilde. Both died, coinci-
dentally, in 1900, on the lip of the new century, Nietzsche in August in
Weimar, Wilde in November in Paris. Both died broken men.
Nietzsche, philologist and philosopher, had contradicted the intellectual establishment with a vengeance, denying that the notion of
history as science had any validity. He had spent the last decade of his
life in melancholia and madness. Yet, his star, faint and unnoticed
before, flared after the onset of his illness. 'The whole of modern
culture is essentially internal', he had said in his criticism of contemporary historiography. History was, in the end, merely autobiography. His invocation to live life dangerously, to glorify titanism
and to scorn the unremarkable, stirred many a young intellectual,
including Gide, by the turn of the century. His aphoristic style, consisting of impulse and impression, was reminiscent of French
thinkers like Montaigne, La Rochefoucauld, and Pascal rather than of
the more exegetical German philosophical tradition. Arguing that
law, custom, and privilege were reflective of power, not of inherent
goodness, Nietzsche would become a prophet of discontinuity,

disruption, and what he himself called 'the great disengagement'. He bequeathed to the twentieth century a vocabulary and imagery of crisis. George Bernard Shaw took the Nietzschean term *Übermensch* and, translating it as 'superman', provided for the popular imagination a whole new dimension of possibility. In his madness Nietzsche, the deicide, had pretended that he was God. At his funeral, his friend Peter Gast read the benediction: 'Hallowed be thy name to all future generations.'

'In this world there are only two tragedies', Oscar Wilde had said, in a formulation befitting the century he never lived to experience: 'One is not getting what one wants. The other is getting it.' Gide first met Wilde in Paris in 1891 and never got over that encounter. '*Il rayonnait*', he said of Wilde. Wilde taught Gide that lust could be spiritual and that, correspondingly, the soul could be carnal. Wilde played out his fantasies in life; he revelled in his own contradictions and brilliance. At the height of his success, he fell. Accused of sodomy and convicted of a lesser charge of indecent behaviour, he fled. He fled home, family, and friends, to die in a decrepit Parisian hotel. Did his vitality and love of contradiction retain a presentiment of doom? 'I was a man', he said of himself, 'who stood in symbolic relations to the art and culture of my age. . . .'

To both Nietzsche and Wilde, myth and legend were more important than history, the subject more luminous than any object. The two died in the year *The Interpretation of Dreams* appeared—what Sigmund Freud called his 'dream book'. In that book the Viennese psychologist argued that dreams were wishes rather than memories and challenged the prevailing consensus that the science of the mind was simply part of the science of physical function. Freud urged that in the study of the mind more emphasis be put on experience than on heredity. The book turned out to be the strategic centre of Freud's psychoanalytic thought and of a good deal of twentieth-century thought as a whole.

Freud himself was less revolutionary than his ideas. He believed that scientific method was the way to decode symbols; he respected causality and suspected caprice. He aimed to tame the human unconscious. Yet these very interests depended on the subjective, the immoral, the impious, and the poetic—what the Austrian writer Arthur Schnitzler called 'impudent wishes'. Like the natural scientists, Freud told the world what it did not wish to hear—to some degree even what he himself did not wish to hear. Freud shocked profoundly.

For this reason alone he was welcomed by some. For modern art as for modern science shock and surprise had become by the early years of the twentieth century an integral part of the cultural landscape. Because it contradicted convention and respectability, surprise was associated with freedom. Picasso's *Demoiselles d'Avignon*, his great brothel composition of 1907, perhaps the most influential painting of the twentieth century, and in turn Igor Stravinsky's 1913 score for the ballet *Le Sacre du printemps*, perhaps the most revolutionary musical composition of the century, were imbued from the outset with shock value. Desecration was their purpose. 'Surprise me, Jean', said Sergei Diaghilev, the Russian impresario who commissioned *Le Sacre*, to Jean Cocteau. The young Frenchman, poet, playwright, cinéaste, rebel, looked on that utterance as revelation.

The avant-garde—adopting an adversarial stance and calling themselves alternately *refusés*, secessionists, or independents—turned art into public performance, into a scene. Publicity, scandal, innuendo created an aura of excitement. The performance itself exuded urgency and involved a declamatory style, often a manifesto. The audience was drawn in; its response, frequently hostile, was essential to the event. The premières, within weeks of each other, of Alban Berg's *Altenberglieder* in Vienna and Stravinsky's *Le Sacre* in Paris brought on riotous behaviour and front-page notoriety. Scandal spelled success.

For the wider public a new medium, the cinema, expressed similar excitement. Its energy was addictive. The guiding principle of most early filmmakers was to keep everything moving, to allow no pause for reflection. Action and violence became staples. Snub Pollard, one of the original Keystone Kops, estimated: 'I figured up once I'd caught about fourteen thousand pies in my puss and had been hit by six hundred automobiles and two trains.'

The British weekly the *New Statesman* noted with prescience in January 1914 that, given the enormous popular success of the 'movies', the world was heading resolutely toward a culture beyond the written word. The cinematograph, it said, 'has already become a serious rival not only of books but of beer'. The cinema was, in other words, threatening not only the library but the cherished pub. The editorialist went on to predict: 'Every man will become his own cinematographer. There will be a cinematograph not only in every street but in every home.'

The artistic and scientific avant-garde intended, of course, to liberate humanity. But as visions of freedom multiplied, so too did those of destruction and terror. H. G. Wells reflected in *The War in the Air* (1908) on what the new technology of flight might do to future conflict: 'There was no time for diplomacy. Warnings and ultimatums were telegraphed to and fro, and in a few hours all the panic-fierce world was openly at war.' The German expressionist Ludwig Meidner painted apocalyptic landscapes of exploding and burning cities, and Italian Futurists, led by Filippo T. Marinetti, applauded war, which they called the only hygiene, a synonym for their aesthetic ambitions. Beauty is aggressive, they said, speed the new morality. Marinetti set out to free the world of 'the stinking gangrene of its professors, archaeologists, . . . and antique dealers'. He called upon his followers to 'murder moonbeams'. To symbolize the break with the past, Marinetti wished to eliminate from his writing all adjectives, adverbs, and punctuation. He evoked 'words in freedom', liberated from the restraints of gravity. In art, the technique of collage, or freely floating images, represented a comparable urge, an urge whereby disjunction was more meaningful than connection, where association replaced cause. The act of creation, like birth itself, had of necessity to be bloody and eruptive. 'Kill John Bull with Art', trumpeted Wyndham Lewis in the summer of 1914 shortly after founding a journal called *BLAST*.

The urge to destroy bourgeois symbols was all-powerful. 'My life has always been war', insisted the sculptor Jacob Epstein. The staid bourgeoisie whose essence was effort, expansion, and achievement was deeply troubled by the violence inherent in this outlook. The turbulence coincided with a growing European self-doubt, as Italy had trouble subduing the Ethiopians, as Spain retreated from its last colonies, as Britain struggled to defeat the Boers, and as Russia was trounced in war by Japan. The geocultural balance of 'the modern' tilted noticeably toward the periphery of traditional power. Germany, on the edge of a long-standing Anglo-French ascendancy, political and cultural, dating back to the age of Louis XIV, embodied much of the revolt. Those hostile to Nietzsche, Wilde, Gide, Picasso, and modern influences as a whole charged that they represented German ideas and perversions. Of the relatively stark lines of the newly constructed

Théâtre des Champs-Élysées in Paris, Alphonse Gosset, an architect, remarked in 1913: 'That the Germans . . . should accept this sort of reclusion is perhaps understandable, but Parisians, avid of bright lights and elegance, no!' 'We often got on the world's nerves', admitted the German Chancellor Bethmann-Hollweg; but this behaviour, he suggested, was motivated less by a desire for world dominion than by 'a boyish and unbalanced enthusiasm'. Britain was the least tolerant of boyish enthusiasm and avant-garde antics. The Russian dancer Nijinsky, who choreographed the revolutionary *Sacre du printemps*, described the English as greedy and cold: 'John Bull eats a lot of money', he noted in his diary. 'The English do not like dancing, because they have a lot of money in their stomachs.'

# The Great War

The war that began in August 1914 embodied this conflict between the forces of innovation and those of order. German intellectuals succumbed to a mood often equated with the revolutionary impulse in France in 1789—poetry in politics. In the early months of the war all Germans seemed to have become poets: Julius Bab, the Berlin critic, estimated that some fifty thousand poems were being penned a day. *Die neue Rundschau*, a German journal that had associated itself with the wave of newness sweeping the land, editorialized in November 1914: 'War! It was purification, liberation that we experienced, and an immense hope. It was of this that the poets spoke, only of this. What do they care for imperial power, for commercial hegemony, even for victory? . . . What inspired the poets was the war itself, as visitation, as ethical exigency.' In 1916 Ernst Troeltsch, theologian and historian, could still speak of 'the wind of the future' that was blowing in, bringing 'storm and world-historical crisis'. The old was about to break up; the new would be issued in with shattering effect. The poet Wilfred Owen used the image of a 'tornado, centred at Berlin'.

The British and the French were, by contrast, determined to preserve a world threatened by an anarchical, immoral thrust emanating principally from Germany. 'Every hour we should remind ourselves that it is our great privilege to save the traditions of all centuries behind us', wrote one British soldier, A. D. Gillespie, to his parents in early October 1914.

From the start this was a war not just of the military and politicians, but of schools, universities, newspapers, football clubs, theatres, art galleries, and opera houses. The Germans called it a *Kulturkrieg*, a war of cultures. It became a word war. Never has so much been written about war. Indeed, never has so much been written—and read—in newspapers, books, circulars, posters, diaries, and private correspondence. In September 1914, one young German wife remarked to her soldier-husband, a middle-aged shopkeeper from Hamburg: 'My dearest, we're now writing to each other more than we ever did when we were courting.'

On all sides, intellectual and emotional engagement in the national cause was intense. Scholars became journalists; clergymen transformed pulpits into rostrums; artists, actors, and filmmakers turned palette, dais, and camera into tools of national purpose. In this effort, the social values associated with the nineteenth-century bourgeoisie—duty, responsibility, hard work, respectability, service, honour—reached an apotheosis. The war was in a sense the grandest achievement of the European bourgeoisie. 'The war revealed the personality of our civilization', wrote the Russian philosopher Nicholas Berdyaev later. Only because of the strength of these social values could the war—this 'love battle' of the European bourgeoisie, as the American writer F. Scott Fitzgerald would call it—last for over four years.

The avant-garde was eager, as always, to look on the conflict in artistic rather than moral terms. The war was part of the drama of life. The French painter and cultural notable Jacques-Emile Blanche suggested that the war was 'staged' by the Kaiser. The implication was that theatricality and performance, image and psychological need, were more important considerations than traditional *raisons d'état* or any moral mandate. Ernst Glaeser, the novelist, would say later that in Germany the war had been 'an aesthetic pleasure beyond compare'. If the nineteenth century had led to the growing secularization of life, the twentieth turned existence into a matter of style, into an aesthetic statement. Life, like art, became a matter of performance.

Language and imagery, already strained by the speed of change in the prewar era, came under wholesale assault because of the unprecedented scale of the war. The crisis of representation mounted.

Artists found it increasingly difficult to render the enormity of the human drama using traditional means. The war, as it developed, became the antithesis of conventional notions of beauty, meaning, and, indeed, history. In his poem 'The Poet as Hero' Siegfried Sassoon wrote: 'My ecstasies changed to an ugly cry'. Wilfred Owen spoke of 'the universal pervasion of *Ugliness*'. Metaphysical notions of truth would never recover from the blows of the war. No Man's Land Owen called 'the abode of madness'. After reading Sassoon's sketches of trench life Owen remarked to his mother: 'Shakespeare reads vapid after these'. By 1916 the Italian journalist Guglielmo Ferrero could say: 'If the war has not yet upset the map of Europe, it has completely changed its spirit . . . How distant the days before the war now seem!'

The war gave the protest, rebellion, and even the artistic abstraction of the prewar era a new urgency. In Zürich, in neutral Switzerland, a group of radical poets and artists—Hugo Ball, Tristan Tzara, and Hans Arp, among others—came together in 1915 and called themselves by the nonsensical name Dada. Rejecting the war and all the impulses that fuelled it, they staged evenings of outrage— 'bruitism'—at the Cabaret Voltaire, insulting their audiences and challenging all notions of stability and purpose, even their own. Dada groups then formed in Berlin, Cologne, Paris, and New York, experimenting alternatively with photomontage, automatic writing, or an abstract assemblage that amounted to street litter as art. Marcel Duchamp took the Mona Lisa, subject of arguably the most famous painting in the gallery of Western civilization, and gave her a moustache, goatee, and new moniker: LHOOQ. When pronounced in French the letters amount phonetically to a vulgarity. The twentieth century would be the century of Dada, with its aesthetics of irony, anger, emergency, and obscenity.

Politically, the revolutionary instincts went off in diametrically opposed directions, but then converged again. The most radical elements espoused a blend of nationalism and socialism. Some were eventually to call their credo 'socialism in one country', others National Socialism. The year 1917 was crucial. The cultural conflicts became more violent. In November, Lenin, who had spent the war years in Zürich, not far from the Cabaret Voltaire, seized power in Russia and turned his Bolshevik experiment into a beacon of hope for the dispossessed, disadvantaged, and dissatisfied everywhere. The artistic community was impressed by the action. Misia Sert, admirer of the *Ballets russes*, thought of the events in Russia as a grand ballet.

Julien Benda was to claim in his famous postwar essay, *La Trahison des clercs* (The Treason of the Intellectuals), that the intellectual community, by soiling its hands in politics and war, had betrayed its trust. For Benda, intellectuals, by definition, had to stay above the fray. But during the war they had not: they had descended from the symposium to the battlefield. Not only had the intellectual and artist descended to the battlefield; intellectuality and creativity had become, by definition, combat. War had become a matter of aesthetics: aesthetics had become a matter of war.

## The Twenties

The end of the war did not bring the epiphany everyone craved. On the contrary, economic dislocation, massive unemployment, inflation and depression, brought political instability and unabating crisis. Pessimism flowered. Pretending to be heroic, Oswald Spengler, whose *Untergang des Abendlandes* (The Decline of the West) had been germinating since 1911 and was finally published in two stages in 1918 and 1922, as the disastrous German inflation spiralled, announced that 'optimism is cowardice'. 'The need for optimism', he said, 'is basically a sentimental and decadent frame of mind . . .' In February 1922 the novelist Thomas Hardy lamented 'these disordered years of our prematurely afflicted century'. The war, he felt, had 'barbarized' taste by encouraging 'a degrading thirst after outrageous stimulation'. Together with Dean Inge of St Paul's Cathedral in London, he spoke of the danger of a return to the Dark Ages. In the same year, Winston Churchill, trapped then and for many years to come in his own political no man's land, commented: 'What a disappointment the twentieth century has been.'

In conversation in October 1923 with the South African statesman Jan Smuts, the German financier Carl Melchior mentioned 'the feeling of hopelessness and national despair' in Germany, and the 'condition of general nervous excitement'. 'Among us', he pointed out, 'eight or nine of every ten men is suffering from nervous illness.' Melchior may have been exaggerating, but dysfunction—particularly as displayed in the condition of shell-shock—became the symbolic condition of the postwar world. In Germany alone over six hundred thousand soldiers had been treated in military hospitals during the war for 'diseases of the nervous system'. The indications of shell-shock were many: morbidity, hysteria, depression, headaches, insomnia, nightmares, hallucinations, ataxy, tics. The condition was widespread, the diagnosis, let alone cure, less certain. Many doctors and officials had been inclined to deny, first, that a military version of 'neurasthenia' might exist and, secondly, that it might have any physical basis. Nervous disorder, the conservative order insisted, was the result of moral inadequacy. War neurotics were derided as self-indulgent social failures, usually with homosexual tendencies. Punishment, not sympathy, was the just dessert of these 'hollow men'.

The culture of the 1920s displayed similar signs. By 1928 the composer Arnold Schoenberg was prepared to admit a connection between musical syntax and the human nervous system. Traditionalists denounced the frenetic dance-steps of ragtime, the paroxysms of the Charleston, the syncopated rhythms of jazz, and even the jiggling of the latest toy, the yo-yo, as emanations of the same moral corruption that had produced shell-shock. 'Tremblers' were by definition 'shirkers'. 'Only uneducated people suffer from such conditions', said one doctor to an officer who had been rendered deaf and dumb by a shell explosion. Only the uneducated and morally defective would indulge in the hedonistic perversions of a modern mass culture, that could celebrate, for instance, a black artiste from the urban jungles of America, Josephine Baker, who would appear onstage in nothing but a skirt of bananas.

Authority, on all levels, came under assault. Life displayed a new energy. Everything—boats, cars, buses, planes, crowds, pictures—seemed now to move, and to move faster. Man and machine became one. Fernand Léger fused human and mechanical features in his art. Charles Lindbergh became the most famous man in the world, overnight, when he flew across the Atlantic in May 1927. His airplane, *The Spirit of St Louis*, received almost as much attention as he did. Lucky Lindy seemed to represent the instincts of an age, an age of action and assertion. Jazz—strident and provocative—was described as 'the sound of speed'. William Faulkner, combining images and sounds, called the twenties 'this saxophone age of flying'.

If flying was alluring as idea, dancing was the thing to do. 'We wanted to forget the war', said Elisabeth de Gramont. 'While eminent men were discussing its consequences, we were dancing.' Dance evoked life, Eros. But the backdrop was death, Thanatos. Eros and Thanatos, apparent opposites, fused. To allow for the freedom of movement necessary for dancing, and indeed for new forms of travel, on land or in the air, skirts rose. Women 'bobbed' their hair; some wore trousers. Fashion took on a perky note: the flowing scarf was *de rigueur* for both driver, pilot, and passenger. Isadora Duncan, whose scarves flowed as freely as her dance, went for a ride in a Bugatti in Nice. Her scarf caught. Her neck snapped. Eros and Thanatos. Many fliers crashed, too, with similar effect. In his journal in 1929, the young English aesthete W. H. Auden wrote: 'The essence of creation is doing things for no reason.'

Action for no reason—what Gide called the *acte gratuit*—usually had a compelling reason: rebellion and provocation of those dedicated to ideas of service, duty, and continuity. Noel Coward, *flâneur* par excellence, loved, like Oscar Wilde before him, to tease the bourgeoisie. 'I am never out of opium dens, cocaine dens, and other evil places,' he told the press with a half-smile. 'My mind is a mass of corruption.' During the war Marcel Duchamp had submitted a urinal to an art exhibition. It was, he said, the one object most likely to be disliked.

But the best expression of movement in the 1920s and in subsequent years was the motion picture. The 'movie' involved the appropriation of the natural world, its breakdown into individual frames, and then its reconstitution in the action-filled images of the film-maker. The poet Ezra Pound said that the cinematograph represented 'the logical end of impressionist art' in that reality was now perceived evanescently. The camera threatened to destroy the eye. In Luis Buñuel and Salvador Dali's surrealist film concoction of 1928, *Un Chien andalou*, a razor slashes an eyeball. If the camera could substitute for the eye, the moving picture could, as Walter Benjamin pointed out, substitute for travelling. Cinema permitted audiences to go on psychological journeys to distant lands, where mystery and vicarious thrill were the essence. 'Our taverns and our metropolitan streets, our offices and furnished rooms, our railroad stations and our factories appeared to have us locked up hopelessly,' wrote Benjamin in his most famous essay, 'The Work of Art in the Age of Mechanical Reproduction'. 'Then came the film and burst this prison-world asunder by the dynamite of the length of a second, so that now, in the midst of far-flung ruins and debris, we calmly and adventurously go travelling.' Travel, with a goal in mind, was old-fashioned; travelling, *sans cesse et sans but*, particularly in one's mind, was liberating.

'Some people go to the movies the way others go to church,' said the Surrealist André Breton; 'it is there that the only *absolutely modern* mystery is celebrated.' The cinema seemed to provide what life, love, and for some even religion no longer offered: mystery, indeed miracle. Breton and Jacques Vaché had met in a military hospital in Nantes in 1916; they had gone movie-hopping regularly on Sunday afternoons, one cinema after another, until their imaginations were charged with ideas and images. Vaché became a hero for the Surrealists, the man who disrupted the opening of Apollinaire's play *Les Mamelles de Tirésias* in 1917 by waving a revolver and threatening to shoot the audience, and whose letter to Breton after the Armistice was memorized by all Surrealists: 'I shall leave this war gently idiotic . . . or rather . . . I shall play a beautiful film!—With crazy automobiles, . . . with bridges that give way, and with large hands that crawl on the screen toward some document! . . . useless and invaluable!'

Cinematic technique improved steadily. By the end of the decade sound had replaced the silent screen. Nevertheless, sentimental drama remained the favourite genre of audiences—in 1927 the Soviet diplomat Ilya Ehrenburg counted no less than twenty-two films with 'love' in their title. But every other aspect of film culture—from the sensuality of the 'stars' to the darkness of the cinema during performance—undermined notions of permanence, tradition, and enlightenment. Sergei Eisenstein, Fritz Lang, F. W. Murnau, G. W. Pabst made films about revolutionaries, misfits, prostitutes, and freaks. Charlie Chaplin, the androgynous little vagabond with the funny gait, led his audiences down endless highways and byways, smacked, kicked, and buffeted by fate. Highbrow or lowbrow, the French loved their Charlot, as they called Chaplin. So did the Germans. So did everyone. He was the most persuasive incarnation of Baudelaire's *flâneur*, a true citizen of the modern world, the survivor, the winning loser. In Germany in 1928 some 353 million cinema tickets were sold; theatre attendance, by comparison, was under fifteen million.

If rapid movement was the most powerful motif of the 1920s, another theme of the increasingly visual culture was the radical rearrangement of space. A cult of the straight line—the shortest distance between two points—emerged, a new directness, in fashion, architecture, and design. This was an ethic not of progress, merely of efficiency or engineering. 'I strive for omission, not addition', said Paul Poiret, who more than anyone else was responsible for the new feminine look of the twenties. The Paris magazine *Le Crapouillot* commented in April 1921 that modern fashion should revolve around the airplane and automobile in the same way that in a previous century it revolved around the Louis XIV chair. With bobbed hair, cloche hat, and sack dress, the flapper looked more like a tube than a woman. Coco Chanel introduced the straightforward 'poor look'; men adopted the shaven, even bald look. Piet Mondrian reduced painting to the fundamentals of rectilinear line and colour; the Bauhaus did the same for design and architecture. Ornamentation, Adolf Loos had said, was a crime. The flat roofs and glass towers of the new architectural style confirmed such sentiment. The nineteenth-century city had expanded horizontally; the twentieth-century metropolis grew upwards.

The commercial advertisement, too, adopted simplicity. Woodbine cigarettes were good for you. A Horch automobile would refresh rather than tire its driver. Wartime propaganda, with its preposterous presumptions, had paved the way for peacetime suggestion. The senses were bombarded, reason outwitted. Politicians took note.

Literature was bound to change under this onslaught against convention and sanity. Language had taken a drubbing during the war. In a conflict where some ten million men died and some twenty million were mutilated, the word casualty was hardly adequate. The philosopher Ludwig Wittgenstein pointed to the chasm that had opened between words and meaning. One needed a whole new vocabulary, a new language even. 'Only the names of places had dignity', concluded Ernest Hemingway in the most famous passage in *A Farewell to Arms*. 'Abstract words such as glory, honour, courage, or hallow were obscene beside the concrete names of villages, the numbers of roads, the names of rivers, the numbers of regiments and the dates.'

If language was undermined and purpose compromised, a writer could no longer—in all honesty—strive toward structure and harmony. James Joyce introduced a 'stream of consciousness' style in *Ulysses*; Marcel Proust termed *À la Recherche du temps perdu* a *roman fleuve.* Time was their subject, and their sense of time had become subjective. Amidst the dissonance, rhyme was a lie. T. S. Eliot's *The Waste Land* was quickly adopted as the poetic expression—in style as well as substance—of the spiritual desolation of the era. An American poet, who had worked as an ambulance driver in France, decided in future to write his name entirely in lower case—e.e. cummings. He eliminated punctuation and capital letters from his poetry. The old rules had no value; they impeded creativity. Ford Madox Ford, author of the tetralogy collected under the title *Parade's End,* became a doubter. 'If, before the war, one had any function it was that of historian', he said. But history had lost its authority. His principal character, Tietjens, loses his memory in the trenches. For Ernst Troeltsch, theologian and historian, the 'essence of modernity' was 'the transformation of history into a game of fantasy'. Fiction was now more important than history.

Franz Kafka, through his life and art, best represented the shifting ground of his age. A Czech Jew, trained in law and employed by a Prague insurance company, Kafka wrote in German about burrows and mazes, guilt and shame. In *The Trial,* the character Joseph K. is convicted of an undetermined crime. Though unaware of the nature of his crime, he feels guilty. A writer with admirable control, Kafka nevertheless found language totally inadequate. The unexpressed was for him more important than the expressed, language a contradiction of its purpose. Still, he continued to write, as if out of self-hatred, not to unburden himself but to wallow in anguish. Kafkaesque became an adjective used to invoke a world of angularity, agony, and negation. Kafka envied extinction. Significantly, his work saw the light of day only after his death in 1924.

Among the themes that obsessed writers like Kafka was the link between disease and art. Critics of cultural modernism assumed that its agents were mentally ill, that abstraction, atonality, and derange-ment went hand in hand, but the moderns themselves luxuriated in the suggestion that madness and brilliance were one and the same. Thomas Mann was convinced that art was rooted in neurosis: he set his novel *Der Zauberberg* (The Magic Mountain) among tubercular invalids in a sanatorium. In his short story 'Ad Astra', William Faulkner has a German say: 'Defeat will be good for us. Defeat iss good for art; victory, it iss not good.' Germany, in its defeat, in its pariah status, in its willingness to reconsider all norms, became the crucible of high modernism. The culture of the Weimar Republic was a culture of catastrophe.

Music of the postwar years articulated both the pain and the quest. Definitions—of music and noise—collided: the force of impact seemed to fuse formerly separate categories. Composers introduced the sounds of urban industrial life into their works—typewriters, whistles, trams. Alban Berg's operas *Wozzeck* and *Lulu*, Kurt Weill's collaborative efforts with Bertolt Brecht, especially on *Die Dreigroschenoper* (The Threepenny Opera), and Paul Hindemith's *oeuvre* culminating in his portrait of a painter, *Mathis der Maler*, captured the existential confusion and violence of the age, in the way that Stravinsky's Dionysian works had represented avant-garde energies in the prewar years. However, Arnold Schoenberg's bold experiments in atonality towered over other composition, at least in daring. The conductor Wilhelm Furtwängler said of Schoenberg: 'The twelve-tone system of Schoenberg . . . as an auditory experience conveys the spirit of chaos but as a method of composition it is the epitome of the world of modern science, the most highly rationalized system imaginable.' This combination of chaos and science bespoke the mood.

Scientific advance continued to accelerate, probing ever further the imperceptibly small and the incomprehensibly large, until infinity and fragment seemed to coalesce. In 1927 Werner Heisenberg, a founder of quantum mechanics, the new physics of the atomic world, concluded that causal logic had to be abandoned. Since one cannot know the precise position and momentum of a particle at any given instant, its future cannot be determined, only a range of possibilities. This came to be known as the uncertainty principle, and for it Heisenberg was awarded the 1932 Nobel Prize for physics. Appropriately, as the idea of uncertainty made headway, the barriers between the sciences crumbled, as had those between various art forms. Psychology, too, reflected the passion for fragment and the move to indeterminacy. The sociologist Georg Simmel remarked: 'The essence of modernity as such is psychologism, the experiencing and interpretation of the world in terms of the reactions of our inner life and indeed as an inner world, the dissolution of fixed contents in the fluid element of the soul, from which all that is substantive is filtered and whose forms are merely forms of motion.' All was now multiplicity and movement.

Freud's prominence grew, and the taboos surrounding sexuality lifted. Life was eroticized. More people were willing to recognize the importance of sexuality in human behaviour and to tolerate, even welcome, its expression. Women could now walk alone, smoke, wear make-up, without being called whores. Movie actors became stars and vicarious partners on the basis solely of physical appearance. A popular song declared: 'The girl I love is on a magazine cover'. The Marquis de Sade was resurrected. Gender roles blurred. Berlin in particular gained a reputation as a netherworld of degenerate sensuality.

Freud's suggestion that human beings were motivated by unconscious urges more powerful than any reasoning faculty intrigued artists, especially the Surrealists. Dada had mimicked chaos. The Surrealists now tried to regain control. Guillaume Apollinaire had coined the word surrealist to describe his absurdist play of 1917, *Les Mamelles de Tirésias*, but it was not until 1924 that André Breton published the first Surrealist manifesto calling for a new conception of life that would transcend necessity and celebrate the power of the marvellous. 'I believe', wrote Breton, 'in the future resolution of these two states, dream and reality, which are apparently so contradictory, into a sort of absolute reality, a *surreality*, so to speak.' The Surrealists painted, wrote, and made films. Their key concept was psychic automatism by which they aimed to free the mind of the constraints of conscious expression. In their attempt to fuse poetry and freedom the Surrealists flirted with communism: some wanted desperately to marry Marx and Freud. But the pairing proved to be incompatible. For the politicians, surrealist environments were worlds of contortion; for the artists, the practical demands of politics chafed. Georges Bataille headed a group that produced a magazine entitled *Acéphale*, or headless man. In the first issue he declared: 'It is time to abandon the world of the civilized and its light. It is too late to be reasonable and educated . . . It is necessary to become completely different, or to cease being.'

Surrealism had its unofficial headquarters in Paris. In Berlin and elsewhere in Europe, Expressionism had more appeal, with its breathless excitement, its extremes of emotion, and its intentional imprecision. Otto Dix, Max Beckmann, Emil Nolde, and Georg Kaiser, among others, built an artistic and literary edifice on 'The Scream' by Edvard Munch—the Norwegian's 1893 painting of sexless, placeless, timeless *Angst*. Joseph Goebbels, propaganda guru of Nazism, had been attracted to Expressionism as a university student. 'I am the most radical. Of the new type. Man as revolutionary,' he had scribbled in his diary. He was to return to these clipped piercing tones in his last radio scripts in 1945, amidst the rubble of Berlin, just before he took the lives of his six children.

These modern manifestations in the arts found little sympathy among the broader public which, for the most part, reacted negatively to what it interpreted as intentional obfuscation, mindless infantilism, or outright perversity. Of the Surrealists the *Daily Worker* wrote: 'The general impression one gets is that here is a group of young people who just haven't got the guts to tackle anything seriously.'

As notions of respectability and social meaning were reconsidered, the individual stood front and centre. Personal experience seemed to be a more valid prism for interpreting life than edicts handed down by timeworn authority. Hermann Hesse's character Demian states: 'I wanted only to try to live in obedience to the promptings which came from my true self.' Autobiography gained in importance as a genre, and a wave of biography swept through literary and historical criticism. A character in André Malraux's *Les Conquérants* asks: 'Aside from memoirs, are there any books worth writing?' The literary generation that had experienced the war answered in the negative. Adolf Hitler was part of that generation. His turgid self-centred tract he entitled *Mein Kampf.*

In the late twenties, after a decade of silence on the subject, books on the war suddenly dominated publishers' lists. The 'war boom' had begun. Most of the books were memoirs or reflections disguised as novels. For several years the public seemed unable to get enough of this material. Robert Graves, Siegfried Sassoon, Richard Aldington, Ernest Hemingway, Ludwig Renn, Franz Schauwecker, and Arnold Zweig were suddenly popular. R. C. Sherriff's war play, *Journey's End*, ran for 594 consecutive performances in London and by the end of 1929 had been staged in twelve different countries. In these accounts the master narrative had disappeared. The sense of purpose had been lost.

Most read of all was Erich Maria Remarque. His novel, *Im Westen nichts Neues* (All Quiet on the Western Front), was serialized in a Berlin newspaper in late 1928 and appeared in book form in January 1929. Within months the thirty-one-year-old Remarque was the world's most famous author. Within a year twenty-eight translations had appeared and world sales were in the millions. His was the first modern bestseller.

# Bolshevism and fascism

In his adaptation of Marxist theory, Lenin emphasized the import-ance of the revolutionary vanguard. It would seize power and govern on behalf of the proletariat until the latter became the largest group-ing in society. History would thus be given a push by an advance guard of inspired leaders.

After the Bolshevik Revolution, in November 1917, many artists and intellectuals in Russia and elsewhere believed that the Revolution would now invariably usher in the victory of the artistic avant-garde as well. Communism would not only eliminate poverty and injustice; it would unshackle creativity. Vladimir Mayakovsky, bard of the Revolution, proclaimed in December 1918: 'It's time for bullets to pepper museums.' Art was to be snatched from the clutches of both the market and the antiquarians and turned into an affair of the square and the street. Under the revolution art became declamation—on posters, in manifestoes, on painted boxcars, in cinematic spectacle. 'We will remake life anew,' wrote Mayakovsky, 'right down to the last button of your vest.' Alexander Blok insisted that the purpose of the Revolution was 'to organize things . . . so that our false, filthy, boring, hideous life should become a just, pure, merry, and beautiful one'. H. G. Wells, who interviewed Lenin in 1920, described him as 'the dreamer in the Kremlin'.

Dreamer he may have been; enthralled by the shock tactics, irreverence, and carnivalesque laughter of the avant-garde he was not. He had more solemn and orderly preferences. He wanted a public art that was accessible; he disliked the products of Cubists and Futurists. Toward his own Constructivists—engineers, scientists, and artists who sought to create a synthesis of body, soul, and machine—he was ambivalent. Aleksandr Rodchenko, Vladimir Tatlin, El Lissitzky excited but did not persuade. The public, too, seemed to demand not avant-gardist experiment but art that provided at one and the same time an escape from and an idealization of daily life.

Although the first decade of Bolshevism remained relatively tolerant of cultural experiment, the power of the apparatchiks grew. Militant in their parochialism, they gradually came to oversee cultural activity. By the late 1920s a new cohort of 'proletarian' cultural sponsors had emerged, their confidence generated by the lower ranks of the party, vigilante groups, proletarian writers, and militant atheists. Anger and hate replaced the earlier fairground spirit. Stalin's consolidation of power at the end of the decade confirmed the shift in both mood and power base. In 1930 Mayakovsky shot himself. Four years later 'socialist realism' was decreed the official art form of the Soviet Union. An art of kitsch, it masked and encouraged, at one and the same time, the brutality of Stalinism.

The Bolshevik revolution in Russia precipitated 'counter-revolutionary' violence elsewhere, an extremism on the right that was driven, nonetheless, by urges and emotions strikingly similar to those on the radical left. Most prominently in Italy in 1922 and Germany in 1933, movements came to power that promoted a fusion of nationalism and collectivism, in theory a spiritual alternative to materialistic communism or self-centred factionalism, but in practice an eruption, often brutal, of frustration. Managerial ideals merged with petit-bourgeois resentment to create a millenarian surge toward a 'brave new world'. Italo Balbo, one of the first to respond to Mussolini's Fascism, said that had it not been for Mussolini, three quarters of Italian veterans would have become communists, because they demanded revolution, of one sort or another. Indeed, there were powerful connections between the revolutionary impulses in politics and in the broader cultural realm. *Tutto osare*, dare everything, was Balbo's Nietzschean motto. In an essay in 1924, the philosopher and historian Benedetto Croce suggested that 'for those with a sense of historical connection, the intellectual origin of Fascism is to be found in Futurism: in the resolve to go down to the piazza, to impose one's own feelings, to shut up the mouths of those who are dissenting'. In Germany, in their desire to break with the past, the Nazis burned books. In place of literary culture they offered images, fantasy, and action. Hitler told the 1933 Party Congress that the Third Reich would institute 'a new style of life, culture, and art'. Poet and soldier would become one.

'The crowd is his element', Baudelaire had said of the modern artist. The crowd was Mussolini's and Hitler's element, too. Fascism turned mass politics into theatre. The rituals of fascism were replete with drama: the balcony address, the Roman salute, the banners, the dialogues with the crowd. The aestheticization of politics was part of a broader development: the loss of confidence in an external world and the resultant tendency to mythologize that world. Architecture, painting, literature, and particularly film were used to promote myths. The Spanish thinker Ortega y Gasset saw in this modern confabulation of life 'a Christianity without God'.

Nazi art, like socialist realism, resorted to cliché, celebrating racial purity, the beauty of work, and the power of nature. In its own terms Nazism was an attempt to move away from the void back to solid ground. Modern art was rejected as degenerate, as 'cultural bolshevism', and in 1937 a huge exhibition of these modern works was assembled in the House of German Art at Munich to show Germans how not to paint and, by corollary, how not to think. Paradoxically, this un-German show attracted more German visitors than any other public display during the Third Reich.

The banal conformism of Stalinist and Hitlerian aesthetics notwithstanding, the totalitarian regimes themselves perpetrated modernist drama, scripted as it were by avant-garde imaginations bent on violent renewal and enamoured of apocalyptic visions. Both were incarnations of the modern impulse.

# The Thirties

Many prominent artists and intellectuals fled the totalitarian regimes of Europe. Large numbers arrived in America. They benefited universities, research institutes, the New York stage, and the Hollywood studios. Others went to England, some to Brazil.

The moderns did not necessarily understand each other. 'I was inclined to regard the Surrealists—who seem to have adopted me as their patron saint—as 100 per cent fools,' remarked Freud. Still, in the summer of 1938, a few weeks after he had fled Vienna for London, he agreed to meet one of these fools, Salvador Dali, or 'The Surrealissimo', as *Time* magazine was to nickname him. How these two giants of modern sensibility communicated is unclear. Dali knew no German and at that stage little English, but true to character he was most animated at the meeting. Edward James was present and described the scene: 'Salvador was looking so inspired, his eyes were so blazing with excitement while he sketched the inventor of psychoanalysis, that the old man whispered in German ... "That boy looks like a fanatic. Small wonder that they have civil war in Spain if they look like that."'

That civil war in Spain, between republican and nationalist forces, concentrated the Western imagination. After the manic activity of the twenties, the economic depression at the end of the decade had doused enthusiasm. But the stunningly rapid consolidation of Nazism in the heartland of Europe once more unleashed chiliastic foreboding. Blackshirts rallied on one street, peace marchers on the next. As Hitler rearmed Germany, the Oxford Union resolved that it would not fight for King and Country. When the Spanish conflict flared, many decided that here was the showdown, left and right doing battle for the future. '*Oggi in Spagna, domani in Italia*', chanted Italian anti-fascists in the Garibaldi Brigade. The ferocity of the Spanish struggle had less to do with options on the ground than with the apocalyptic phantasms that the European crisis had disgorged. André Malraux, George Orwell, Arthur Koestler, Stephen Spender, W. H. Auden, and many others went either to fight or to look. The first English volunteer to die was a woman, the painter Felicia Browne. All thought they were journeying to a frontier that led to the centre of the world. Picasso's *Guernica*, commemorating the German bombing in April 1937 of the Basque town and expressing more broadly the disjointed anguish of modern life, would become one of the most celebrated paintings of the century.

Melodic history, Paul Valéry had said in the wake of the Great War, was gone. Fascism and communism tried in theory to restore melody to history; however, in practice—in that their violence was so pervasive—they furthered only cacophony. Gottfried Benn, medical doctor and poet, spoke of the dissolution of history. In 1936 the Berlin critic Walter Benjamin, who by then had fled to France and a few years later would commit suicide on the border to Spain, asserted that the alienation of mankind had reached such proportions that self-destruction was to be perceived as 'an aesthetic delight'.

Spain turned out to be merely a prelude. The furore in men's minds mounted. Near the end of his verse play *Trial of a Judge* Stephen Spender, outwardly gentle but 'eyes the violent colour of

196 | MODRIS EKSTEINS

bluebells' (Isherwood), wrote the lines: 'And the aerial vultures fly/ Over the deserts which were cities./Kill! Kill! Kill! Kill!' In August 1939 Hitler and Stalin signed their pact of non-aggression and in the process divided up Eastern Europe between them. When Stalin said that the pact was sealed by blood, the aerial vultures flapped their wings in anticipation.

## The Second World War

What the Great War had undermined, the next major conflagration extinguished—the omniscient imperial idea that once was Europe. In the Second World War the ironies were as monstrous as the devastation. After Hitler turned on his blood brother Stalin in June 1941, capitalism and communism were compelled to become allies. It was Soviet Communism that now put up the stiffest resistance to Nazi Germany and in the end saved the world—for capitalism. Auden, who had fled the Old World for the New early in 1939 caught the mood in his New Year reflections of 1940: 'The situation of our time / Surrounds us like a baffling crime.'

As many as seventy-five million people died in this war. If the First World War, as it was now known, had been presented as a civilizing mission, the leaders of the West in the Second World War employed a related if more subdued vocabulary, but to most of those involved the conflict was simply a struggle for survival. It was a question of 'them or us'. Ivor Rowbery, a private in the South Staffordshire regiment, wrote to his mother just before the battle of Arnhem. She received the letter after her son had been killed on 17 September 1944. On the envelope Rowbery had written 'To the Best Mother in the World'. In the letter he said: 'England's a great little country—the best there is—but I cannot honestly and sincerely say "that it is worth fighting for". Nor can I fancy myself in the role of a gallant crusader fighting for the liberation of Europe. It would be a nice thought but I would only be kidding myself. No, Mom, my little world is centred around you and includes Dad, everyone at home, and my friends.' In thirty years, from 1914 to 1944, the social implications of duty and responsibility had shrunk drastically: from King and Country, to Mom, Dad, and friends. Many Germans thought in similar terms. 'Never before in our history have we faced such deadly peril,' remarked Joseph Goebbels, 'nor have the German people as fully realized the peril.'

Extermination or survival. Those seemed the only options. The polarities and contradictions of modernism reached their apotheosis in the Second World War. The *Vernichtungskrieg* on the Eastern Front, the genocidal assault on European Jewry, the saturation bombing of cities, and at the end the atomic attacks against Japan are as telling of the Second World War as the battles of Ypres, Verdun, and the Somme on the Western Front were of the First. Herbert Read, poet and soldier, commented: 'It is not war in the ordinary sense which we are enduring but a world revolution in which all conventions, whether of thought or action, break down and are replaced— not by new conventions . . . —but by provisional formulas . . .' Toward the end of his life, in 1945, H. G. Wells concluded that '*homo sapiens*, as he has been pleased to call himself, . . . is played out'. For Gertrude Stein the war had made everything 'really unreal'.

Faced by events so unprecedented and incomprehensible, the literary and artistic imagination fell silent. What could one say in response to a Second World War that had not been said in response to the First? Milton Acorn, a Canadian poet, sensed the dilemma: 'This is where we came in; this has happened before/Only the last time there was cheering.' Theodor Adorno expressed the predicament in his famous formulation that after Auschwitz poetry was impossible. He meant that literature and imagination and perhaps even history, as they had been known before, were impossible. 'All the poems which sustained me before are as rigid and dead as I am myself,' wrote Mathilde Wolff-Mönckeberg, wife of a professor of English in Hamburg. The great ideas that had animated Western civilization lay among the ruins of Rotterdam, Coventry, Hamburg, Dresden, and Hiroshima. The muses had been silenced by the ashes of Auschwitz. Modernism, like everything else, had shattered. Arnold Schoenberg never finished the third act of *Moses and Aron*. Only mathematical equation had survived, yet this too conjured up a vision of the ultimate void. On witnessing the successful testing of his atomic bomb in the New Mexico desert, J. Robert Oppenheimer, head of the Manhattan Project, whispered verse from the *Bhagavad Gita*: 'I am become death, the destroyer of worlds!'

Only the second rate had the courage to speak. Only the mindless claimed to understand. 'Everything was false,' wrote Charlotte Delbo, a survivor of Auschwitz, 'faces and books, everything showed me its falseness and I was in despair at having lost the faculty of dreaming, or harbouring illusions; I was no longer open to imagination, or explanation.' The Rumanian thinker, E. M. Cioran, was so revolted by the carnage of his age that he dreamed 'of a provincial *ennui* on the scale of the universe'. He wanted history to stagnate. The postmodern age had begun.

Perhaps the most powerful literary voice eventually to come out of the experience of the Second World War was that of the poet Paul Celan, a Jew from the Bukovina, a part of Rumania that Stalin had seized in 1940. After Hitler's invasion of Russia in 1941 Celan's parents were exterminated. Celan, however, had gone into hiding and survived. After the war he moved to Paris. Yet his verse he wrote in German. For Celan as for Kafka, words turned out to be barriers, not means of communication. The 'final solution' he called 'that which happened'. On Hitler's birthday, in 1970, in 'the city of light', he committed suicide.

# 8

# Conclusion

Julian Jackson

## 1945: Year Zero?

The historian Alan Bullock, biographer of Hitler, recalled visiting Germany at the end of the war: 'I remember going to the Ruhr—this was the heart of Europe as far as industry was concerned—and there was silence everywhere. There wasn't a single smokestack. There were no cars, no trains.' This literal silence at the industrial heart of Europe offers a kind of parallel with the literary silence which was felt by some writers to be the only appropriate response to the horror of the events which had occurred. Germans called 1945 *Stunde Null*, hour zero. Roberto Rosselini made a film called *Germany Year Zero* which was shot in what remained of Berlin after the end of the war. One of the chapters in this volume ends in the rubble of the city of Cottbus, about 100 kilometres from Berlin; the next book in this series opens in the rubble of Berlin itself.

It is tempting to see 1945 not only as the Year Zero of Germany but of Europe as a whole. Thus the uncertainties expressed in the introduction about the most appropriate starting date for this volume do not seem to arise so acutely in regard to its ending. Yet in many respects 1945 was not a turning point. It did not represent the end of fighting in Europe since civil war went on in Greece until 1948. The division of Europe into two blocks, which were to define the framework of European politics for the next forty years, did not fully take shape until 1948 when the Communist Party in Czechoslovakia seized power in a bloodless coup: only from this point was the whole of eastern and central Europe was under Soviet control. As for the disintegration of the Empires, this occurred gradually, and 1945 is not in itself a significant date in that process. Perhaps, as David Stevenson writes, the real turning point of European history was not 1945 but 1947 when the Americans launched the Marshall Plan: this signified American readiness to provide economic aid and security commitments to Western Europe, and made possible the future reconciliation between Germany and France which was to be the motor of future European integration (up to 1947 the French had hoped to keep Germany down and had looked to the Soviet Union to help them do this). In short, 1945 is almost as arbitrary an ending to this volume as 1900 is an arbitrary beginning.

# 1900–1945 in perspective

It emerges very clearly from the preceding chapters that the first half of the twentieth century was a period of terrible violence, instability, and fragmentation. There was the cultural fragmentation associated with modernism, the political fragmentation which resulted from the collapse of the Austro-Hungarian, Russian, and Turkish Empires and the economic fragmentation which followed the disintegration of the monetary system which had provided stability to the nineteenth-century economy. Harold James's chapter shows how a world integrated through the mobility of capital, goods, and people—in short a world of what we would today call globalization—broke up as result of the Great War and the Depression; the result was a retreat in the 1930s into varieties of economic nationalism. Similarly, Raj Chandavarkar's chapter shows how the increasing contestation of the Empires of the European powers by their imperial subjects undermined a system which had functioned as a means of 'underwriting the process of expansion and integration of the world economy'.

Yet the same authors also notice at the end of the period the emergence of conditions making possible the reconstruction of a global economic system in a new form. Out of the Second World War, emerged, especially in America, the idea that 'only economic internationalism could provide a remedy against the world of political nationalism and war'. Chandavarkar notes that although formal empire was becoming obsolete as a means of sustaining the integration of the capitalist economy, it was replaced by other kinds of intervention which worked more efficiently. Multi-national enterprises were sophisticated and powerful enough to defend their own interests without requiring the protection of formal empires. The history of Europe after 1945 is characterized, as Mary Fulbrook notes in the introduction to the following volume in this series, by a process of progressive integration occurring within an international context of globalization and internationalization. In this perspective, then, perhaps the first half of the century will be seen merely as a nightmarish parenthesis between two eras of globalization and integration.

# Witness to the Age: John Maynard Keynes (1883–1946)

No one wrote more eloquently about that first era of globalization, or worked more tirelessly at the end of his life to recreate it, than the great economist John Maynard Keynes whose adult life almost exactly spans the years covered by this book. In the celebrated opening pages of his phillipic against the Treaty of Versailles, *The Economic Consequences of the Peace*, Keynes wrote:

What an extraordinary episode in the economic progress of man that age was which came to an end in August 1914! The greater part of the population, it is true, worked hard and lived at a low standard of comfort, yet were to all appearance reasonably contented with this lot. But escape was possible, for any man of capacity or character at all excelling the average, into the middle and upper classes, for whom life offered, at low cost and with the least trouble, conveniences, comforts, and amenities beyond the compass of the richest and most powerful monarchs of other ages. The inhabitant of London could order by telephone, sipping his morning tea in bed, the various products of the whole earth, in such quantity as he might see fit, and reasonably expect their early delivery upon his doorstep; he could at the same moment and by the same means adventure his wealth in the natural resources and new enterprises of any quarter of the world, and share without exertion or even trouble, in their prospective fruits and advantages . . . He could secure forthwith, if he wished it, cheap and comfortable means of transit to any country or clime without passport or other formality . . . But most important of all, he regarded this state of affairs as normal, certain and permanent, except in the direction of further improvement, and any deviation from it as aberrant, scandalous and avoidable. The projects and politics of militarism and imperialism, of racial and cultural rivalries, of monopolies, restrictions and exclusion, which were to play the serpent to this paradise, were little more than the amusements of his daily newspapers, and appeared to exercise almost no influence at all on the ordinary course of social and economic life, the internationalisation of which was nearly complete in practice.

Keynes's conceived the ultimate purposes of his activity as an economist to create—or rather recreate—the conditions for the living of the 'good life' as he, and Bloomsbury, conceived it before 1914. He was only too aware, as he put it to Virginia Woolf in 1938, that civilization was a 'thin and precarious crust'; it was a 'miraculous construction made by our fathers . . . hard to come by and easily lost'. Economists, as he put it on another occasion, were 'trustees not of civilisation, but of the possibility of civilisation'. Believing that there was no return to laissez-faire capitalism, but convinced also of the 'profound connection between personal and political liberty and the rights of private property and private enterprise', he sought an equilibrium between collectivism and individualism: his heart inclined towards the latter and his head towards the former. In 1943, reading *The Road to Serfdom*, the anti-planning polemic published by his old adversary Friedrich Hayek, Keynes wrote to Hayek expressing his admiration for much of the book, but he criticized Hayek's failure to draw a satisfactory line between freedom and planning:

you admit that it is a question of where to draw the line. You agree that a line has to be drawn somewhere, and that the logical extreme is not possible. But you give us no guidance as to where to draw it . . . As soon as you admit that that extreme is not possible . . . you are on your own argument done for, since you are trying to persuade us that so soon as one moves an inch in the planned direction you are necessarily launched on the slippery slope which will lead you in due course over the precipice . . . I should therefore conclude your theme rather differently. I should say that what we want is not no planning, or even less planning, I should say that we almost certainly want more. But the planning should take place in a community in which, as many people as possible, both leaders and followers, share your own moral position. Moderate planning will be safe if those carrying it out are rightly orientated in their own minds and hearts to your moral position.

Keynes's own resolution certainly has its problems—who is to ensure that those carrying out the policy will be 'rightly orientated'?—but the debate, which Keynes and Hayek never had the chance to engage fully, is certainly one of the crucial themes of twentieth-century political economy.

Keynes wrote his letter to Hayek in June 1944 while on board the ship taking him to the Bretton Woods conference to discuss the setting up of a new international monetary system after the war. For much of the interwar years, Keynes, in despair at the consequences of Versailles, had been an economic nationalist; but the last five years of his life were to see him deeply involved in the efforts to build a new international monetary order which might provide an improved version of the system prevailing before 1914. Keynes can therefore also be said to have been one of those who helped to lay the foundations of the new globalization which emerged after 1945. But in participating in these negotiations he was also a sad witness to the fundamental shift in the balance of world power which had taken place during his lifetime. The plan which emerged at Bretton Woods was much closer to the version proposed by the Americans, in the form of Harry Dexter White, than to the version proposed by the British, in the form of Keynes. At the end of 1945, Keynes went on another visit to the United States to try and negotiate a loan for the bankrupt British economy after the end of Lend Lease. After extremely arduous negotiations, which finally destroyed his precarious health, Keynes obtained a loan much less large than he had hoped, and with humiliating conditions attached. 'May it never fall to my lot to have to *persuade* anyone to do what I want, with so few cards in my hand' wrote Keynes to his mother in November 1945. Six months later he was dead.

The new internationalism was, then, very much on American terms. This is hardly surprising: by 1945, the United States produced over half the world's manufactured goods, it was the home of the most productive technologies, and accounted for four fifths of the world's exports of manufactured goods. Looked at in this perspective, perhaps we should see the first half of the twentieth century not so much as a parenthesis between two eras of globality as a era in which occurred a tectonic shift in the power away from Europe towards the super powers, and ultimately America. This was a shift in cultural power every bit as much as in economic power: when the French came to negotiate their American loan in 1946, they were forced to accept conditions requiring them to import a certain quota of Hollywood films. Since 1945 Europe has been simultaneously fascinated by, and resentful of, America, and at least in the minds of some of European leaders, the process of European integration has come to be conceived, in part, as a form of resistance to American economic and cultural hegemony. Whether this enterprise succeeds in such an objective, only the twenty-first century will tell us.

# Further reading

## General

There are a number of recent general histories which treat part or all of the period covered in this book: Eric Hobsbawn, *Age of Extremes: the Short Twentieth Century 1914–1991* (London, 1994); Mark Mazower, *Dark Continent: Europe in the Twentieth Century* (London, 1999); Richard Vinen, *A History in Fragments: Europe in the Twentieth Century* (London, 2000); Clive Ponting; *Progress and Barbarism: the World in the Twentieth Century* (London, 2000). There is still a lot to be learnt from James Joll, *Europe since 1870: an International History* (London, 1980). Norman Stone, *Europe Transformed 1878–1919* (London, 1983) is excellent on the period to 1919.

## International relations

W. Keylor, *The Twentieth-Century World: an International History* (3rd edn., London and New York, 1996) is the best general survey of twentieth-century international history.

On the origins of the Great War, James Joll, *The Origins of the First World War* (2nd edn., London and New York, 1992) is the best short synthesis, and Huw Strachan (ed.), *The Oxford Illustrated History of the First World War* (Oxford and New York, 1998) probably the best one-volume introduction to the history of the war itself. M. F. Boemeke, G. Feldman, and E. Glaser (eds.), *The Treaty of Versailles: a Reassessment after 75 Years* (Washington DC and Cambridge, 1998) is an important new collection of essays on the making of the peace.

On inter-war international relations, Sally Marks, *The Illusion of Peace: International Relations in Europe, 1919–1933* (Basingstoke, 1976) is very useful on the 1920s, but is ageing slightly and should be read in conjunction with Jan Jacobson, 'Is There a New International History of the 1920s?', *American Historical Review*, 88, 3 (1983), 617–45 which summarizes a mass of new research; and Stephen Schuker, 'France and the Remilitarization of the Rhineland, 1936', *French Historical Studies*, 14, 3 (1986), 299–338 which is wider than its title suggests and important on the origins of French appeasement. Philip Bell, *The Origins of the Second World War in Europe* (2nd edn., London and New York, 1997) is the best short synthesis of this topic (it is in the same series as the volume by Joll); and Robert Boyce (ed.), *Paths to War: New Essays on the Origins of the Second World War* (Basingstoke, 1989) contains several valuable contributions.

Gerald Weinberg, *A World at Arms: A Global History of World War II*

(Cambridge, 1994) is the fullest and most up-to-date one-volume introduction to World War II. David Reynolds, '1940: Fulcrum of the Twentieth Century', *International Affairs*, 66, 2 (1990), 325–50 is excellent on the global significance of the Fall of France; V. S. Mastny, *Russia's Road to the Cold War: Diplomacy, Warfare, and the Politics of Communism, 1941–1945* (New York, 1979) is still the best study of Soviet war aims; and Richard Overy, *Why the Allies Won* (London, 1995) is a very stimulating reassessment, though still controversial.

## Economy

The best overall survey of the pre-1914 economy is W. Arthur Lewis, *Growth and Fluctuations 1870–1913* (London, 1978). On the interwar period, see W. Arthur Lewis, *Economic Survey 1919–1939* (London, 1949), which is still the best 'Keynesian' survey of the period, and Charles P. Kindleberger, *The World in Depression, 1929–1939* (2nd edn., Berkeley, 1986), which looks at international transmission mechanisms in a fascinating and illuminating way, as does the more recent and authoritative Barry Eichengreen, *Golden Fetters: The Gold Standard and the Great Depression 1919–1939* (New York, 1992). Peter Temin, *Lessons from the Great Depression* (Cambridge Mass., 1989), is stimulating and provocative. Beth A. Simmons, *Who Adjusts? Domestic Sources of Foreign Economic Policy During the Interwar Years* (Princeton, 1994), offers the considerable insights of a political scientist.

On migration, see Brinley Thomas, *Migration and Economic Growth* (Cambridge 1954); Dudley Baines, *Emigration from Europe*, (Cambridge, 1995). On technical changes, see David Landes, *The Unbound Prometheus: Technological Change and Industrial Development in Western Europe from 1750 to the Present* (Cambridge, 1969).

On unemployment, see W. R. Garside (ed.), *Capitalism in Crisis: Responses to the Great Depression* (New York, 1992). For national histories of the depression, on Britain: H. W. Richardson, *Economic Recovery in Britain, 1932–39* (London, 1967). On France, Julian Jackson, *The Politics of Depression in France 1932–1936* (Cambridge, 1985); Kenneth Mouré, *Managing the Franc Poincaré: Economic Understanding and Political Constraint in French Monetary Policy 1928–1936* (Cambridge, 1991). On Germany, Gerald D. Feldman, *The Great Disorder, Politics, Economics, and Society in the German Inflation 1914–1924* (New York, 1993); Harold James, *The German Slump: Politics and Economics, 1924–1936* (Oxford, 1986). The most detailed history of Soviet planning is E. Zaleski, *Planning for Economic Growth in the Soviet Union 1918–1932* (Chapel Hill, NC, 1971). A less technical history is provided by Alec Nove, *An Economic History of the USSR 1917–1991* (London, 1992).

Finally, perhaps the best way of understanding the economics of the period is to understand the leading economist of the century, and a major figure in what was still the central economy of the world, the Cambridge (UK) born John Maynard Keynes. The standard source is the three volume biography of Keynes by Robert Skidelsky: *John Maynard Keynes: Hopes Betrayed 1883–1920* (London, 1983), *John Maynard Keynes: The Economist as Saviour 1920–1937* (London, 1992), *John Maynard Keynes: Fighting for Britain 1937–1946* (London, 2001).

## Politics

Two celebrated works which each offer a powerfully argued if controversial thesis are Arno J. Mayer, *The Persistence of the Old Regime: Europe to the Great War* (London, 1981) which argues that European politics before 1914 were dominated by the old regime nobility, and that bourgeois liberals had been corrupted by this aristocratic spirit, and Charles Maier, *Recasting Bourgeois Europe: Stabilization in France, Germany and Italy in the Decade After World War 1* (Princeton, NJ, 1975) which argues that the bourgeoisie re-established its power after the Great war by abandoning traditional liberalism for 'corporatist' negotiations between organized interests.

On women and politics, Richard J. Evans, *The Feminists: Women's Emancipation Movements in Europe, America and Australasia 1840–1920* (London, 1977) is an informative survey, which makes some excellent comparative points, although sharing the same 'liberal-modernization' approach to history as Mayer. Despite the post-communist over-optimism that characterizes the views of some contributors, *Women in Central and Eastern Europe*, Special edition of *Women's History Review* Louise A. Tilly (ed.), 5, 4 (1996) contains useful information on women's political influence. Victoria De Grazia, *How Fascism Ruled Italian Women: Italy, 1922–1945* (Berkeley, Los Angeles and Oxford, 1992) is essential for anyone interested in fascist attitudes to women and the role of women in fascist movements. For socialism and women, see Helmut Gruber and Pamela M. Graves, *Women and Socialism, Socialism and Women* (Providence, RI, 1998).

Peter Fritzsche, 'Did Weimar Fail?', *Journal of Modern History* 68, 3 (1996): 629–56 offers a thought-provoking review of recent works on Nazism. George Luebbert, *Liberalism, Fascism, or Social Democracy: Social Classes and the Political Origins of Regimes in Interwar Europe* (Oxford, 1991) is a stimulating comparative treatment of the 'social basis', of European regimes in the first four decades of the century, showing how political, religious, class, and town/country cleavages influenced the course of political history in the first half of the century. Mária M. Kovács, *Liberal Professions and Illiberal Politics: Hungary from the Habsburgs to the Holocaust* (London and Washington DC, 1995) is a brilliant account of professional and ethnic tensions involved in the breakdown of liberal politics in Hungary. See also Tim Kirk and Anthony McElligott (eds.), *Opposing Fascism: Community, Authority and Resistance in Europe* (Cambridge, 1999). For a brief survey of the history of fascism, see Kevin Passmore, *Fascism: A Very Short Introduction* (Oxford, 2002).

On labour and politics see Stephen Salter and John Stevenson, *The Working Class and Politics in Europe and America, 1929–1945* (London, 1990) and Marcel van der Linden (ed.), *The Formation of Labour Movements, 1870–1914,* 2 vols., *Contributions to the History of European Labour and Society* (Leiden, 1990). On the Soviet Union see Sheila Fitzpatrick (ed.), *Stalinism: New Directions* (London, 2000), a fascinating collection of recent innovative research on Stalinism, and Ronald Grigor Suny, 'Nationality and Class in the Revolutions of 1917: a Re-examination of Social Categories', in *Stalinism: Its Nature and Aftermath. Essays in Honour of Moshe Lewin,* edited by Nick Lampert and Gábor T. Rittersporn, (London, 1992), 211–42.

## Society

Paul Thompson, *The Edwardians. The Remaking of British Society* (2nd edn., London, 1992) is one of the first substantial oral-history based studies, a pioneering work which has become a classic. On the impact of the First War see Richard Wall and Jay Winter (eds.), *The Upheaval of War. Family, Work and Welfare in Europe, 1914–1918* (Cambridge, 1988) an excellent collection of essays on the social and demographic effects of the war across Europe; and Jay Winter, *The Great War and the British People* (London, 1986), a standard work on the effects of the First World War on the health and demography of the British population. On the aftermath of the war, H. Clout, *After the Ruins. Restoring the Countryside of Northern France after the Great War* (Exeter, 1996) is a superb study of the reconstruction of northern France after the devastation visited upon it during the 1914–18 conflict; and George L. Mosse, *Fallen Soldiers. Reshaping the Memory of the World Wars* (New York and Oxford, 1990) is a stimulating and pioneering discussion of the ways in which the 'myth' of the fallen soldier and the memory of world war was shaped and manipulated.

Orlando Figes, *A People's Tragedy. The Russian Revolution 1891–1924* (London, 1997) is a widely acclaimed, readable account of the Russian revolution; and Richard Pipes, *Russia under the Bolshevik Regime 1919–1924* (London, 1994) an incisive and damning account of the first years of Bolshevik rule. William J. Chase, *Workers, Society, and the Soviet State. Labor and Life in Moscow, 1918–1929* (Urbana and Chicago, 1987) contains some fascinating glimpses of the hard lives of workers during the early years of Soviet rule; and Moshe Lewin, *The Making of the Soviet System. Essays in the Social History of Interwar Russia* (London, 1985) contains a collection of essays by one of the most insightful analysts of the Soviet Union under Lenin and Stalin. Victoria de Grazia, *How Fascism Rules Women, 1922–1945* (Berkeley, Los Angeles and

Oxford, 1992) is a pioneering work, offering new insights into the nature of the fascist regime and the lives of people under it.

For the impact of the Depression see Marie Jahoda, Paul F. Lazarsfeld, Hans Zeisel, *Marienthal. The Sociography of an Unemployed Community* (London, 1972), the translation of a sociology classic which provides a detailed study of the lives of the unemployed in a small Austrian town at the depths of the Depression in 1930; and Kate Nicholas, *The Social Effects of Unemployment on Teesside, 1919–39* (Manchester, 1986), a solid local study of how unemployment affected people in the north of England between the wars.

Roy Porter, *The Greatest Benefit to Mankind. A Medical History of Humanity from Antiquity to the Present* (London, 1997) is a wide-ranging, informative, and immensely readable account of the social history of medicine; and Colin Chant (ed.), *Science, Technology and Everyday Life 1870–1950* (London, 1989) is a useful collection on key subjects in the social history of science and technology during the period.

## Imperialism and the European empires

J. A. Gallagher, *The Decline, Revival and Fall of the British Empire: the Ford Lectures and Other Essays* (edited by Anil Seal) (Cambridge, 1982) has elaborated the framework within which the history of imperialism has been analysed for several decades. F. Cooper and A. Stoler (eds.) *Tensions of Empire: Colonial Cultures in a Bourgeois World* (Berkeley and Los Angeles, 1997) is a lively collection of essays which examines the impact of the colonies in shaping metropolitan society and the consequences of imperial rule for colonial cultures.

On the British Empire, the most recent comprehensive treatment is J. M. Brown and W. R. Louis (eds) *The Oxford History of the British Empire, Vol. IV, The Twentieth Century* (Oxford, 1999) while P. Cain and A. G. Hopkins, *British Imperialism*, (London, 1993) 2 vols., offers a revisionist account of the Empire's rise and fall which gives centrality to the metropole, and especially the role of finance and banking, in explanations of imperialism. On the French Empire, Jacques Marseille, 'Phases of French Colonialism,' in A. N. Porter and R. F. Holland (eds.) *Money, Finance and Empire, 1790–1960* (London, 1985) summarizes important findings which this author has published at greater length in French.

On India and Southeast Asia, see: C. J. Baker, *An Indian Rural Economy: the Tamil Countryside, 1880–1955.* (Oxford, 1984), a seminal study which sets the Depression of the 1930s in a long historical perspective; J. A. Gallagher and A. Seal (eds.) *Locality, Province and Nation: Indian Politics, 1870–1940* (Cambridge, 1973), an influential collection of essays on Indian political responses to the changing structure of colonial government; James C. Scott,

*The Moral Economy of the Peasant in Southeast Asia* (New Haven, 1976) an innovative study of peasant responses to the Depression of the 1930s; A. Stoler, *Capitalism and Confrontation in Sumatra's Plantation Belt, 1870–1979* (New Haven, 1985) an excellent study of labour and gender relations under colonialism; A. Jalal, *The Sole Spokesman: Jinnah, the Muslim League and the Demand for Pakistan* (Cambridge 1985), a persuasive analysis of the strategy of Jinnah and the Muslim League; B. R. Tomlinson, *The Political Economy of the Raj, 1914–1947: the Economics of Decolonization in India* (London, 1979), an important investigation of the changing relations between the British and Indian economies in the decades leading up to decolonization.

On Africa see: J. Iliffe, *The Africans: the History of a Continent* (Cambridge, 1995), a compelling and encyclopaedic survey of the history of the African peoples and their environment since their origins; B. Berman and J. M. Lonsdale, *Unhappy Valley: Conflict in Kenya and Africa* (London, 1992), 2 vols., a seminal study of the political economy and political culture of Kenya in the twentieth century; P. Gifford, and W. R. Louis (eds.), *The Transfer of Power in Africa, 1940–1960: Decolonization, 1940–1960* (New Haven, 1982), an important collection of essays which offers a comparative dimension; D. Killingray and R. Rathbone (eds.) *Africa and the Second World War* (Basingstoke, 1986), a valuable collection on the impact of the war upon Africa; and D. Prochaska, *Making Algeria French: Colonialism in Bone, 1870–1920* (Cambridge, 1990) a fascinating study of a small town in Algeria under colonial rule.

On the Middle East, E. Monroe, *Britain's Moment in the Middle East, 1914–1956* (Baltimore, 1963) is an excellent survey of British policy. J. Darwin, *Britain, Egypt and the Middle East: Imperial policy in the Aftermath of War 1918–1922* (London, 1981) is a valuable study of British policy after the First World War. M. J. Cohen, *Palestine, Retreat from Mandate: the Making of British Policy 1936–1945* (London, 1978) is a careful investigation of the political history of Palestine in a critical period. Philip S. Khoury, *Syria and the French Mandate: the Politics of Arab Nationalism, 1920–1945* (Princeton, 1987) is an excellent account of French rule and the nature of Syrian nationalism.

Decolonization is covered in many of the works mentioned above, but in general see W. R. and R. E. Robinson. 'The Imperialism of Decolonization' *Journal of Imperial and Commonwealth History*, 22, 3 (1993), pp. 462–511.

## Culture

For an overview, see Peter Conrad, *Modern Times, Modern Places* (London, 1998), a brilliant and invigorating survey, but not for the uninitiated. Also stimulating is Frederick Karl, *Modern and Modernism: The Sovereignty of the Artist 1885-1925* (New York, 1985). On the pre-1914 period, Carl Schorske, *Fin-de-siècle Vienna: Politics and Culture* (New York, 1980) is a landmark study, and Stephen Kern, *The Culture of Time and Space 1880–1918* (Cambridge, Mass., 1983) is an exceptionally imaginative cultural history. On the impact of the Great War see Paul Fussell, *The Great War and Modern Memory* (London, 1975), a highly influential study of the literary reverberations of the war, and Modris Eksteins, *Rites of Spring: the Great War and the Birth of the Modern Age* (London, 1989) an attempt at a modernist history.

On particular countries, Steven. E. Aschheim, *The Nietzsche Legacy in Germany, 1890–1990* (Berkeley, 1992) is the best overview of the enormous influence of Nietzsche on twentieth-century Germany; Detlev Peukert, *The Weimar Republic: The Crisis of Classical Modernity* (London, 1991) is a model analysis in its ability to link economic, social, and intellectual developments; Samuel Hynes, *The Auden Generation: Literature and Politics in England in the 1930s* (London, 1976) is a fine study of the English intellectual landscape during that 'low dishonest decade'; Richard Sites, *Revolutionary Dreams: Utopian Vision and Experimental Life in the Russian Revolution* (New York, 1989) is the best survey of the culture of Bolshevism.

Among biographies, see John Richardson, *A Life of Picasso* (2 vols.) (New York, 1991–6) an admirable study of a life in its time; David Robinson, *Charles Chaplin: His Life and Art* (London, 1985) a fine study which evokes the significance of Chaplin; and Peter Gay, *Freud: A Life for Our Time* (New York, 1988) an impressive biography by a great historian.

Finally, Zygmunt Bauman, *Modernity and the Holocaust* (Cambridge, 1989) is a path-breaking interpretative study by a sociologist; and, in a lighter vein, Robert Wohl, *A Passion for Wings: Aviation and the Western Imagination, 1908–1918* (New Haven, 1984) is an entertaining account of the symbolism of early flight.

# Chronology

| | |
|---|---|
| 1912–13 | Balkan Wars |
| 1914 | Outbreak of First World War (August) |
| 1915 | Dardanelles expedition (April–November) |
| | Italy enters the war (May) |
| | Dada formed in Zurich |
| 1916 | Battles of Verdun and Somme |
| | Easter Uprising in Dublin |
| | Sykes–Picot Agreement |
| 1917 | America enters the war (April) |
| | Russian Revolution |
| | Balfour Declaration (November) |
| 1918 | President Wilson's fourteen points (January) |
| | Germany sues for armistice (November) |
| | Montagu–Chelmsford Reforms in India |
| 1918–20 | Russian Civil War |
| 1919–20 | Greco-Turkish War |
| 1919–21 | Russo-Polish War |
| 1919 | Revolution in Germany |
| | Founding of Weimar Republic |
| | Treaties of Versailles (Germany), St Germain (Austria), Neuilly (Bulgaria) |
| | Wafdist Revolt in Egypt |
| | Massacre in Amritsar |
| | Bauhaus founded in Weimar by Walter Gropius |
| 1920 | Treaties of Trianon (Hungary) and Sèvres (Turkey) |
| | United States Senate fails to ratify Versailles Treaty |
| | Rebellion in Iraq |
| | Release of *Cabinet of Dr Caligari* |
| 1921 | Formation of Little Entente |
| | Partition of Ireland |
| | New Economic Policy in Soviet Union |
| | Abd'el Karim insurrection in Morocco |
| 1922 | German–Soviet Treaty of Rapallo (April) |
| | Mussolini comes to power in Italy (October) |

|      | James Joyce's *Ulysses* published in Paris |
|------|---|
|      | T. S. Eliot's *Wasteland* published |
|      | BBC begins broadcasting |
| 1923 | France and Belgium occupy Ruhr |
|      | Primo de Rivera Coup in Spain |
|      | German hyper inflation |
|      | Self government for Southern Rhodesia |
| 1924 | Dawes Reparation Plan approved |
|      | Death of Lenin |
|      | First Surrealist Manifesto Published |
|      | Death of Franz Kafka |
| 1925–7 | Druze revolt in Syria |
| 1925 | Locarno Treaties signed (December) |
|      | Great Britain returns to Gold Standard (April) |
|      | Founding of Étoile Nord-Africaine in Paris |
|      | Release of Eisenstein's *Battleship Potemkin* and Chaplin's *Gold Rush* |
|      | Berg's *Wozzeck* premiered in Berlin |
| 1926 | Germany enters League of Nations |
|      | Piłsudski coup in Poland |
|      | Smetona coup in Lithuania |
|      | Stabilization (de facto) of French franc |
| 1927 | Lindbergh flies across the Atlantic |
| 1928 | Kellogg–Briand Pact (August) |
|      | Nationalist Unification of China |
|      | Release of Luis Bunuel and Salvador Dali's film *Le Chien Andalou* |
| 1929 | Young Plan (reparations) approved |
|      | Royal dictatorship established in Yugoslavia |
|      | Wall Street Crash (October) |
|      | Arab–Jewish riots in Palestine |
|      | Remarque's *All Quiet on the Western Front* published |
|      | The talkies arrive in the cinema |
| 1930–1 | Roundtable conference on India in London |

1930    Briand Plan for European Union
        Allies evacuate Rhineland
        Royal government established in Romania
        Establishment of Spanish Second Republic
        Civil Disobedience in India

1931    Gömbös becomes Prime Minister in Hungary
        Failure of Creditenanstalt (Austria) (May)
        Hoover Moratorium on reparations
        Formation of National Government in Britain
        Suspension of sterling convertibility (September)
        Statue of Westminster defines dominion status

1932    Lausanne conference ends reparations
        Social Democratic administration in Sweden
        Salazar dictatorship in Portugal
        Imperial economic conference Ottawa
        Iraqi independence

1933    Hitler becomes chancellor of Germany (January)
        Germany leaves League of Nations and disarmament
        conference (October)
        Dollfuss dictatorship established in Austria (May)
        United States leaves the gold standard (April)
        World Economic Conference in London

1934    Extreme right riots in Paris (February)
        Päts dictatorship in Estonia
        Army coup in Bulgaria
        Ulmanis dictatorship in Latvia
        Attempted Nazi coup in Austria
        Foundation of Neo-Destour Party in Tunisia

1935    Saar plebisicite (January)
        Stresa front (April)
        Italy invades Abyssinia (October)
        Nuremburg Anti-Semitic Laws in Germany
        Colonels' dictatorship in Poland
        Devaluation of Belgian franc (April)

|      | Government of India Act provides for provincial autonomy |
|------|-----------------------------------------------------------|
| 1936 | Germany remilitarizes Rhineland (March) |
|      | Election of Popular Front government in France (May) |
|      | Civil War in Spain begins (July) |
|      | Metaxas establishes dictatorship in Greece |
|      | Beginning of Great Purge in USSR |
|      | Publication of Keynes's *General Theory* |
|      | France abandons gold standard (September) |
|      | Anglo-Egyptian Treaty |
|      | Peel Commission on Palestine |
|      | Release of Charlie Chaplin's *Modern Times* |
| 1937 | Italy joins anti-comintern pact |
|      | Hossbach conference (November) |
|      | Guernica bombed (April) |
|      | Nazis organize exhibition of degenerate art |
|      | Provincial election in India: Congress wins seven provinces |
| 1938 | Germany annexes Austria (March) |
|      | Sudeten crisis and Munich agreement (September) |
|      | Crystal Night Pogrom in Germany (November) |
|      | Singapore naval base completed |
| 1939 | Germany invades Czechoslovakia (15 March) |
|      | Nationalists win Spanish Civil War |
|      | Britain and France guarantee Poland (31 March) |
|      | Nazi–Soviet Pact (23 August) |
|      | Britain and France declare war on Germany (3 September) |
|      | Sigmund Freud dies |
| 1940 | Churchill becomes British Prime Minister (May) |
|      | Germany defeats France (May–June) |
|      | Italy enters war (10 June) |
|      | Italy invades Greece (October) |
|      | Release of Chaplin's *Great Dictator* |
| 1941 | Lend Lease Act (March) |
|      | Germany invades Yugoslavia and Greece (April) |
|      | Germany invades Soviet Union (June) |

Atlantic Charter (August)

Japan Attacks Pearl Harbor (December)

Shostakovitch writes Symphony No. 7 during siege of Leningrad

1942      Wannsee Conference formalizes Holocaust (January)

Fall of Singapore (February)

Battle of Stalingrad begins (October)

Battle of El Alamein (October)

Americans land in French North Africa (November)

Congress launches Quit India movement

Greer Garson stars in *Mrs Miniver*

1943      Casablanca Conference decides unconditional surrender (January)

German surrender at Stalingrad (February)

Warsaw ghetto uprising (April)

Allied defeat of U Boats in Atlantic (May)

Battle of Kursk (July–August)

Allies invade Italy (September)

Fall of Mussolini (September)

Famine in Bengal

1944      Germay occupies Hungary (March)

Normandy landing (June)

Brazzaville Conference

1945      Yalta Conference (February)

Death of Roosevelt (April)

German surrender (May)

Potsdam Conference (July–August)

Atomic bombs dropped (August)

Civil War in China

Sétif massacre in Algeria (May)

# Maps

**Map 1** Europe in 1914.

EDEN

Stockholm

Baltic
Sea

St Petersburg

ESTONIA

LIVONIA

LATVIA

COUR-
LAND

LITHUANIA

EAST
PRUSSIA

Posen

Niemen

Tannenberg

CONGRESS

KINGDOM

OF POLAND

SILESIA

USTRIA

Vistula

GALICIA

Vienna

AUSTRIA–

Budapest

HUNGARY

Danube

ROMANIA

Bucharest

BOSNIA

ALMATIA

Belgrade

Sarajevo

SERBIA

MONTENEGRO

Sofia

BULGARIA

ALBANIA

Adriatic
Sea

GREECE

Aegean
Sea

Athens

Volga

Moscow

RUSSIA

Don

Kiev

Kharkov

Donets

Dnieper

UKRAINE

Odessa

CRIMEA

Sebastopol

Black Sea

Constantinople

OTTOMAN
EMPIRE

CYPRUS
(Britain)

--·-- International Frontiers, *c.*1926

----- International Frontiers, 1914

Rhineland Zone under Allied Occupation after 1919

1. Saar Plebiscite Area (under League of Nations, 1919–35

2. Limit of Rhineland Demilitarized Zone after 1919

3. Danzig Free City

4. Memel Territory (to Lithuania, 1923)

5. Klagenfurt Territory (to Austria, 1920)

6. Burgenland Territory (to Austria, 1921)

7. Fiume Free State (1920–4)

**Map 2** European Territorial Changes after 1918. (Source: D. Stevenson, *The First World War and International Politics* (Oxford, 1988))

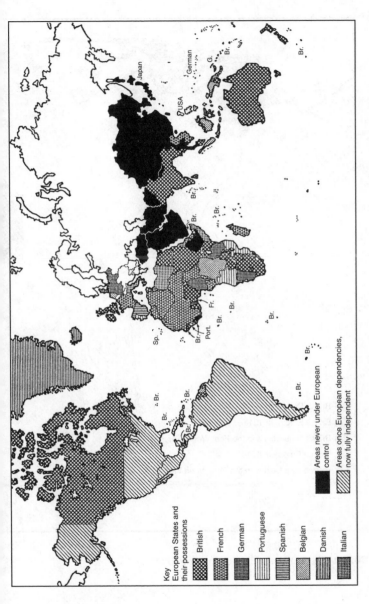

**Map 3** The colonial empires in 1914. (Source: D. K. Fieldhouse, *The Colonial Empires: A Comparative Survey for the Eighteenth Century* (London, 1965))

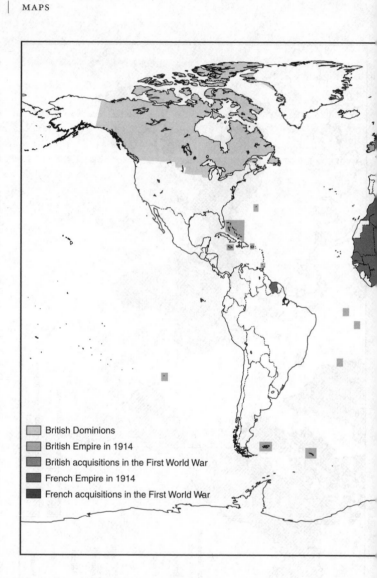

**Map 4** The British and French Empires in 1930.

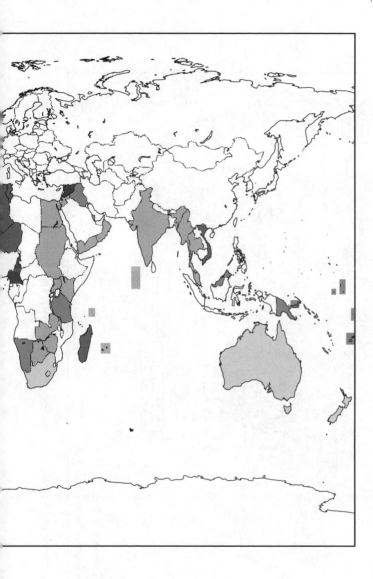

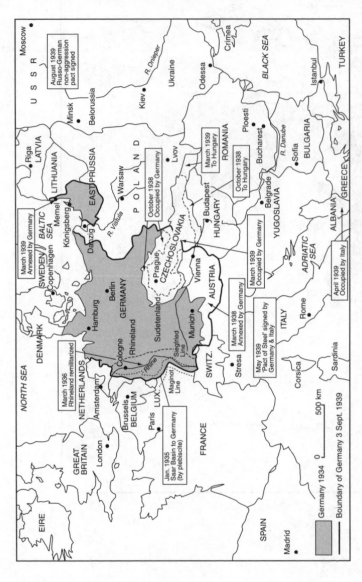

**Map 5** Germany and central Europe, 1933–9. (Source: R. J. Overy, *The Origins of the Second World War* (London, 1987))

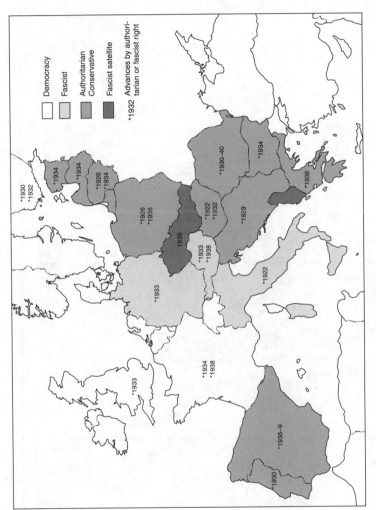

**Map 6** Europe on the eve of war: the retreat of democracy.

Democracy

Fascist

Authoritarian
Conservative

Fascist satellite

*1932 Advances by authori-
tarian or fascist right

*1930
*1932

*1934

*1934

*1926
*1934

*1926
*1935

*1930–40

*1934

*1936

*1922
*1932

1939

*1929

*1933
*1938

*1933

*1922

*1934
*1938

*1933

*1936–9

*1930

**Map 7** Territorial changes in eastern Europe, 1939–47. (Source: J. Wheeler-Bennett and A. Nicholls, *The Semblance of Peace: The Political Settlement after the Second World War* (London, 1972). By permission of Palgrave Macmillan.)

# Index

Laporte, Maurice 99
Larkin, Philip 5
La Rochefoucauld, François 6th Duc
de 176
Latin America 66, 155
see also Argentina; Uruguay
Latvia 6, 81
Lausanne Treaty (1923) 8, 23, 29
Lawrence, D. H. 4
League of Nations 20, 23, 24, 25, 27, 33,
54, 55
Economic and Financial Section
73
Germany enters 28
Germany walks out of 30
Japan leaves 31
Soviet Union joins 32
World Economic Conference (1927)
58
Lebanon 22, 147
Le Corbusier (C.-E. Jeanneret) 4
left-wing politics 3, 5–6, 78, 80–8, 93,
94, 95, 108
destruction of 105, 107
failure of 96–101
radical 193
resistance movements 112
symbols of 104
united 110
use of fascists against 104
Léger, Fernand 175, 184
leisure 11, 14, 105, 109
mass 137
Lena Goldfield massacre (1912) 6, 88
Lend-Lease Act (US 1941) 39, 42, 203
Lenin, Vladimir I. 6, 15, 22, 24, 71, 85,
93, 97, 98
adaptation of Marxist theory 192
admonition of Zetkin 99
seizure of power in Russia 182
Leopold II, king of Belgium 144
Leopoldville 165
Levi, Primo 1–2
Lewin, Moshe 14, 130
Lewis, Wyndham 179
Ley, Robert 13

liberal democracy 4, 79, 92, 93, 113
disillusion with 95
threat to 102
weakened 114
Liberal party (Britain) 87, 89, 94
liberalism 53, 77, 89, 91, 106
decline of 96
economic 74, 75
feminism not synonymous with 83
laissez-faire 10
left 5–6, 78, 85, 86–8, 93, 95
working-class 84
Libya 159
life expectancy 118, 134
Lindbergh, Charles 136, 184
linguistic nationalism/particularism
80, 87
Linlithgow, Victor, A. J. (2nd
Marquess) viceroy of India 158
liquidity 155
Lissitzky, El 192
literature 187–8, 191, 194, 197
Lithuania 80
Little Entente (1920–21) 23, 27
Litvinov, Maxim 32, 36
'living space' 30
living standards 41, 58, 118, 119, 122, 132
Lloyd George, David (1st Earl) 24, 25,
27, 53
loans 27, 31, 33, 39, 54, 203
recalled 29
reconstruction 44
Locarno treaties (1925) 28, 29, 34
London 35, 108, 136, 194
Shoreditch and Spitalfield 139–40
St Paul's Cathedral 183
London Magazine, The 174
London Schedule of Payments (1921)
26–7
Loos, Adolf 187
Louis XIV, king of France 179, 187
Louvain 8
Low Countries 35, 37, 43
see also Belgium; Luxembourg;
Netherlands
Ludendorff, Erich 21–2, 23

modernity/modernism 4, 120
  polarities and contradictions of 197
  essence of 188, 189
  'Janus face of' 3, 132
  subversive potential of 15
modernization 77, 168
Moellendorff, Wichard von 9, 53
Molotov, Vyacheslav M. 36, 38, 44
Mombasa 165
Mona Lisa 182
monarchists 7, 89, 90, 96
Mondrian, Piet 187
money, see currency
monoplane fighters 35
Montagu–Chelmsford reforms (1920s)
  151
Montaigne, Michel Eyquem de 176
morality 11, 179
Morgenthau, Henry 75
Morocco 18, 149
mortality 118, 165
Moscow 15, 43, 129, 130
Mosley, Sir Oswald 105
movie stars 190
multilateral payments system 74
Munch, Edvard 190
Munich:
  conference (1938) 30, 34, 35, 42
  House of German Art 194
murder 105, 106, 111, 117
  mass 121
Murnau, F. W. 186
music 15, 178, 184, 189
Muslims 149, 151, 160, 166
Mussolini, Benito 3, 6, 10, 12, 27, 30, 55,
  107, 193
  climate of fear and hatred in which
    he succeeded in seizing power 121
  conquers Abyssinia 33
  conversion to Catholicism 103
  March on Rome (1922) 104
  ousted 40
  pact with Hitler (1939) 33, 160
  'quota novanta' 62
  resistance to Nazi control of Austria
    32

unprepared for hostilities 38
writing history 'with fist, not pen'
  94
Mustafa Kemal Atatürk 23, 152
Myrdal, Gunnar 60
myths 177, 194

Nairobi 165
Nantes 186
Napoleonic Wars (1805–15) 117
natalists 94
national honour 143
National Socialism 182
  see also Nazism
nationalism 11, 43, 77, 82, 87, 88, 92, 93,
  148, 152, 155, 166
  anti-semitic 6
  Arab 149
  collectivism and 193
  economic 71–4, 75, 200, 203
  ethnically homogenous 103
  liberal 80–1
  political 200
  populist 6
  racist 104
  radical 169
  revolutionary 104
  right-wing 6, 84, 91
  social underpinning for 165
nationality 58, 104, 112
nationalization 98
naturalization 153
navies 21, 23, 139
Nazi–Soviet Pact (1939) 35, 36, 38, 42,
  112
Nazism 4, 11–15 passim 32, 40, 75,
  131
  appeasement 29
  attempt to move back to solid
    ground 194
  attempted coup in Austria 30
  autarky 73
  campaign of mass murder 121
  communist resistance to 109
  demonstrations against 108
  expansionist policies 104, 108